The Practice
of
Public Relations

The Institute of Public Relations defines public relations practice as 'the deliberate, planned and sustained effort to establish and maintain mutual understanding between an organization and its public'.

The Practice
of
Public Relations

Edited by

Wilfred Howard, M.A., M.CAM., F.I.P.R.

Second Edition

Published on behalf of
the CAM Foundation and
the Institute of Marketing

HEINEMANN : LONDON

William Heinemann Ltd
10 Upper Grosvenor Street, London W1X 9PA
LONDON   MELBOURNE   TORONTO
JOHANNESBURG   AUCKLAND

First published 1982
Second edition 1985
© The Communication Advertising and
Marketing Education Foundation Ltd
and Institute of Marketing 1982, 1985

British Library Cataloguing in Publication Data

The Practice of public relations.—2nd ed.
1. Public relations
I. Howard, Wilfred
659.2   HM263

ISBN 0–434–90785–5

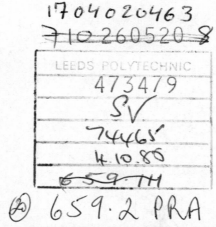
Filmset by Willmer Brothers Limited, Birkenhead, Merseyside
Printed in Great Britain by Redwood Burn Limited, Trowbridge, Wiltshire
and bound by Pegasus Bookbinding, Melksham, Wiltshire

Preface to the Second Edition

This book is intended in the first instance for the guidance of CAM students of public relations. It has been designed therefore to cover broadly the subject matter with which CAM certificate students are expected to be familiar, but it is hoped that it will also provide a useful introduction to the practice of public relations for a wider range of readers, including those pursuing courses in communications, marketing and other business studies.

Public relations has to keep pace with the changes in the world in which it operates and with the problems of the organizations it serves. But though the problems may change, the principles which the authors set out will remain valid.

I should like to record my debt to a team of busy practitioners, each of them an expert in the area he or she has covered, for the time and trouble they have taken to help construct this compendium. The leaders of the profession have for many years been generous in the time they have given to the instruction of their successors and these pages provide yet another example of that tradition. 'Let such teach others who themselves excel.'

This second edition incorporates essential up-dating, but has not changed the basic approach of the original text.

W.P.H.

v

Contents

hand-prepared artwork. Three-dimensional media: signs, displays, models. Composite media: special events, press conferences, sales presentations, facility visits, exhibitions, export promotions. Sponsorship. Educational activities. Acknowledgements.

and TV, information services, publications and graphic design, visits and visitors, finances

List of Illustrations

Biographical Notes

PHILIP BARRON, MIPR started his career in advertising, but has been involved in journalism and public relations for over twenty years. Since heading Oxfam's PR operation for several years in the early 1960s, he has paid special attention to the promotional problems of charities and currently advises a number of voluntary agencies. He is a member of the Institute of Public Relations and a past chairman of the Voluntary Movement Group. Aged forty-nine, Mr Barron is married and has two teenage daughters. He is a member of the Society of Friends (Quakers).

PAT BOWMAN, FIPR, MAIE entered public relations after thirteen years as a journalist, becoming public relations officer and editor to the Industrial Society in 1957. After two years there, two years as press relations officer to Bowaters and eleven years as press and public relations officer to British Aluminium, he was appointed head of public relations to Lloyds Bank in 1972. He has been Chairman of the Press and Public Relations Branch of the NUJ, a member of the board of examiners and of the professional practices committee of the IPR and a committee member of the City and Financial Group of the IPR. He was joint editor (with Nigel Ellis) of the *Handbook of Public Relations* (Harrap, 1963) and joint author (with Nigel Ellis) of the *Manual of Public Relations* (Heinemann, 1969, revised 1977). Aged fifty-six, he is married with two sons and two daughters.

JOHN COLE-MORGAN, B.Sc (Agric.), DIP.CAM, FIPR graduated in agriculture from the University of Reading in 1960 and after a year as a farm manager in the North of England joined the Public Relations Department of the Animal Foods Division of Spillers Ltd. Specializing in agricultural public relations, he subsequently worked for the Agricultural Engineers' Association, Astral

Public Relations as agricultural account manager and Fisons before entering Government service as Head of Information of the Agricultural Research Council in 1971. In 1975 he went, on promotion, to the Department of Trade as Head of Publicity for the British Overseas Trade Board and in 1979 became Deputy Head of Information for the Department. He has been a member of Council of IPR and Chairman and Vice-Chairman of its Education Committee. From 1981 to 1984 he was Director of Public Relations to the British Council. In 1984 he became a director of Bloy Eldridge Ltd., communications consultants.

KENNETH J. COOK, Dip.CAM, FIPR is a former Chairman of the Professional Practices Committee of the Institute of Public Relations. He was first elected to the Council of the Institute in 1969 and served for seven years. He was elected a Fellow in 1975 and for a second term on Council in 1978. He holds the CAM Diploma in Public Relations and has acted as an examiner for the diploma. After national service with the RAF he began his career in the advertisement department of BBC Publications and moved to BEA Public Relations in 1960. He became a member of the department's management team in 1969 and joined British Airways Public Relations as Chief of Information Services in 1973. He is now a senior member of the Public Affairs department. He is a past Chairman of the Airline Public Relations Officers Organisation. He is married with two sons.

JAMES PARKYNS DERRIMAN Dip.CAM, FIPR, Barrister, retired in 1982 as Secretary and Group Personnel Director of Charles Barker ABH International Limited. Following war service with the Merchant Navy, he was a journalist for ten years with the *Daily Herald*, Reuters, and the *News Chronicle*. He entered public relations in 1955 while working for J. Walter Thompson and subsequently joined Charles Barker in 1962 to form the public relations business now carried on by Charles Barker City Ltd. He was the President of the Institute of Public Relations 1973–74 and President's Medallist of the IPR in 1978. He is an Honorary Vice-President of CERP, the European Confederation of Public Relations, and a past President of CEDAN (the federal committee of European national associations for the public relations profession within CERP). He is also author of *Pageantry of the Law* (1955), *Discovering the Law* (1962), *Public Relations in Business Management* (1964), *Company-Investor Relations* (1969) and joint editor (with George Pulay, MIPR) of *The Bridge Builders* (1979).

WILFRED HOWARD, MA, MCAM, FIPR was educated at the City of London School and at Exeter College, Oxford, where he read honour classical Moderations and Greats. During the war he was commissioned into the King's Royal Rifle Corps (60th Rifles), was wounded in Italy and then served as a staff instructor at the Royal Military College, Camberley, and on the staff in

Burma. After management training with Bakelite Limited he was that company's press officer from 1949 to 1951 when he left to become deputy to the Chief Press Officer of GEC. He joined Turner & Newall in 1956, when he was appointed Publicity Manager of Ferodo, a T&N subsidiary. In 1961 he was asked to set up a Public Relations Department at Turner & Newall itself, and had managed it until his retirement in 1982. Turner & Newall makes a wide range of industrial materials and components. In the IPR he was a Council Member from 1967–76 and President in 1974–5. He was awarded the President's Medal in 1971. He is a member of the CAM Society, and was a Governor of CAM from 1972 to 1974 and again from 1978 to 1980. Other activities have included Chairmanship of the NW Publication Committee (1964–5), PRO to 'Operation Springclean' (Civic Trust for NW), Council Member of Buxton & District Civic Association, Chairman of Buxton's 'Save the Woodlands' Fund, Chairman of Buxton Playhouse Supporters' Club 1963–4, Buxton Parochial Church Council 1959–1972, Chairman of Buxton Parish Christian Stewardship Campaign 1960–61, Secretary of Buxton and District Christian Aid Committee 1958–74 and currently Chairman, Buxton Musical Society.

HENRY L. JAMES, CB, F.CAM. FIPR, FRSA, during forty years in the Government Information Service has been press and public relations adviser to four prime ministers and was seconded to the Rt. Hon. Margaret Thatcher, MP, for the initial six months of her Administration. On leaving the public service he joined Vickers Limited as Public Relations consultant and is now Director-General of the National Association of Pension Funds. He was Deputy Chairman of CAM from May 1979 and President of the Institute of Public Relations in 1979. He became a Member of the Council of the RSPCA in 1980. He was awarded the President's Medal of the Institute of Public Relations in 1976 and was Alumni Guest Lecturer, Gustavus Adolphus College, Minnesota in 1977.

FRANK JEFKINS BSc(ECON), BA (HONS), MCAM, FIPR, MInstM, MAIE has probably written more books on communication subjects than any other writer in the English language. For five years he was Rentokil's PRO, then managed Scientific Public Relations. He has run his own School of Public Relations since 1968, and in addition to running courses in the UK, has taken courses to Belgium, Egypt, Kenya, Ghana, Holland, Indonesia, Malaysia, Nigeria, Singapore, South Africa, Sweden, Trinidad, Zambia and Zimbabwe. The first person to gain the CAM Diploma in Public Relations, he was also the first to hold CAM Diplomas in both Public Relations and Advertising. He holds honours degrees from London and the Open Universities. His Fellowship of the Institute of Public Relations was awarded in recognition of his 'educational services, especially overseas'. He serves on the IPR Council, and has served on the Membership, Professional Practices, International and Education Committees. He is married and his son and daughter are both graduates.

GRAHAM KEMP, MIPR is chairman of KMS Partnership Ltd, a Windsor-based group specializing in marketing and employee communications, research, contract publishing, conference management and publicity. He was, for twelve years, head of public affairs at Birds Eye, where he introduced in 1970 the first really open newspaper published by private industry in Britain. He also played a large part in that company's development of consultative councils. He is the author of *The Company Speaks* and *British Eating Out*; he was an industrial editor in his twenties and has devoted a considerable amount of time during the past few years to the problems of employee communication.

GEOFFREY LEWIS, FIPR began working life as an apprentice journalist on a London suburban weekly newspaper. After war service he returned to journalism and worked for the *Daily Mail*, the *Evening Standard*, the *Sunday Express* and the *Woman's Mirror*, and was a regular contributor to a programme on the BBC overseas service. In 1961 he became Press Officer for the Institute of Practitioners in Advertising and joined the London County Council three years later as Chief Press Officer, transferring to the Greater London Council on its inception in 1964. When he retired from the GLC in 1982, he was its Director of Public Relations. Mr Lewis is a Past President of the Institute of Public Relations, a past Chairman of its Local Government Group and a founder Member and Past President of the London Government Public Relations Association. He has lectured extensively on local government public relations and has written a book on the subject.

DAVID MORGAN REES MA, LLB (CANTAB), MIPR, DIPCAM was born in South Wales in 1930, but is a Yorkshireman by adoption since 1965 when he joined Bridon Limited, wire, wire rope and cordage manufacturers, as Group Information Manager. Based at the Group's headquarters in Doncaster, he is responsible for corporate public relations and for running an information service to employees in this country and overseas, as well as advising on management communication problems. Before his present position he was Joint Managing Director of a small family business in South Wales with a particular interest in export. With a legal training at Cambridge, he has also studied at the Harvard School of Business Administration. He was High Sheriff of Breconshire (now Powys) in 1963. He has written and broadcast on a variety of topics.

MICHAEL MORLEY, DIP.CAM, MIPR started his career in local newspaper journalism after National Service (officer, Royal Artillery). He joined W. H. Smith & Son Ltd. (Publications Department) and later became an editor of a group of magazines at Maclaren's, the trade and technical journal publishers. In 1959 he joined Harris & Hunter Ltd, the leading PR consultancy, and a year later was elected to the Board. While at H&H he planned, controlled and implemented PR programmes for several leading international companies, among them Aspro-Nicholas, Dornay Foods, Warner-Lambert, Libby's, Fisons Pharmaceuticals and Cheesebrough-Pond's. He left Harris & Hunter in 1967 to start Daniel J Edelman Limited in the UK and to develop DJE's capability in Europe. He is a past Chairman of the Member Services Committee, the Education and Training Committee and a past member of the Board of the Public Relations Consultants Association, and is a graduate holding the Public Relations Diploma of the Communications Advertising and Marketing Education Foundation. In 1978 he was created Knight First Class, Order of the Lion by the President of Finland in recognition of ten years' service on behalf of the Finnfacts Institute. He is married with three children. His special interests include honorary activities for GAP, an organization which arranges jobs in foreign countries for students in their 'gap' year between school and university.

WARREN NEWMAN, DIP.CAM, MIPR entered public relations via industrial journalism as a reporter/photographer with the John Lewis Partnership. He then went into local newspapers and edited the South Londoner series. He has spent the rest of his career in public relations with London Boroughs. He headed the PR unit at Hounslow Council before joining his present authority, Southwark, in 1978. He has been Chairman of the Institute of Public Relations Education and Public Relations Committees. He is a guest lecturer on PR for Non–Commercial Organisations at the College for the Distributive Trades. He has a CAM Diploma in Public Relations and the Diploma of the British Association of Industrial Editors. Warren is married with two children. His special leisure interests are photography and personal computing. With his wife, Avril, he is developing a range of educational software for young children.

RAY PALIN, MA, MCAM was educated at Oxford University (Honours Degree in Applied Mathematics with Electricity). He joined Armstrong Siddeley Motors Limited as Control Systems Engineer in 1956 and in 1958 was commissioned as Air Electronics Officer in the Royal Air Force. From 1962 to 1964 he was a PR Account Executive with Roles and Parker Limited, working on Components and Dynamics Groups, Plessey Company Limited. For three years after that he was Publicity Officer with English Electric Company Limited, then in 1968 he was appointed Deputy Publicity Manager,

Engineering Division, Tube Investments Limited. In 1970 he joined Marsteller Limited as Senior Account Executive and was promoted to Account Director in 1973. He returned to public relations in 1976 as Director, Burson-Marsteller Limited.

BRIDGETT SHEARER at the time of writing was an associate director of Charles Barker, Watney & Powell, part of the Charles Barker Lyons public relations company specializing in parliamentary affairs. She was born in 1950 and educated at Wimbledon High School, Benenden, and Bristol University, where she got a Combined Honours degree in Politics, French and German. She attributes her initial interest in politics to her family and particularly to her late cousin and godmother, Betty Harvie Anderson, the first woman Deputy Speaker. After university she spent two years working in the European Department of a firm of stockbrokers and then joined Charles Barker immediately after the October 1974 Election to work under Conrad Voss Bark, the former BBC parliamentary correspondent. Then just three people, the parliamentary side of Charles Barker now numbers fifteen, covering both Westminster and Europe for over one hundred clients. Whilst following many subjects for her clients she has developed a particular interest in legislation affecting food manufacturing companies and the horseracing industry. In 1981 she married Dennis Walters, Conservative MP for Westbury, and is now a consultant to Charles Barker, Watney & Powell.

DAVID WOOD, MIPR, MIPRA was educated in Yorkshire and joined *The Yorkshire Post* in Leeds following National Service with the Royal Air Force. He later joined the Diamond Corporation's Information Department in London after which he spent three years as a freelance feature writer for UK and foreign publications. He joined Pilkington in 1963 as a Press Officer and later became Chief Press Officer. He joined the company's advertising department on a special assignment before being appointed Group Public Relations Co-ordinator in 1971. He was additionally appointed Group Publicity Co-ordinator in 1978 with specific responsibility for corporate advertising. As well as co-ordinating the Pilkington Group's world-wide public relations activities, David Wood is responsible for the Group's Exhibitions and Photographic Departments, the Pilkington Glass Museum and the Theatre Royal, St. Helens — the only commercial theatre in Britain owned and operated by a manufacturing company. He is a member of the Council of the Merseyside Chambers of Commerce and Chairman of the St. Helens Chamber of Industry, Trade and Commerce and has been a member of the committee of the IPR's City and Financial Group.

Introduction

The Plight of the Pianist

Henry L. James, CB

It is a common habit of mind, having announced the intention, to assume the deed. How often do we hear a proud fanfare of achievement immediately after the Queen's Speech with a whole session of Parliament to come before enactment, and executive interpretation?

It is a form of self-delusion not confined to politicians. All of us are guilty of it from time to time; and it is a frequent cause of the credibility gap of which politicians and leaders in other fields complain. The root cause is a contradiction of time-scales. For each institution has its own discipline. Central government, local government, industry, unions, pressure groups, the media — all are working under different constraints and to different deadlines. Failure to appreciate this, or at any rate to make adjustments for it, frequently leads to misunderstanding or incomprehension.

Those of us in the middle of the communications chain are familiar with the problem. We know, too, the professional dangers — especially the temptation to shoot the pianist. Indeed in the communications business, as in politics, the execution of the pianist is part of the ritual of failure. In soccer, it is the manager. In the media, the editor. In any other case it is the hapless public relations officer, press officer or adviser.

We all believe in communications. We keep saying so. We also say that any management which endorses good communications — in-house and externally — is enlightened. Why anyone should be regarded as enlightened in simply propagating and explaining their own policy or point of view escapes me. It must be pointless to work in the dark, or, pursuing a relentless *cliché*-ridden train of thought, to hide your light under a bushel. Which is where *we* come in, professionally.

But we must come in at the beginning. It is simpler, cleaner, more efficient and more credible to get the story right from the outset. It is much more difficult to try to get it changed after it has been misrepresented and the myth created. It is often said that there is nothing more *passé* than yesterday's headlines; that yesterday's paper is good only for fish and chips. This is the untruest *cliché* of all. The fact is that there is nothing more durable than yesterday's cuttings. The yellower they get, the more hallowed they become. And the more authoritative.

That is the evidence of history. What did Nelson say to Hardy? A good PRO would have got it right; and a lot of harmless fun would have been lost. Who was the dark lady of the sonnets? Good unattributable briefing at the time would have destroyed a wealth of scholarship. Our world of instant communication does not make for instant understanding. The science of words is not an exact science. Those in the communications business tend to be bad communicators. We have to remind ourselves of this daily.

If the Press get it wrong, and they often do, we have to ask why. And we should not shoot the pianist without trial. Look to the composer or even the piano tuner. Unless the pianist knows the score, the score is musically sound and the piano in tune, the result must be discord. To confuse the metaphor, unless the communicator is an integrated part of the policy-making machine — unless indeed a communicator has properly assigned responsibilities — the audience will not catch the tune. 'I shot an arrow into the air; it fell to earth I know not where' illustrates what all too often masquerades as an information policy.

Government on the whole has learned this lesson — though not necessarily the politicians themselves. There is often a statutory obligation on governments and government departments to explain in unequivocal terms the impact of policy and the creation of new rights and new responsibilities. Every government assuming office declares its belief in open government, whatever that may mean. Successive governments have tried to off-load their responsibilities by stressing the responsibilities of the media. But the media in principle and practice accept only an intellectual responsibility for seeking and publishing the truth: though even that might be seen sometimes as a doubtful premise.

It follows that there is a natural instinct to protect the decision-making process. I respect this. No cook likes to take the cake out of the oven too soon or too often; with light concoctions the result can be disastrous. Ministers can reasonably claim their right to change their minds in private. But when the ultimate defence is that the Press got it wrong, the case is lost.

We have seen in the Swinging 'Sixties and the Shifting 'Seventies the denigration of authority. The process has been accelerated in public life by major and much publicised misdemeanours or, in the current jargon, cover-ups. In most of these cases there has been a superfluity of contradictory advice from numerous, frequently undisciplined and less than well-informed sources. The critic or commentator, of course, needs more than one source of information; this provides a perspective. But if he is prepared to accept guidance only at the lowest intellectual level, the outcome is likely to be disastrous. We may frequently complain that the media is prepared to pay undue attention to guidance at that level and that this is professionally intellectually dishonest. But before we have justice on our side we should be able to show that guidance was available at a higher or appropriate level. And this is not always so.

The captain of the ship is ultimately responsible for that ship. But particularly with modern technology, the line of command may be so impersonal as to threaten morale. The analogy extends to industry where the gap between board room and shop floor has widened over the years.

Multi-disciplinary, multi-national companies suffer most. The romantic vision of the works manager who knows everyone on the shop floor from foreman to floor-sweeper by his Christian name and joins them for darts at the local is probably so romantic as to be fictional. But the vision of efficient, cost-effective, instant communication through line management by every modern device from Tannoy to television, is equally fictional. The reality lies somewhere between the two.

It is probably true that nowadays we face the greatest threat to industrial democracy. The company which berates the government of the day for secrecy is probably most guilty of the same offence. Indeed the word 'secret' has become a term of opprobrium. If there is a right to know, there is also a right to confidentiality. The main discretion left in terms of open government and open management is the timing of publication — and the method. It is here that professional advice is most needed, which brings us back to the pianist. Unless he knows the composer's intention, the range of his instrument, and the intellectual level of his audience, he is lost. The good impresario chooses the pianist with all these in mind.

The analogy now ends; and we get down to defining lines of communication and of responsibility. *The Observer* once recorded, after my briefing — extensively and explicitly — on behalf of a prime minister, that they wanted the organ-grinder, not the monkey. *The Times* will not publish a letter signed by a public relations officer or adviser. Thirty-two years of government information services have not established credibility. The reason for that lack of credibility is frequently because the media are not satisfied that the spokesman is sufficiently part of the policy-making machine to be wholly acceptable or believable.

In that statement there should be seen no criticism, real or implied, of the public relations consultant whose value is that he provides the objective external view with clear terms of reference as devil's advocate. His professional role is clear and he brings with him the extra dimension of access to worlds not normally part of the conscious public of the employer. But the voice of the company can carry weight only if the adviser is an integrated part of the management team and is seen to be so. And he will sustain authority if it can be shown that he has played a part in policy formation.

The consequences of instant policy are that the adviser or spokesman becomes fully occupied in what can only be called *post eventum* rationalization. In fact he becomes merely an interpreter. Those organizations which work on the basis of 'need to know' present the public relations man with a rigid case. The concealment of formal policy from him until the last moment will limit his effectiveness. Only in listening to, and contributing to, the cut and thrust of policy formulation can a perspective be gained and the strengths — and weaknesses — of the case be identified. At that stage the man in the front line — Bernard Braden's Arnold Spokesman — is on his own: constant reference back dissipates the confidence he is trying to create. If we are to have faith in management, it must be assumed that management at any rate tries to foresee all eventualities. Government without contingency plans is non-government. The management that does not study the permutations and combinations of probable public response is unworldly. Reference back invites the supposition of uncertainty.

The public relations man is not just an image-creator, despite popular belief. Images evolve and public relations men find it easier to take advantage of them than to create them. The public relations man is not a social secretary to the chairman; he is the *alter ego* of the company. The image depends on the performance of the company as a whole. In turn, performance is affected by *amour-propre* and *amour-propre* is sustained through knowledge.

It is valid to argue that each individual member of the company contributes by his own attitude not only to the performance of the company, but also to its image. Which is why internal communications are so important. British management over the last decade has failed in its frequent abdication from that responsibility. It would be interesting to enquire in any company — and it has been done — from what source the individual employee gets information about changes of policy or about the happenings within the company. Is it through line management, through gossip, through unions, through foremen, through house magazines, through broad sheets, through direct mail? And which would he prefer?

Experience shows that management, in seeking the goodwill and co-operation of the unions, has tended to use *them* as channels of information on what are more properly management themes. This process undermines the position of the line manager. Most people want to hear through management about policies which will affect themselves — not necessarily from the managing director or the chairman, but from their immediate superior. Unfortunately there is some evidence that this line of communication is no better than, and frequently not so good as, the line of communication through the union hierarchy. Small wonder, in these circumstances, that there has been a shift in the balance of power.

Public relations is an intellectual exercise, but one of surprising simplicity and common sense. It is to tell a story in such a way that the listener, viewer or reader understands it within his own terms of reference.

Patience is called for. Teaching by rote did, after all, produce children who could be regarded basically as literate or numerate, or sometimes both. Repetition is valuable, but you do need to choose the right language for the audience, to get the score right. We are back to my initial metaphor: don't shoot the pianist — play it again, Sam.

1

Operational PR

Ray Palin

A truly original public relations idea, like a footballer whose talent changes the course of an entire tournament, arises but rarely. Success in planning and implementing a PR campaign is more likely to spring from logical thought, meticulous attention to detail and the sound application of time-tested methods, than from any sudden breakthrough or gimmick. In other words, hard work gets results. Genius in public relations is undoubtedly 'an infinite capacity for taking pains'. How true that is we shall see in this chapter which discusses how a public relations campaign is planned and executed. The first step is to set down what it is we are hoping to achieve, how we are hoping to achieve it, over what period the work is to be done and how much it is expected to cost. A typewritten 'plan', simply and clearly drafted by the public relations staff or consultancy, is the normal way of presenting this information.

A written plan is fundamental because there are normally many people involved in the approval and implementation of a PR plan and they must all be carried along. In complex business situations which are the norm, the plan will be broken down into a number of sections or 'sub-plans' which list and describe the individual actions or events (such as new product launches or press briefings) which will make up the public relations programme for a given period, normally twelve months.

A public relations plan can be compared to, and is most often developed in parallel with, other plans such as those concerned with marketing and advertising. The precise relationship of public relations with these activities and its developing role in other areas, such as employee communications or investor relations, will depend on circumstances. The modern view is that public relations considerations should be part and parcel of almost every business decision. It will be found, however, that the extent to which this is accepted (and hence planned) varies widely in different organizations and indeed within outwardly similar ones.

1

tering a wider appreciation of these varied aspects of public relations and
as a management function is perhaps one of the most important tasks
facing the profession.

For brevity this chapter takes as its basis public relations in support of
marketing objectives, since this is its most common area of operation. The
business-like approach demanded here will however be a useful pointer to
good practice in others. In what follows, each topic is discussed in the same
order that would normally be followed in an actual public relations plan,
beginning with problem analysis.

Problem analysis

Every well-planned public relations programme must begin by asking the
simple question, why? What do you want your improved communications or
public relations to achieve? Is there an obvious problem or specific marketing
objective to take as our starting point? If there isn't, we must delve deeper.
Lacking a specific task, we shall be either wasting money outright or at best
guilty of using the powerful weapon of public relations at random, hoping that
we may hit the target in the course of scattered fire.

Sometimes the objective will be stated, but in general terms. One hears that
PR is to build goodwill, improve an image, or — vaguest of all — sell more
products. Of course, the great majority of organizations desire these ends: but
we must probe more carefully before we can begin to detail our plan.

A professional method of eliciting the kind of information we need is by
carrying out a 'communications audit'. This can be quite short, or long and
complex involving many individual interviews, depending on circumstances.
In its simplest form, the audit compares the impressions and experience of
users or prospective users of a product or service with that of those who are
providing that product and who are seeking public relations help.

As a shorthand method of sampling opinion without the expense of a great
number of interviews, journalists' or other opinion leaders' views can be
sought on the reasonable assumption that they will form a guide to public
opinion.

Most often, what is called a communications 'gap' is uncovered. For
example, a product may be thought expensive because its true value is not
appreciated. The proper use of a new offering may not be understood as well as
its manufacturer would like; or an alternative may be preferred because of
some factor like size, design or availability, the importance of which has not
been appreciated. Reconciling these differing attitudes then becomes the
thrust of the PR programme.

A more complex audit will involve interviews with various levels of
management concerned with a spread of activities and locations. Again these

findings are contrasted with the opinions held about the organization by important target audiences — which could extend to business partners such as independent distributors, retailers and suppliers and to shareholders, trade union leaders, the local community and so on.

On completion of the questioning, the public relations team is able to analyse the communications needs of an organization and prepare a comprehensive programme to deal with the problems thrown up.

It should be noted that a communications audit as described does not, and is not intended to, constitute a formal piece of market research which quantifies precisely market shares or the percentage of respondents holding a particular view. The audit may, however, point up areas where, from a marketing standpoint, for example, knowledge is insufficient and there is a need for research. If so, the public relations team should be involved in planning the research and developing the questionnaire to ensure that PR needs are also met.

What we are concerned with in formulating our public relations programme, in a nutshell, is finding out people's attitudes towards a product or company; and then in devising a programme of communication which will seek to modify those attitudes in such a way as to create understanding and win preference.

Objectives

It is sometimes said that if the objectives are defined clearly enough, the problem solves itself. While not strictly true in public relations planning, which requires strategy, targeting and methods, we can learn something from this adage. A well-defined objective or set of objectives makes obvious precisely what needs to be done and thus leaves a clear bridge for moving on to targets and methods. Equally, on completion of the project, or the year's activity, a carefully set objective provides a benchmark for measuring what we have achieved.

In setting objectives, try to keep the following in mind:

1 Make the objectives measurable. Pompous, inflated objectives can be spotted and removed even by the relatively inexperienced eye, but it takes a little more experience to put together measurable objectives. 'To increase awareness' is a flabby objective. Give it some muscle by adding more facts. Of what, by whom? (See how you are led right into your targets.) And watch out for the objective that is not an objective at all. Staging a press briefing is not an objective — it is one of the many tools that could be used to help meet an objective.

2 Make the objectives realistic and pertinent to the activity. While no one

would advocate narrow, arcane goals of interest only to those in public relations, it needs to be said that a communications plan requires objectives of a communications nature. Thus do not, in a limited PR programme dealing with a national brand, set as an objective to increase sales of that brand. Except in a few odd cases, there would be no direct correlation between sales and the attainment of PR objectives. Bringing a certain message to x number of people of a certain type in a certain area is more to the point.

3 At the same time, the communications goals must clearly and absolutely contribute to overall business objectives. Simply generating publicity may not help the company's business goals. As public relations matures, it is having to take a wider view of its activities than ever before and practitioners who are promotional technicians rather than business strategists will be left by the wayside.

4 Make the goals attainable. Do not try to influence all men earning over £10,000 with a £500 budget and a series of news releases, even if the writing does sparkle. This type of thinking is especially necessary in an environment that is unfamiliar with the workings of PR. If you set an objective that is unattainable, you will be seen to fail by others even if you have done a superb job.

Targets

The process of public relations has sometimes been likened to throwing a dart at a wall and then drawing a target around it. However successful may be the end result, this technique does not go down very well in business-like public relations practice.

It should be evident that targeting a PR programme is crucial. After deciding in the 'objectives' section what to say, and before deciding in the 'methods' section how to say it, the missing link is targeting: to whom and through whom to send the message. As most communications are not direct to the target audience, we must also give equally serious consideration to what are called 'communications targets' — the channels which link the source of the information to its ultimate end-user or 'audience'.

Communications targets include the Press, television, radio and magazines. They may include conference organizers that are of interest to the target audience. They may also include opinion leaders, who will pass the message on to the target audience. But for most intents and purposes, communications targets are those in the communications industry who will carry a suitable message to the target audience.

The target audience for the message itself may be more obvious, or certainly built into the equations you are given. This is often the case in marketing. 'Our product is designed to appeal to all AB businessmen', or 'Our product is designed for women 35-45 living in the Midlands'. Again the more specific the definition of the target, the more obvious it will be how to reach them. Where do they live? What are their habits? How much do they earn? What makes them different? What publications do they read and respect? What do they do with their free time?

Once these questions are laid down and answered, the communications targets should become more apparent. There will necessarily be other considerations, such as the likely frame of mind the target will be in when the message is received, but these can be considered only once an analysis of targets has been made. Perhaps the biggest trap in public relations work is to get so immersed in throwing the darts that you forget the target you are aiming at.

Programme planning

Having clarified what we want to achieve, we must now turn to the second of the questions listed in the introduction: how are we going to achieve it? In deciding on the methods we plan to use, it will help to divide public relations activity into twelve basic channels of communication. They are:

1 The Press:
   (a) Trade journals and magazines.
   (b) Consumer, national, regional and local newspapers and magazines.
   (c) House journals.
   (d) Club, society and institution magazines.
2 Radio and television.
3 Demonstrations:
   (a) In stores.
   (b) In homes.
   (c) At exhibitions.
   (d) At clubs, societies or public meetings.
4 Sponsorships in sport, the arts or publishing (books, audio-visual and other media).
5 Activities directed at educational establishments.
6 Exhibitions.
7 Lecture panels.
8 Information services.
9 Print and corporate design.
10 Promotions.
11 National and regional competitions.
12 Direct mail.

These channels enable us to transmit the message from the 'source' to the 'receiver', to use terms from communications theory. In some cases, note that communication is direct; in others, it is via a third party, for example an opinion leader or journalist. It is this fact that provides us with one of the principal advantages of public relations, the familiar 'third party endorsement' which substantially enhances the credibility of the message in the mind of the receiver. It is more believable when someone else talks about us and our achievements. If we use the same glowing terms about ourselves (as advertising must do), our action is felt to be predictable and the message to an extent discounted.

A further important point lies in the very existence of multiple channels. Research has shown that a message received independently through a number of channels is more often remembered (and hence acted upon) than one which arrives via a single source. So, it will usually be best to employ as many channels as possible. The skill lies in tailoring the message to the channel.

Planning usually kicks off with an 'ideas' session. Begin by getting clear in your mind the essential pattern that the plan must follow when it is finally assembled: situation, objective, target audience, action.

From this starting point, we must gather the ideas that will form our plan. The important factor here (if you're not one of those rare people to whom ideas just seem to come from nowhere) is not to sit with a blank sheet of paper, but to work at the problem. There are many techniques of idea generation; choose those which you find most productive.

A simple one is to start with the basic media you have at your disposal (print, Press, etc.) and try to think of one idea in each area. It need not be a marvellous idea: the important thing is to keep working towards a target, rather than waiting for that blinding flash that comes so rarely. If there is a team of people, let each think up one idea for each channel and then choose the best. A group, if you can arrange one, will always out-perform individuals working alone because there develops a kind of 'momentum' in which one idea builds on another.

It will help considerably if you are familiar with the principles of lateral thinking (Edward de Bono has written a number of books which you ought to read). The basic idea of lateral thinking is to 'jump' to a new idea and then to try to justify it, rather than going forward step by step as we do in traditional thinking.

To make the unpredictable jump that can begin the birth process of a workable PR action, try one of the following lateral thinking methods:

1 Look at a quota of alternatives. Give yourself a target number of ideas and suspend judgement on any one of them until it is complete. This is really an extension of our first simple method.

2 Use random stimulation. If you are up against a tricky problem, go and talk to people working in entirely different fields, take in an exhibition which has nothing to do with the subject or simply walk down a busy shopping street. The parade of things that catch your attention may spark off a useful thought. (It is well worthwhile keeping an ideas file for just this purpose.)
3 Play with the key words. One needs something to be getting on with while helping the 'big idea' to come. So write down the objective and try to divide it up word by word, and then each word into its component ideas. Put down the opposite, or reverse it. Remember we're not looking for sense, but for inspiration.

Finally, a simple suggestion that many successful PR people are not too proud to employ. Read and study what other people are doing. Perhaps there's no profession in which successful ideas can be more readily, legitimately and effectively re-applied in other situations.

You can keep in touch through participation in IPR (Institute of Public Relations), PRCA (Public Relations Consultants Association) or CAM events and by dipping into the many books and journals that are published on PR strategy and methods.

Strategy and method

Having arrived at the actions we propose to carry out, we write them down to form the central core of our public relations plan.

A strategy paragraph should first state simply the basic rationale for the method. The strategy is the thread that links the individual actions proposed in the method section and provides the reader with an insight into the planning process which led to the selection of those methods.

Perhaps the hardest part of a plan to conceive and express, it is nevertheless the essential bridge between a statement of the objectives discussed earlier and the means of achieving them through a planned sequence of PR activities. A programme of even quite original ideas will lack cohesion and hence effectiveness, rather like an orchestra of brilliant players without a conductor, if no clear strategy exists.

The method section of the plan, sometimes called the 'action plan', lists the individual elements that will form the programme during the period. The method section should give not only a short description of each type of activity, e.g. writing and distributing releases, producing consumer print, arranging interviews and so on, but also their priority and target number planned over the period.

Of course there will be unforeseen additions and perhaps changes; but that fact does not remove the need to plan rather than to rely on chance.

In the case of a major event, for example a conference or sponsorship, a separate document .or appendix may be necessary to provide the required detail.

Finally, a month-by-month timetable shows at a glance when each activity will occur.

Costing and budgetary control

Before we can expect to get approval for any public relations programme, we must be able to provide an answer to that immediate and important question: how much will it cost?

There are broadly two types of cost which occur in planning and implementing a PR programme. Firstly there is the value of the executive time involved (salary plus overheads) and secondly the expenses which are necessarily incurred. These latter cover payments to suppliers or other third parties.

Public relations executives spend time in planning, writing, making editorial contact, maintaining internal or client liaison and in the implementation of the public relations programme. Depending on the content of the work they are asked to carry out, there may also be significant time involved in special events, conferences, lunches or meetings with advertising agencies, trade associations and others.

Expenses can include a wide range of items such as photography, design, printing, audio-visual production, press-cutting and monitoring services, travel, entertainment, telephone, telex and postage. And it must be remembered that simply because we are in the communications business, the use of such bought-out services is likely to be heavy and continuous.

The method of accounting for public relations costs will differ according to whether the work is carried out externally by a public relations consultancy or internally by staff employed directly by the company or organization on whose behalf the work is being done.

To be profitable a consultant has to maintain a careful record of how his executives' time is spent and time sheets are used for this purpose. These are not usually employed in-house; instead, staff are simply assigned to areas of responsibility or specific projects.

It is also important, in consultancy and in-house work equally, to track expenses on each project. This can conveniently be done on a budget control sheet which lists the expected costs, printing estimates and so on, associated with each part of the programme. By this means the sum remaining from the original allocation is always accurately known, so that action in curtailing the programme or obtaining permission in advance for an overspend may be taken before it is too late.

Public relations as a management tool will be successful to the degree that it is seen to be run on a business-like basis. The last thing that senior management likes are surprises, and so the importance of accurate and realistic costing and strict budgetary control in public relations cannot be overestimated.

Make sure you request sufficient budget to carry out the plan effectively. Nothing is more wasteful than too many activities spread too thinly. If good results are not obtained, it will be too late to request a budget increase. And however successful we are, the gilt is off the gingerbread if costs get out of hand.

Case presentation

Whenever possible, the opportunity should be taken of presenting a completed PR plan personally to those who must approve it. The reason for this is that a meeting will enable you to explain it to management in a way that is far more effective than a written document can ever be — even assuming it gets read at all closely, which may not always be the case.

If the contribution of PR is to be better understood and receive the management's attention and hence the budget it deserves, a face-to-face presentation will also be invaluable in discussing any questions which may arise and in helping to deal with lingering unfavourable attitudes towards PR that may exist, perhaps as a result of experience elsewhere.

If it is a small meeting, you may decide simply to 'talk through' the plan, having provided an advance copy. If it is a larger meeting, the presentation is a long one or it has to be repeated a number of times, it will probably be worthwhile to consider some sort of visual aid.

Simple, handwritten flipcharts can be used to highlight the key points in the plan, to provide a visual focal point during the meeting and to reinforce what is being said.

Boards or overhead projectors are also commonly employed, particularly where complex charts or visuals form an essential part of the plan.

In consultancy presentations slides are very often the chosen medium and — done well — they can be extremely effective, though somewhat more costly than the other media. A darkened room can however be a disadvantage in that the opportunity to maintain eye contact with the audience may be lost.

A common fault in slidemaking is to display long passages of text, while simply reading them out or, worse still, saying something other than what is on the screen. This adds nothing to comprehension of the plan.

Exactly the same guidelines should apply to the use of visual aids in presenting a PR programme to management as in the case of audio-visual productions designed for external audiences.

But whatever is decided upon in the way of aids, remember one old but valuable maxim: content is more important than format.

Finally, always rehearse and rehearse again. Justice will not be done to a good plan if you are not confident, well-drilled and completely *au fait* with your material.

Execution

With our plan costed and approved, we are ready to put it into operation. A consultant will assign the work to one or more account executives, each of whom takes day-to-day responsibility for the implementation of the programme. Titles vary, but he or she will probably report to an account director or manager, while in a big agency there will also be a board director who is ultimately responsible to the client for the satisfactory progress of the work. In a small agency this will generally be the managing director.

Well-trained, able secretaries can undertake a good deal of the time-consuming, detailed work upon which a successful programme depends. There will be agendas to prepare, meetings to arrange, minutes to be taken, estimates to be obtained from suppliers and follow-up telephone calls made to journalists or clients. The brightest of these girls often become first-class account executives after a period of operating experience and successful examination results.

In-house PR departments, while they differ from consultancies, generally recognise the same three broad areas of responsibility. There will probably be a press officer or officers, aided by assistants or secretaries, who report to a public relations manager or chief press officer.

As before, the third tier — overall direction of the PR effort — will usually be the responsibility of a board director. Titles such as director of communications, director of public affairs or publicity director will be encountered as well as the more usual director of public relations. Where the PR department is concerned only with product PR it often reports to the marketing or sales director. This method, though still quite common, has the disadvantage that it does not readily allow public relations to contribute as it should in areas outside marketing communications.

The PR team should meet regularly so that the progress of the work can be discussed and any unforeseen problems dealt with. The best work is almost always the result of a team effort where the skills and experience of each member are welded together to contribute to a smooth-running, efficient and carefully directed operation.

It is common practice to compile check lists for often-recurring circumstances in PR work. Such lists can be developed in-house or culled from outside sources, such as text books or articles. They are great time-savers and, by ensuring that no detail is overlooked, can often mean the success of a project that might otherwise be 'hit or miss'. There is no need to reinvent the wheel on every occasion after all, and by using such lists, much collective experience can be harnessed to such tasks as planning an exhibition or organizing a press conference.

Despite the most careful planning, there will inevitably arise unforeseen situations in which action needs to be taken: either reactive, to deal with a disaster, emergency or other unexpected event; or positive, to capitalize upon a PR opportunity that suddenly presents itself. The team therefore needs to be able to meet or to get in touch with each other at short notice, even at unexpected times. Home telephone numbers are an essential part of the agency or staff PR team's internal communications.

By its very nature, public relations generates a good deal of paper work. It is also labour intensive and subject to more than average peak workloads at times of special events or unexpected happenings. It is therefore important that modern office equipment is available to reduce effort and maximize efficiency. This should certainly include adequate telephone and telex facilities, copying machinery and generous filing space. For monitoring purposes access should be available to radio and television receivers — the latter equipped to receive the newly developing teletext information services.

Dictating and recording equipment, telecopier, slide viewing and storage equipment, addressing and duplicating machinery for release production are also usually provided in a large PR department or consultancy. Type composing and offset printing machinery are useful and TV camera and video recorder find a place in the comprehensively equipped organization.

Storage typewriters or, increasingly, modern screen-based word processing systems are capable of very greatly improving typing productivity and have particular importance in PR work, making it easy to personalize letters, prepare releases in many different versions, store copy and organize mailing lists.

Public relations people need frequent recourse to outside services or other departments whose work is necessary to the programme. Working under the direction of the PR team, and at times forming an integral part of it, specialists such as designers, photographers, film and audio-visual producers, freelance writers and researchers will require careful briefing (and some appreciation of their work) if they are to give of their best. Considerable skills are needed by the PR practitioner to select, monitor and judge the work of such specialists.

Where outside services are used, it will be found best to choose a relatively small number of firms who can be given significant amounts of work. Every PR man or woman builds up a list of such specialists whose work they have learned to rely upon.

Reporting

In addition to the simple 'contact report' which serves to record major decisions and summarize important conversations, it is normal practice to produce at regular intervals a public relations progress report. Depending on the intensity of the work, this can be done monthly or less often, say quarterly as a minimum — but though it may sometimes seem a chore it is not one to neglect. It will pay dividends to maintain a business-like standard of reporting in an area which is thought by some to be undisciplined. We shall succeed the better if we document our actions to no less a standard than in other professions.

The progress report should be a simply worded narrative and since it is intended to be read by general management, assume neither a knowledge of PR jargon, nor of previous reports. Each one should stand alone, as should each item in the report.

A satisfactory format, which can be adapted as necessary to meet individual requirements, includes highlights of the month, actions completed, work in progress, future events and recommendations. Although important cuttings will be circulated immediately, it will often be convenient to include with each report a record of press mentions or other results of specific actions in the programme.

Monitoring of competitive activity, issues and outside events affecting the organization is an important public relations function and if not reported on separately should form a section of the monthly report.

A special report is often prepared following a major event such as an exhibition, press conference or VIP visit, so that management can assess the results and examine opportunities for improvements.

Send the report to all those managers who may be concerned with the programme and its results. It is the ambassador for the PR department and its best defence against ill-informed criticism.

Assessment of results

At the end of every year the overall PR programme should be assessed against its objectives. We need to ask, how much of our plan did we complete, what unforeseen events arose, how well did we cope with them and what have we learned that will enable us to improve our programme next year?

Public relations is very much concerned with the achievement of long-term objectives and we need also to consider whether we should not in the light of experience modify or extend those objectives. We must also deal with the often-asked, but seldom answered, question, how effective is our PR programme?

It is usually acknowledged that PR has made a contribution, but how much can only be guessed. This is because our target audience is generally exposed to communications from many sources — advertising, competitive activity and sales calls, for example — and reacts to the cumulative effect of these messages, rather than to any one in isolation.

It is accepted that an editorial or piece of press publicity, coming as it does from a third party, is likely to be more believable and thus many times more effective than, say, an advertisement. But there is no established measure for this improvement in PR effectiveness over advertising.

Sometimes one can calculate how many people in the target group have been reached by a PR action. We can also assess the quality (not just the column inches) of press mentions received over a period compared with a previous period. Computer programmes exist that can provide a measure of this in terms of exposure to specific audiences of specified messages.

Another recommended technique is to repeat at intervals a simple audit among a group of representatives of mass opinion, for example journalists or other opinion leaders. This can be a very useful benchmark in judging the success of our communications programme in changing attitudes to a company, organization or a specific issue — and, insofar as the Press is often our primary communications target, can point to the effectiveness of the work done. Other measures can sometimes be devised and written into the PR plan.

Perhaps no area of PR practice has been given more thought than the question of measuring effectiveness — and a good deal of work is still going on. Though we cannot yet answer the question rigorously, a proper use and appreciation of the importance of research and the need to be both cost-conscious and results-orientated will not be lost on management when budgets are being considered.

For the sceptic, there abound successful PR case-histories that would convince even Scrooge. They are part of our profession — so do not hesitate to make use of them.

2

Types of Media

David Wood

In the context of this chapter the term media can be defined as follows:

> 'Any means through which a message reaches an audience; any combination of such means.'

The Spoken Word

Human speech, allied to gesture, is the most fundamental form of communication. It has a unique facility for emphasis and has never been displaced as the principal weapon of advocacy.

The ability to speak clearly, coherently and convincingly can secure commitment to programmes in which the media available to the communicator can be deployed. It is therefore an essential attribute, yet many people of great ability and with mastery of their subjects suffer a feeling of inadequacy when called upon to express their views verbally.

Public speaking

Few people have inhibitions about talking spontaneously to those they know. They do not begin to feel inadequate until they are cast in a didactic role where there is an expectation on the part of an audience that the speaker will:

1 Convince.
2 Inform.
3 Instruct.
4 Clarify.

Proficiency in public speaking is most likely to be attained through formal training and repeated practice. Training is available through a variety of agencies and through the internal training services of larger companies, although no teacher will promise to produce an accomplished speaker as a result of a short period of intensive training.

All forms of training will emphasize:

1 The importance of continuing practice.
2 The acceptability of notes.
3 The importance of being the master of one's subject.

There are no effortless solutions for those who wish to become competent public speakers. There are, however, two elements which through *practice* can be developed in each of us:

1 Greater fluency.
2 A conviction of self-competence.

Presenting a formal paper is technically more amenable to the disciplines that improve speaking skills than is a less structured meeting where a degree of opportunism must be allied to all other qualities.

A formal paper allows the presenter to draft and refine what he wishes to say before he is required to deliver his speech, and he has a reasonable expectation that he will be allowed to deliver it without interruption.

The structure of a paper — the order in which facts are presented so as to produce a coherent message — will depend upon the nature of the talk and the pace at which a speaker wishes to disclose information to his audience. Ground rules are therefore difficult to define beyond stating that a logical, brick-on-brick structure encourages clarity; and that the number of concepts advanced should be limited so that each can be elaborated sufficiently to make the speaker's views clear.

The old dictum that the speaker should 'say what he is going to say, say it, and say what he has said', remains relevant. The speaker should outline the territory he proposes to cover, cover it in detail, and then summarize the main points of what he has said.

In preparing his speech, the speaker can legitimately use circumlocutions to avoid expressions that inhibit him in impromptu speech. He can practise timing, noting in his text the pauses and emphases that will express his message most clearly. He can then, should he wish, stick to the letter of his script so that his message is delivered in the form that he intended.

This is not generally to be recommended. A preferred alternative is the use of prompt cards on each of which is a single point that requires to be made, perhaps with two or three sub-points if the subject is complex. Successful use of prompt cards requires careful rehearsal so that each prompt calls immediately to mind the arguments that it represents.

A useful means of rehearsing is by use of a cassette recorder. Having recorded the speech it can be played repeatedly at home or in the car. Listening to the tape will reveal whether the speech is clear, concise, and complete.

It will also enable the speaker to assess whether the cadence of his speech could be improved and, by repeated practice and re-recording, the speaker will achieve a familiarity with his text and an improvement in his style. This approach allows the style of the speech to evolve rather than remain frozen in its initial form, so that it emerges as a reflection of the speaker's personality.

Familiarity with the text will enable the speaker to spend most of his time looking at the people to whom he is speaking. It will also allow him to employ those gestures of head and shoulders which we unconsciously use in spontaneous speech, but which the reading of a speech inhibits.

In a formal paper, therefore, fluency can to an adequate extent be ensured through careful preparation.

The second element is a conviction of self-competence. This can only derive through the speaker's familiarity with his subject and the extent to which he is convinced of the legitimacy and relevance of what he has to say. It differs from self-confidence in that it accepts that, while public speaking may cause a sense of unease or alienation, the merits of what the speaker has to say will secure an interested hearing.

Visual aids for the speaker abound and the principal forms are described later in this chapter. Used appropriately, they clarify and reinforce the content of a speech; used indiscriminately they distract audience attention and increase the possibility of the presentation being sabotaged by electrical or mechanical failure.

The speaker should therefore choose carefully and sparingly the visual aids he proposes to use, ensure that they will be compatible with the equipment available at the conference and, if at all possible, rehearse the audio-visual side of his presentation together with those who will be operating the equipment.

Speaking in committee

Less structured meetings, with clients or colleagues, are often less stressful than the public platform if only to the extent that a significant number of those present will be known to each other and all are present to achieve an agreement.

Factors that were considered in discussing the formal speech remain relevant however: written notes can list key points the committee member wishes to make or to have made; and careful preparation for the meeting, including mastery of topics on which the member might be expected to profess a view, should provide an adequate assurance of competence.

The additional factor called for, and one which is unnecessary at a formal presentation other than in a question and answer period, is a degree of opportunism. The cut and thrust of a committee meeting requires a spontaneity and cogency that will seek and exploit opportunities to turn the current of conversation in the desired direction. The 'good committee man', present in most organizations, is invariably a good listener as well as a good speaker, so that his interventions can be timed to greatest effect.

Somewhere between him and bottom-shuffling dumbness lies the middle ground that, through preparation, practical experience, and mastery of the subject, can be occupied by the majority.

Being called upon to chair a meeting appears to combine the horrors of platform speaking and committee work with one or two of its own. It has the high visibility of the platform, the participative element of the committee, and the judicial element of the bench. Good chairmen therefore are few. In recognising this, it is not uncommon for an executive to assign the role of chairman to a colleague who is better able to exercise the role, in favour of a place in the body of the meeting from which he need intervene only on substantive matters.

Similarly, chief executives who are diffident about their ability to conduct meetings or conferences, or who simply dislike the task, are increasingly seen on the right-hand of a celebrity or of a colleague more adept at the role when their presence is required at, say, a major product launch.

This is simply a recognition that the best end-result is most likely to derive from the best deployment of resources.

In summary:

1 Master your subject.
2 Seek the assistance of those qualified to teach public speaking.
3 Use notes if they help you.
4 Above all, practise.

TV interviews

'Many corporate spokesmen are convinced that today's news media . . .
are imbued with a fundamental bias against business.'
Burger, C. 'How to meet the Press', *Harvard Business Review* July–August,
1975

'Industry does not see public opinion as its task and so it tends to leave [it]
to other people.'

Catherwood, Sir F. 'European Management Forum', *Davos*, February
1978

'Nowhere does the businessman's case go by default more than on
television.'
Bland, M. 'You're on next', *Kogan Page*, 1979

Mycock, B. 'Don't be afraid of the box', *CBI publication*, August 1974

The average Briton views twenty hours of television each week, and the
probability is that during that time he will not see an industrialist.

British industry's unwillingness, often perceived as inability, to counter
adverse publicity and to promote a more constructive and forceful image has
attracted a barrage of criticism. It is an unwillingness that can descend to
obduracy when the media available are radio and television.

The reluctance can occasionally be attributed to a company's culture,
which may be inward-looking and secretive, but it more often stems from the
fear of being made to appear inadequate at the hands of an experienced
interviewer.

The fear is not irrational and can be compounded by concern about letting
down one's organization, especially in the eyes of colleagues who constitute a
particularly knowledgeable audience.

To the public relations adviser the problems and opportunities posed by
radio and television are more in the area of guidance than of participation. It is
his advice rather than his presence before the cameras or the microphone that
is required.

If a company agrees to give an interview following consideration of the likely
benefits and disadvantages in consultation with its public relations adviser, it
is important that the interviewee should be the line or functional executive
with the greatest mastery of the subject.

It is difficult to envisage circumstances under which the public relations
adviser might be an acceptable substitute. Not only is he unlikely to be as
familiar with the subject as the line or functional manager, but his presence as
an obvious intermediary can lead the critical viewer to regard him as an
apologist for those who might more usefully have appeared. And the
interviewer, having failed to secure the primary interviewee, is likely to feel less
hesitant about challenging the expertise of a surrogate.

The three principal concerns that should exercise the public relations
adviser are:

1 The validity of the company or client's position in relation to the topic.
2 The weighing of advantages/disadvantages in terms of advancing the
   company/client's position by granting an interview.

3 Ensuring that the executive put forward has been given the opportunity to learn the fundamental techniques that will enable him to approach the interview with an enhanced chance of acquitting himself well. This is overwhelmingly important.

Failure to deal professionally with any of these concerns could harm the cause the interview is intended to help and might seriously undermine the professional credibility of the public relations adviser within his organization.

What, then, should the public relations adviser do when asked whether his company can provide someone to be interviewed?

He can, firstly, gauge the merits of his company's case and, if he feels justified, suggest ways in which the company might modify its posture on the issue so as to reduce its vulnerability.

He can also advise on the likely effect of having the topic aired, bearing in mind that valid arguments will not guarantee a sympathetic audience.

But before he does any of this he must already have accomplished one key task without which any other efforts might be frustrated: he must have ensured that executives who might one day have to appear on radio or television have been given professional training.

While books and pamphlets on how to prepare for and take part in interviews are widely available and are a useful adjunct to training under studio conditions, they are not a substitute. The Confederation of British Industry (CBI) and Institute of Directors, as well as industrial training boards, will organize courses and there are numerous consultancies offering training in London or at the client's own premises.

Formal training, reinforced at, say, annual intervals, teaches interviewees to avoid the pitfalls that might otherwise negate any benefit an interview may offer. Training also enhances the ability to exploit an interview to the company's advantage.

Happily there is a school of thought within industry which believes that attitudes to radio and television are unnecessarily negative and which sees those media as integral with other media, e.g. newspapers, as a platform for favourable publicity.

The British Insurance Association (BIA) is probably the most successful exploiter of television and radio. Regional representatives are trained by Television Interview Training Consultancy each year and the managers are responsible for identifying opportunities for favourable publicity and securing interview time. The BIA regularly secures hundreds of constructive appearances each year.

The greater, and longer term, benefit for BIA has been the establishment of a nucleus of potential top management with practical and positive experience of television and radio.

Before discussing briefly the requirements of and opportunities provided by radio it is worth summarizing some of the advice offered to prospective interviewees by television training consultancies and in existing literature.

It cannot be overstated, however, that a theoretical knowledge of what is required is almost valueless compared with practical interview training.

The following guidelines are an amalgam of advice offered by experienced professionals.[1]

Before going to the studio

1 On receiving the approach, establish:
a The name, position and telephone number of the caller.
b The names of the director, producer, programme.
c The time of recording and/or broadcast.
d Whether the programme will be live, live-down-the-line, or recorded.
e What led to the programme or item being scheduled.
f Whether film, pictures, or models will be shown, and whether your interviewee will be able to have a preview.
g Whether, if useful, your company will be able to show its own film, pictures, or models and, if so, when can a rehearsal and scripting session take place?
h Whether others will be appearing, and if so who?
i Will there be a studio audience?
2 Know what you are going to say before the interview by anticipating what questions will be asked and by preparing the two or three points you would like to cover.
3 Avoid spokesmen, i.e. press officer, information officer, public relations adviser. Choose the man in charge who need not necessarily be the top man in the hierarchical sense. It may be the company's man-on-the-spot, known in the region and familiar with its problems, rather than the man from a remote head office.
4 Wear clothes that are appropriate to the interview: conventionally this would be a business suit. Middle tones are preferable to dark ones, and a dark suit/white shirt combination should be avoided, as should horizontal stripes or pronounced checks which produce a dazzling effect called strobing. Ladies should be prepared to remove items of jewellery which might flash distractingly at the camera.
5 Do not drink alcohol before an interview.

At the studio

6 Allow the make-up girl to do her job. She knows what to do to complement studio lighting. Street make-up is not suitable.

[1] Tidman, P. Television Interview Training Consultancy Limited; Mycock, B. 'Don't be afraid of the box', CBI Publication, August 1974.

7 Ask to meet the interviewer before going on camera.

8 When invited to 'say a few words for sound balance', don't say 'one, two, three, four — is that enough?' Tell them how you got to the studio, what you had for lunch — it gets your voice going and relaxes your tension.

9 Pay no attention to which camera is on you — look at the person to whom you are speaking.

10 Make each viewer feel as if you are speaking to him personally by using the personal pronoun, you.

11 Do not fall for the 'pregnant pause' gambit where the interviewer allows you to answer a question and then withholds comment or a further question in the hope that you will go burbling indiscreetly on. The onus is on the interviewer to keep things flowing.

12 Be clear about the key points you wish to make and make them. This may involve answering the occasional question tangentially, after which the interviewer might ask his question again. Do not, however, blurt out your key points irrelevantly. If you are sufficiently skilful you could drop them into the 'pregnant pause'.

13 Never say 'I think' on television. It is not positive enough and viewers will get the impression you do not know the answer. 'No comment' is totally unacceptable: if you cannot give the interviewer an answer, say why. The matter could be *sub judice* for example.

14 Do not hesitate too long in answering a question. No matter how honest your reply is you will come across as indecisive and uncertain.

15 Let nothing go by default. If the interviewer makes a mistake, correct him. By remaining silent you appear to agree.

16 Try to be conversational — you are not addressing a public meeting.

17 Avoid jargon — the public relations adviser can normally suggest alternative expressions in advance of the interview. Speak as if to a 12- to 14-year-old of average intelligence.

18 Avoid notes other than for complex figures or quotations, then use them openly and, having used them, put them aside.

19 Do not move your chair or touch the microphone.

20 Do not rise from your chair at the end of the interview — the camera may still be on you. You will be told when it is all right to get up.

21 Do not smoke.

22 Above all concentrate! Listen to the question, answer it succinctly and add that extra point which strengthens your case.

Doorstepping

23 If there is a possibility of 'doorstepping' — interviewing you on emergence from a meeting, say, then be clear what you will say when you walk into the lights and the microphone is thrust at you.

Radio interviews

All that has been said about television interviews, with the exception of strictures about dress and physical mannerisms, is equally relevant to radio interviews.

A distinction which is perhaps surprising is that the radio studio is likely to offer more distractions than the television studio where background clutter and activity is obscured behind the studio lights. In a radio interview, technicians are visible in the control room, researchers and assistants pass notes to the interviewer, and there is generally an air of controlled chaos. It is nevertheless considered less daunting by potential interviewees and can offer a means of easing executives towards the brighter lights and greater rigours of television.

Radio's appetite for interviewees has increased with the advent of BBC and independent local stations. Each offers an admirable platform, and management reluctance to give interviews is often diminished by the knowledge that they will be heard by a relatively restricted audience.

Universal News Services (UNS) has created a series of packages to assist industry and others in making constructive use of radio.

In essence, the client company's public relations adviser identifies a topic that will provide the subject for a radio inverview or feature. UNS then provides an interviewer and liaises with the client up to the stage where an edited tape of perhaps three minutes' duration is prepared and approved.

If using the basic service, the tape is mailed, with cue sheet, to twenty-five selected, named producers/presenters at twenty-five radio stations. The comprehensive radio service gives coverage of all BBC and independent radio stations, as well as selected English-speaking stations overseas.

The system has the advantage that the client need not appear in the programme. Often, instead, he acquires the services of a specialist whose convictions parallel those of the company and who is prepared to be interviewed about them. The system can be used in an effort to redress the balance when a client feels he has been unfairly dealt with by other media and has failed to secure adequate rebuttal.

Its possibilities are beginning to be appreciated by public relations advisers who are persuading clients and companies to take the first faltering steps towards using radio and television to advance a constructive and forceful image of industry.

The Central Office of Information (COI) offers a similar, and free, service which reaches forty different countries with stories of British economic, industrial, and scientific achievements. The COI also has a service covering television stations throughout the world.

By telephone

A relatively recent innovation in spoken communication extends the usefulness of a company's internal telephone network so that it becomes com-
plementary to internal information systems.

This is achieved by acquiring, usually on rental, a telephone answering
device whose recorded message is simultaneously accessible to up to five
direct-dial callers, or up to one hundred callers by using slave units. The
Robophone Communicator V is one such device that has been installed by a
number of British companies.

A relatively simple system, costing around £500 a year, would comprise a
recording/answering device, a microphone, and fixed-duration cassette tapes
of thirty seconds to, say, ten minutes. Communicator V automatically records
the number of calls it receives.

Editorial responsibility for the content of broadcasts usually rests with the
company newspaper editor, and a standard broadcast would not normally
exceed two minutes.

Once a system is installed, it is important that changes in the content of the
tape should be scheduled at fixed intervals, just as radio and television
schedule their news broadcasts. In this way, users know at what time of day to
expect a new tape, and the system's credibility as a *news* service is reinforced.

The intervals at which tapes are changed varies according to the user,
ranging from once to three times a day. Tapes can however be re-recorded at
any time to encompass newsworthy developments.

It is customary to have around ten well-publicised numbers giving access to
the system, and it is not unusual for access to be denied to callers who are not
on the direct-dial system, obviating use of the service by geographically distant
locations which would incur telephone charges.

Topics typically covered on such systems embrace personnel changes,
company share price, local road/weather conditions, recreation club fixtures
and results, and 'running' industrial relations stories. The service tends to
reflect the contents of the company's newspaper.

The system has also been used as an electronic press release by the National
Equestrian Centre (NEC). The NEC provides a specialist results service to
sportswriters, recording the results of UK and overseas horse shows on a
twenty-four-hour basis.

The Printed Word

If the spoken word is the most persuasive method of communication, then the
printed word is the most pervasive: as editorial (newspapers, periodicals),

press advertising, direct mail, internal and external company publications, point-of-sale material, handbills, posters and bulletins. Only the forms of print that particularly concern the public relations practitioner are discussed here.

Newspapers

There are around 1,200 newspapers in Britain, discounting the growing number of freesheets (newspaper format publications, often displaying a cover price, supported by advertising and delivered free to households in defined areas).

The six principal categories are:

1 National daily newspapers.
2 National Sunday newspapers.
3 Provincial/regional daily and Sunday newspapers.
4 London evening newspapers.
5 Provincial/regional weekly and bi-weekly newspapers.
6 Free distribution newspapers (freesheets) — usually weeklies.

National daily newspapers

All national daily newspapers are printed in London. Some are also printed in Manchester, and the *Financial Times* is printed in Frankfurt as well as in London.

Newspapers such as *The Scotsman*, which claims to be the national newspaper for Scotland, are for public relations and advertising purposes grouped with the provincial Press. This is not to deny their national character in the geo-political sense; it is a recognition that for planning purposes such newspapers offer a mainly regional coverage.

The national dailies can be sub-divided into broadsheet and tabloid. Broadsheets are the large page format newspapers: the *Financial Times*, the *Morning Star*, *The Times*, *The Daily Telegraph* and *The Guardian*. The tabloids are the *Daily Mirror*, the *Daily Express*, the *Daily Mail*, the *Daily Star* and *The Sun*. The broadsheets are characterized as 'heavy' and the tabloids as 'popular'; their importance as editorial outlets for the public relations practitioner will vary according to the nature of the activity he is attempting to publicise and the audience he is attempting to reach.

Selection and preparation of editorial for newspapers are described elsewhere in this book, but it is worth noting here that each newspaper has recognizable and often proclaimed characteristics which should be borne in mind when considering its usefulness or relevance as a channel of communication and in considering the newspaper's own requirements.

The following comments are not exhaustive and are intended only to demonstrate that differences exist which should be weighed when considering the role that newspapers might play in reaching the public.

The letters 'ABC' after the newspaper circulation figures refer to the Audit Bureau of Circulations, a newspaper industry organisation set up to verify publishers' circulation claims by two annual audits, each covering a six-month period.

The Financial Times — Established 1888; publishers, The Financial Times Ltd, part of Pearson Longman Group; printed in London and Frankfurt. One of the world's leading business newspapers, it is an indispensable outlet for news of a financial and business nature. The *Financial Times* has writers specializing in all major areas of industry and commerce, as well as specialist financial writers.

Colour advertising: yes
Circulation: 215,570 (ABC January–June 1983)

The Daily Telegraph — Established 1855; publishers, The Daily Telegraph Ltd; printed in London and Manchester; associate, the *Sunday Telegraph*. An 'independent Conservative' newspaper, it offers perhaps the most comprehensive coverage of home and foreign news of any of the national press. Detailed city and business coverage.

Colour advertising: no
Circulation: 1,266,069 (ABC January–June 1983)

The Guardian — Established 1821; publishers, Guardian Newspapers Ltd; printed in London and Manchester; associate, *Manchester Evening News*. Once a Liberal newspaper with a capital 'L', now more widely perceived as liberal, it is the most widely read newspaper among students. Good City and business coverage, if occasionally censorious. High social awareness.

Colour advertising: yes
Circulation: 437,222 (ABC January–June 1983)

The Times — Established 1785; publishers, Times Newspapers Ltd (The Thomson Organisation Ltd); printed in London; associate, *The Sunday Times*. Also publishes *Times Literary*, *Times Educational* and *Times Higher Education* supplements. Oldest of Britain's national newspapers and politically independent. Highest circulation of any within managerial, administrative and professional social groups. Good City and business coverage.

Colour advertising: yes
Circulation: 336,189 (ABC January–June 1983)

The Morning Star — Established 1930; publishers, Morning Star Co-

operative Society Ltd; printed in London. Britain's sole communist daily and opposed to private industry and commerce.
  Colour advertising: no
  Circulation: 33,952 (Willings Press Guide February 1983)

  The *Daily Express* — Established 1900; publishers, Express Newspapers Ltd; printed in Manchester and London; associates, the *Sunday Express*, the *Daily Star*, *The Standard* (London). Right of centre, pro-Commonwealth, anti-EEC. Less detailed City and business coverage than the broadsheets, but authoritative.
  Colour advertising: yes
  Circulation: 1,891,270 (ABC January–June 1983)

  The *Daily Mail* — Established 1896; publishers, Daily Mail Ltd (Associated Newspapers/Northcliffe Newspapers Group Ltd); printed in Manchester and London; associate, *The Standard*; right of centre; authoritative City and business coverage. *Money Mail* (Wednesdays) is a widely read, family-orientated guide to financial matters.
  Colour advertising: yes
  Circulation: 1,806,022 (ABC January–June 1983)

  The *Daily Mirror* — Established 1903; publishers, Mirror Group Newspapers Ltd (Reed International Ltd); printed in Manchester and London; associates, the *Sunday Mirror*, the *Sunday People*. 'A little way left of centre' and the popular though not uncritical voice of moderate Labour and trade union opinion. Limited amount of objective City and business coverage.
  Colour advertising: no
  Circulation: 3,315,070 (ABC January–June 1983)

  The *Daily Star* — Established 1978; publishers, Express Newspapers Ltd (Beaverbrook Newspapers Ltd); printed in Manchester and London; associates, the *Sunday Express*, the *Daily Express*, *The Standard* (London). Newest national newspaper. Less serious than its sister paper, the *Daily Express*, with minimal City or business coverage.
  Colour advertising: yes
  Circulation: 1,337,486 (ABC January–June 1983)

  The Sun — Established 1964; publishers, News Group Newspapers Ltd (News International Ltd); printed London; associate, the *News of the World*. Politically independent, but supported Tories in 1979 General Election. Introduced nudity as a regular feature of British daily journalism. Minimal City or business coverage.
  Colour advertising: no
  Circulation: 4,170,909 (ABC January–June 1983)

National Sunday newspapers

The national Sunday newspapers also divide into broadsheet and tabloid, 'heavy' and 'popular', although unlike the dailies, broadsheet does not always correspond with 'heavy'. The fact that they publish only once a week means that pressure on space is far greater than for national dailies. They therefore represent a more exclusive medium for public relations purposes.

'Campaigning' journalism, which may be 'pro' or 'anti' a current social phenomenon, is the hallmark of Sunday newspapers which therefore represent potentially powerful allies in 'advocacy' public relations.

The six with colour magazines — the *Sunday Telegraph*, *The Observer*, the *Sunday Express*, *News of the World*, *The Sunday Times*, and the *Mail on Sunday* — are interested in the possibility of giving exclusive coverage to industrially sponsored events, e.g. fine art exhibitions, which have strong pictorial possibilities.

The broadsheet/tabloid division between the papers is:
broadsheet: the *News of the World*, *The Observer*, the *Sunday Express*, the *Sunday Telegraph* and *The Sunday Times*
tabloid: The *Mail on Sunday*, the *Sunday Mirror* and the *Sunday People*

The *Mail on Sunday* — Established 1982
Circulation: 1,307,060 (ABC January–June 1983)

The *News of the World* — Established 1843; publishers, News Group Newspapers Ltd; printed in London and Manchester; associate, *The Sun*. Notable for having the largest circulation of any newspaper in the western world, its concern with man's seedier preoccupations should not obscure the fact that it campaigns forcefully on moral issues. City coverage is irregular but family money matters are dealt with. A colour magazine was introduced in 1981.
Colour advertising: magazine
Circulation: 4,070,424 (ABC January–June 1983)

The Observer: Established 1791; proprietors, The Observer Ltd; printed in London. Claims 'an authoritative role in the country's social, cultural, political, intellectual and business life'. Has three parts: news, *Observer Review*, and a colour magazine. Left of centre; high 'social awareness' — which most newspapers would probably claim — comes through clearly.
Colour advertising: magazine
Circulation: 783,068 (ABC January–June 1983)

The *Sunday Express* — Established 1918; publishers, Express Newspapers Ltd; printed in London and Manchester; associates, the *Daily Express*, the *Daily Star*, *The Standard* (London). Colour magazine. A British — mainly

middle-class — institution. Best City and business coverage of the popular
Sunday newspapers. Contains a colour supplement magazine.
Colour advertising: magazine
Circulation: 2,616,825 (ABC January–June 1983)

The *Sunday Mirror*—Established 1915 (as the *Sunday Pictorial*); publishers,
Mirror Group Newspapers (Reed International Ltd); printed in London and
Manchester; associates, the *Daily Mirror*, the *Sunday People*. Dominant among
young marrieds; 'politically independent but philosophically supports
Labour'. Deals briefly but cogently with money — rather than City — matters.
Colour advertising: no
Circulation: 3,512,228 (ABC January–June 1983)

The *Sunday People* — Established 1881; publishers, Mirror Group Newspapers Ltd (Reed International Ltd); printed in London and Manchester;
associates, the *Sunday Mirror*, the *Daily Mirror*. 'Marginally left of centre';
genuinely fearless exposure of vice, corruption and 'commercial skulduggery'.
Colour advertising: no
Circulation: 3,392,746 (ABC January–June 1983)

The *Sunday Telegraph* — Established 1961; proprietors, The Sunday
Telegraph Ltd; printed in London; associate, *The Daily Telegraph*. Colour
magazine. Follows the 'independent Conservative' line of its sister paper.
Good City and business coverage.
Colour advertising: magazine
Circulation: 738,193 (ABC January–June 1983)

The Sunday Times — Established 1822; publishers, Times Newspapers Ltd
(The Thomson Organisation Ltd); printed in London; associate, *The Times*. A
four-parter: news; *Weekly Review*; *Business News*; colour magazine — Britain's
first. Tends to out-page the rival serious Sunday newspapers. Impartial, but
not afraid of attacking industry. Powerful investigative reporting.
Colour advertising: magazine
Circulation: 1,288,448 (ABC January–June 1983)

Provincial newspapers, daily and Sunday
There are around 120 UK regional newspapers appearing daily and six that
are published on Sundays. They include associates of national newspaper
groups, members of provincial newspaper groups, and a decreasing number of
independents which often have a series of weeklies and bi-weeklies in their
areas. The category includes what in geo-political terms might be regarded as
'national' newspapers, e.g. *The Scotsman*. They constitute a fertile ground for

product publicity and a more questioning observer — through their greater regional awareness — of corporate behaviour, than do the national press.

London evening newspapers

There is only one London evening newspaper. Operating in the capital and in proximity to the City, its appetite for industrial and financial news from the major industries and institutions is comparable to that of the national Press.

The Standard — Established 1827; proprietors, Evening Standard Co. Ltd (Beaverbrook Newspapers Ltd); printed in London; associates, the *Daily Express*, the *Daily Mail*, the *Daily Star*, the *Sunday Express*.
Colour advertising: yes
Circulation: 506,998 (ABC January–June 1983)

Provincial weekly and bi-weekly newspapers

Numbering more than 1,000, the provincial weekly and bi-weekly newspapers are by far the most numerous of any category. They range from small independent publications with minimal staff to substantial provincial groups affiliated to daily newspapers.

Free distribution newspapers

Free distribution newspapers, known for convenience — though often disparagingly — as freesheets, have been part of British publishing for many years. They have recently proliferated and in many regions they pose a serious threat to established paid-circulation newspapers.

As an editorial outlet they are unsurpassed in their readiness to accept copy from the public relations profession. This is not to say that their critical faculties are less developed than those of the established Press; it is a reflection of the fact that freesheets exist on advertising revenue alone. Their circulation is guaranteed by them and not by public interest, and no amount of editorial brilliance will affect it. Their requirement is an acceptable standard and percentage of editorial content without the necessity for an editorial team capable of upstaging an opposition.

It remains a frustration to the advertiser and a source of solace to the established newspaper that freesheets tend to market their product in terms of circulation rather than of readership.

At the time of going to press the Audit Bureau of Circulations had put to publishers of local free distribution newspapers a proposal for a circulation monitoring system called Verified Free Distribution (VFD). It was hoped to have the system in operation by the end of 1981.

The indications are that such publications are here for the foreseeable future and it is up to the public relations practitioner to resolve the problem of whether he can capitalize on their editorial appetite without compromising himself in the eyes of his traditional customers, the paid-for regional Press.

Periodicals

Periodicals include general and special interest magazines, the trade Press, guides and directories, with publication intervals ranging between one week and a year. They are so diverse in nature and content that it would be impractical to attempt to analyse their differing characteristics.

It is essential that those responsible for dealing with the media should isolate from the more than 2,000 titles available those that are relevant to their industry or business. These should then receive the same degree of consideration when selecting circulation lists as do all other media.

Each story, if examined for factors that might extend its interest to a wider audience, can be sent to a supplementary list of periodicals derived so as to reach the eyes of those to whom the company's activities are not customarily relevant.

Details of the technical Press and UK newspapers are published in *Willing's Press Guide*, *Benn's Press Directory*, and *PIMS Media Directory*.

Overseas newspapers and periodicals

Many overseas newspapers and magazines are represented by London-based editorial staff who are as accessible as their colleagues in the UK newspaper industry.

Companies having large investments or other interests in overseas countries normally ensure that the London correspondents of the relevant newspapers receive their more important press releases. They do so not only when the story relates to the correspondents' own countries, but also when the subject of the release will help to educate the correspondent about the company's broader activities.

Dealing directly with the overseas offices of the foreign Press is somewhat more complex.

Careful research will reveal the journals that are directly relevant to the specific industry, and these can be added to existing press lists. It is in identifying the less obvious outlets that problems arise.

An effective though not inexpensive means of locating and communicating with these outlets is through agencies such as EIBIS International. EIBIS, which is based in London, maintains a detailed record of the world's newspapers and periodicals. In consultation with the client company, they will translate and distribute press releases and photographs or will place technical features overseas on a nationally exclusive basis. EIBIS also informs the client of the results of its activities.

Internal journals (see Fig. 1)

Internal journals, also known as house or company newspapers, are even more numerous than periodicals: there are approximately 2,300 (source: British Association of Industrial Editors) in the UK. They are mostly published as magazines or tabloids in an approximate 65/35 ratio, the trend being towards tabloids.

Other differences between company newspapers concern their volume, attitudes to advertising, and methods of distribution and printing. Research[2] carried out by Lansing Bagnall (now Lansing Ltd) gives the latest available analysis of these differences.

At that time 25% carried display advertising which occupied 5%–40% of available space. Classified advertising, carried by one-third of the respondents, was free of charge in the majority of cases.

Distribution was for the most part by internal mail and pick-up points, with a minority (12·5%) posting publications to employees' homes.

Eighty-seven per cent were printed by offset-litho (sheet and web-fed), the remainder by letterpress. Pages ranged from four to forty, with eight pages (48%) and 12 pages (23%) being the most popular. More than 90% of papers were issued free of charge, while production costs per copy ranged from 2·49p to 25p plus, the average being 6·47p (1975 prices).

Monthlies were most represented (50%), followed by bi-monthlies (17%) and quarterlies (11%).

Circulations ranged from less than 2,500 to more than 175,000.

The newspaper's role within a company depends on that company's culture: if it is an authoritarian organization it will have one kind of journal; a participative organization will have another kind. Some may have no journal, either because they are too small to warrant one or because they have failed to identify a need for one.

Whether or not a journal is used effectively it is potentially a key medium in internal communications, its precise role being affected by the company's overall attitude to communications and by the effectiveness of alternative means of communication.

There are principally two schools of thought about the house journal's role. Firstly, it may be seen as a mixture of births, marriages and deaths which occupies that part of the communications vacuum that might otherwise be filled by an unofficial, possibly anti-company journal produced by disaffected employees.

Secondly, it may be seen as an integral part of a company's communications network capable of dealing equally with the sensitive topics of negotiation and

[2] *Survey of Selected Employee Journals produced by Members of the British Association of Industrial Editors, 1975.*

consultation as well as with social topics. Such a journal is also expected to deal intelligently with product stories and personnel movements and to serve as a platform for policy statements on matters of employee interest.

Pressure for disclosure has tended to push the first category somewhat unwillingly into a more creative posture if only to the extent of publicising the company's results, but the effective company journal has most of the attributes of the second category.

Even here there is a wide disparity in approaches and debates tend to arise around questions of editorial freedom: can any company journal be editorially free and, more important, be seen to be impartial when it is paid for by the company? And, from line management's point of view, can a journal be allowed to be free when one careless editorial comment could complicate a negotiation?

The existence of an editorial committee offers safeguards, but is often seen as a fettering of editorial freedom. If the committee is properly constituted and alert to its opportunities, there is no reason why this should be so.

From a survey of ten European countries' house journals,[3] Britain's industrial editors appear to have less to fear from this direction than colleagues in other countries:

Country	Editorial Committee for company newspaper		Nature:	
	Yes	No	Advisory	Directive
Austria	42·9%	57·1%	31·0%	69·0%
Belgium	57·1	42·9	35·7	64·3
Denmark	84·2	15·8	59·6	40·4
France	45·8	54·2	36·4	63·6
Holland	69·9	30·1	55·4	44·6
Norway	69·0	31·0	58·6	41·4
Sweden	63·3	36·7	51·2	48·8
Switzerland	58·2	41·8	40·5	59·5
United Kingdom	*27·0*	*73·0*	*22·5*	*77·5*
West Germany	44·2	55·8	35·0	65·0

In reality most UK companies approach their journals with a large degree of pragmatism.

Industrial relations stories tend to move at a pace faster than the journal is capable of reflecting, because of publication intervals and the gap between final copy date and publication date. Journals therefore tend to deal with these issues in cautious terms that will allow for a dispute having been solved, or a

[3] *The European Inventory '79*. Federation of European Industrial Editors

negotiation having been concluded, between the time the journal goes to bed and the time that it is circulated.

Running stories — those that have not reached a conclusion — are likely to be more effectively dealt with by rapid response bulletin systems.

It is of considerable importance to the credibility of the newspaper that where time constraints permit, it should be the principal written communication for employees. Communications programmes can and should be formulated to ensure that wherever practicable the company newspaper 'breaks' a major story first. Only where external factors are insurmountable, as they might well be at times of, say, a takeover bid, should the newspaper take other than first place.

A further area of debate concerns the right — or duty — of the company journal to publish letters or stories that are critical of the company or its management.

Some publish a column of the 'You ask . . .' nature in which employees are invited to put questions or criticisms to senior executives who must then reply through the journal.

Such features give a refreshing appearance of openness to a journal, but the editor and the company must keep three further considerations in mind, particularly if there is implicit or direct criticism of an individual:

1 If the criticism were of a plumber's mate in the factory, would the letter be printed?
2 Would normal information-seeking procedures, e.g. through line management, be more appropriate?
3 What will the effect be when the company journal lands on a journalist's desk, as most of them do?

Among larger companies the transition has by now almost been completed whereby the journal's place within an organizational structure has passed from the personnel function, where many journals first saw the light of day, to the public relations or public affairs function. This permits a close working relationship with others who are fulfilling a communications role and assures a close working relationship with the Press Office which should be a prime source of stories. The latter consideration is particularly valuable as it offers the journal an opportunity to affect the timing of press releases, especially major ones, in its own favour.

Staffing levels on company newspapers and the allocation of tasks among those available vary from the one-man operation to an organizational set-up which reflects that of a substantial local newspaper.

The role of editor, once regarded as a sinecure for journalists displaced by upheavals in the provincial and national newspaper worlds, is increasingly passing to trained specialists whose journalistic experience is tailored to the industrial world. The British Association of Industrial Editors (BAIE), which has done much to increase the expertise and standing of the specialist industrial editor, has a membership of over 11,000. The BAIE offers a variety of courses on newsgathering, writing, sub-editing and layout which are relevant to all but the seasoned journalist.

The credibility of the editor and his team depends on the interest, relevance and accuracy of their publication and on their ability to create anticipation among regular readers around the publishing date. Publications appearing at random intervals sacrifice the latter ability and their relevance and credibility as a communications medium suffer accordingly.

For companies which, for whatever reason, prefer not to produce their own journals, there is the option of using one of a number of specialist organizations which exist to take the client's editorial copy and turn it into a company journal. This is presumably a frustrating experience for those whose job it is to supply copy to the consultant, perhaps together with an indication of each story's relative importance, but it can have practical advantages for a tightly-staffed holding company wishing to produce slip editions of a group journal.

The economics of a company journal will vary. The 1980 budget reproduced here is for an eight-page web-offset tabloid using a second colour and with a fortnightly print-run of 30,000.

	£
Salaries	27,560
Travel	2,500
Entertaining	200
Photography	4,000
Postage	20,000
Production costs	41,700
	95,960
Less: advertising revenue	3,000
Total	£92,960

The journal in question plays a key role in communicating with 20,000 UK employees and 6,000 pensioners. Costs work out at 12·8p a copy or a little over 1·6p a page.

Bulletins

Bulletins offer rapid transmission of important information to all employees or to categories of employee.

Systems vary, and that described here has been developed to suit one company with more than a dozen UK locations.

The two categories of bulletin used by the company are:

General interest

Industrial relations.

The general interest bulletin is used to keep all employees in close touch with topical events, from takeovers to appointments. These are issued in advance of any major announcement to the Press. Headings are available in six different colours, each colour being used in turn. The appearance of each new colour is sufficient to distinguish it from its predecessor on a notice board or elsewhere.

Circulation at the head office and adjacent factories is by hand via personnel departments, and the nature of the circulation, e.g. 'All employees', is indicated on each bulletin. The contents are simultaneously telecopied or telexed to remote sites where they are run-off on the appropriate colour of bulletin paper for circulation.

Industrial relations bulletins are typographically distinctive from the general interest bulletins. Each carries the name of one of the company's central negotiating bodies, and the bulletins are used principally for circulating an agreed management/union statement following negotiations and other meetings. The circulation methods are the same as for general interest bulletins, with the option of confining circulation to the members of the union represented on the negotiating body and to the management concerned.

The system permits each UK employee to see a bulletin within a little over two hours of its publication.

External journals

External journals at the glossy end of the range are one means by which a company transmits its news, views and opinions in order to influence key publics outside the organization. These can include suppliers, customers, government, civil service, and local government.

It would be futile to produce an external journal without a clear knowledge of the audience for which it is intended and the purpose for which it is being published. In terms of quality of paper and use of colour, external journals often represent very much up-market cousins of the house journal and costs are correspondingly greater.

The two questions to be answered when devising circulation lists are:

'Would we like them to know this?'

'Would they like to know this?'

The end result is often an amalgam of corporate and general interest stories. The first imperative is therefore to reconcile the topics the journal will be likely to cover with the possible audiences to see whether the project looks viable.

If the indications are encouraging, and some trimming of the balance between content and audience may be required, it is then advisable to sketch out the contents of each monthly or quarterly edition — intervals vary — for at least one year ahead. At this stage one might assume one topical article, the nature of which will emerge nearer to the publication date. This is an important discipline for it establishes at an early stage the likely difficulties that the editor will face and the probable viability of the publication.

Launching an external journal without giving sufficient thought to its evolution and continuity could lead to missed publication dates or even the post-launch abandoning of the project with considerable embarrassment.

External journals are most widely relevant and most likely to be successful when they avoid emulating the Sunday colour supplements and opt instead for a more practical role. They might be designed specifically for customers, for instance, and deal with practical matters concerning products and their applications, rather than with general interest topics not tailored for a particular audience and of uncertain appeal to any.

Such journals can supplement the role of the salesman in making known changes in the range of goods available and in the sales climate:

1 They can put the marketing expertise of large organizations at the disposal of smaller organizations.
2 They can demonstrate a concern for the customer and his problems that is both genuine and helpful in sales terms.
3 They can create a sense of cohesion among widely dispersed small businesses by advocating solutions to problems which the supplier can identify as being more usually encountered than the individual retailer or small wholesaler might suspect.

Where the glossy external journal might provide a general interest feature by recruiting an economic guru to produce an analysis of the business climate over the ensuing twelve months, the less ambitious publication might deal with subjects such as:

1 Shop/warehouse layout and design.
2 The latest mechanical aids for goods handling.
3 How modern display techniques can improve sales.

Each type of publication — the glossy and the more practical — exists in profusion. Therefore, if the right questions about effectiveness are being asked, each must appear justified.

On balance, the glossy external journal is best left to the large battalions to whom it represents a single instrument in an orchestrated campaign to influence opinion.

Direct mail

Direct mail means just that: communicating with people by post.

According to the USA's Direct Mail Marketing Association, there are forty-nine ways of using direct mail which can be compressed into ten categories[4]:

1 Preparing the way for the salesman.
2 Obtaining an order.
3 Following up enquiries.
4 Getting a product specified.
5 Sample distribution.
6 Communicating with the distributive trades (see: *External Journals*, above).
7 Announcing a new product to likely customers.
8 Research.
9 Fund-raising.
10 Building goodwill.

The Post Office, which has a vested interest in a healthy direct mail business, defines the advantages and limitations of direct mail in a pamphlet[5] which may be summarized as:

1 Direct mail is selective and allows for selection to a degree no other medium can offer. It should therefore be used only where the market can be clearly defined.
2 It should seldom be used in isolation. Although there are times when direct mail must be the only medium, its full effect, and the greatest benefit to the advertiser, accrues when it is planned and put into effect as part of the total campaign.
3 It should not be regarded as a one-off or shot-in-the-arm form of immediate business fillip.
4 Although direct mail is the one medium where short term results can be most easily measured, this should not be the only criterion. The steady building up of an awareness of the (advertiser's) product or service can be of more permanent benefit than the immediate enquiries.

[4] Ford, L., Director, British Direct Marketing Association
[5] *Direct Mail does what other media can't do*, Post Office publication

5 20–25p per approach by mail compares favourably with the average salesman's cost of £15 per call.
6 Direct mail is an adjunct to, not a replacement for, the sales force.

Users of direct mail joined together in 1976 to form the British Direct Marketing Association whose 500-plus members range from credit card companies, through mail order and publishing houses, to the National Computing Centre and the World Wildlife Fund.

More than fifty of the advertising agencies specializing in servicing the industry belong to The Direct Mail Producers' Association. The agencies provide services covering consultancy, creativity and design, print management, production and mailing, mailing list research and list booking, fulfilment (responding to leads produced by direct mail), competitions, packaging, automatic letter writing, and computer services.

Direct mail is a highly specialized activity and the majority of even the largest industrial and commercial organisations use outside services in this area rather than attempting to duplicate them.

Press advertising

Display advertising — as distinct from classified (including recruitment) advertising — is the principal source of revenue for the vast majority of publications and can be broadly categorized as corporate advertising, financial advertising and manufacturer's consumer advertising (MCA).

In 1980, display advertising expenditure in the UK Press totalled £724,900,000, whilst TV advertising accounted for £762,530,000.

Conventionally a company retains one or more advertising agencies to handle its MCA campaigns — the advertising of products to the consumer — from inception, through implementation to assessment of effectiveness. This pattern has been broken in recent years by the parallel growth of creative consultancies and media buying 'shops' whose joint services allow the advertiser to sidestep the established full-service agency and retain part of the 15% or lesser commission which the agency would otherwise absorb. This is what Philip Kleinman, advertising's Edmund Burke, describes as 'advertising à la carte'.[6]

While this leaves the advertising or publicity manager apparently financially better off, much of the saving can be eroded by the costs of the creative consultancy and the to-ing and fro-ing that has to be undertaken by the client to bring together the efforts of the two services.

Another new factor in the relationship between client and agency is the abolition from January 1979 of the fixed commission agreement.

[6] Kleinman, P. *Advertising inside out*, W. H. Allen & Co. Ltd, 1977

This stemmed from the 1973 Fair Trading Act which was extended in 1976 to cover services. The result has been to introduce a fee basis for remunerating agencies as an alternative to — not instead of — the commission system. At present this relates only to advertising placed in printed media; it does not apply to radio, television, cinema, and poster advertising.

Of the three types of display advertising, corporate advertising is perhaps the least understood, yet its objective is simple in conception, if difficult to achieve. Its rationale is that public awareness of an organisation and its activities should be of a nature and at a level that might be expected to work positively for a company at all times, and more particularly when:

1 It is under external pressure by, say, takeover or public criticism.
2 It is seeking to acquire other companies.
3 It is trying to improve efficiency.
4 Its goods or services are offered for sale in competition with technically/ aesthetically comparable products or services.
5 It wishes to introduce new products.
6 Institutional investors are contemplating sale or purchase of its shares.

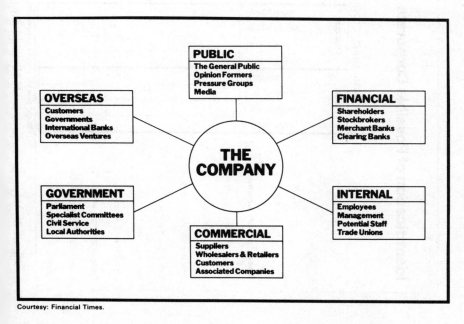

Courtesy: Financial Times.

Figure 2 A company and its publics: some of the potential audiences to whom corporate advertising might be addressed.

Identification of Possible Corporate Advertising Needs

	THE COMPANY'S POINTS OF CONTACT																							
	Public				Financial				Internal				Commercial				Government				Overseas			
Uses of Corporate Advertising:	General Public	Opinion formers	Pressure groups	The Media	Shareholders	Stockbrokers	Merchant Banks	Clearing Banks	Employees	Management	Potential Staff	Trades Unions	Suppliers	Wholesalers & Retailers	Customers	Associated Companies	Parliament	Specialist Committees	Civil Service	Local Authorities	Overseas Customers	Foreign Governments	International Banks	Overseas Ventures
Improve or restore confidence with																								
Indicate social responsibility to																								
Underline stability and potential to																								
Correct misconceptions by																								
Plead a case with																								
Improve attitudes and opinions of																								
Create understanding with																								
Establish special relationships with																								
Counter criticisms and attacks to																								

Please tick those areas where the achievement of objectives on the left with those areas across the top could benefit the company's business operations.

Based on a design by the Financial Times

Figure 3 What the company would like to achieve (vertical axis) and in whose eyes (horizontal axis).

Corporate advertising can increase that level of awareness for a wide range of audiences.

The list is not exhaustive, nor does it ascribe a useful function to corporate advertising on the higher levels of finance where decisions on loan rates are made, or where conclusions are reached by financial analysts. Those involved in such deliberations are not however immune from exposure to, and the effects of, corporate advertising.

It is known from comparative image studies among companies that the better known a company is, the more favourably it is perceived. There are exceptions; for example, when a company has been involved in a major scandal or other problem it may become notorious rather than familiar. But the rule has been widely demonstrated to be generally valid.

As the *Financial Times* corporate advertising brochure winsomely proclaims: ' "Understanding is the beginning of approving" — André Gide.'

The desired effect of corporate advertising is to change opinions about an organization and to make it more widely known, and this presupposes a datum line against which shift can be measured. Unlike MCA, it cannot be measured in terms of the movement of tins and packets off the supermarket shelf. A pre-requisite is therefore detailed research among target audiences before a campaign begins, followed by research at the end of each phase to assess its effectiveness.

Roger Stubbs, of Market and Opinion Research (MORI) states: 'Changes in opinion are effected glacially, not incrementally.' MORI has conducted countless image surveys for many of Britain's leading companies and their experience, as well as that of advertising agencies and clients, shows clearly that only sustained campaigns are capable of effecting changes that are statistically significant. The exception to this is where attitudes to a topical issue are to be affected: Amoco, Bristol Channel Ship Repairers and the clearing banks have mounted intensive and successful short-term campaigns on such issues.

Corporate advertising campaigns are therefore relatively expensive — £100,000 to £300,000 a year would be a reasonable appropriation for a medium-sized company, yet they are capable of improving the background of opinion in areas to which MCA is directed.

Nor is corporate advertising confined to newspapers and periodicals: it has been used extensively on television by STC, ICI, Philips, Glynwed, Tube Investments and others.

Financial advertising, once dismissed as a *quid pro quo* for charitable editorial mentions in the City pages, is today veering towards corporate advertising in style. Where it was once considered sufficient to feature the Chairman's photograph, together with a several-hundred-word extract from his statement to shareholders, plus the salient figures from the accounts, it is today becoming less turgid and more attractive.

The Chairman's message is often reduced to a few key points either narratively or displayed, his photograph is slowly being abandoned, and the visual aspect of the advertisement is devoted to graphics putting the financial concepts across crisply or to an illustration that attempts to synthesize the stature or diversity of the organization.

The optional use of colour in advertising increases the cost of space by between 30% and 50% in return for an increase in the impact of the advertisement. This dates from the inception of colour advertising when research showed that the 'noting value' for colour advertisements was 30% to 50% higher than for black and white. Mechanical costs increase by around 33⅓% to 50% and a further cost is incurred through the requirement that stand-by black and white plates must also be provided.

Despite the added costs, pressure on colour space in the nationals that provide the option (*The Times*, the *Financial Times*, *The Guardian*, the *Daily Mail*, the *Daily Express* and the *Daily Star*) is fairly intense. Although only 80–90% of a print-run is guaranteed to be in colour, the guaranteed figure is normally exceeded by a fairly wide margin.

Numerous provincial newspapers, for the most part broadsheets, also offer colour.

Posters (see Fig. 4)
Posters are a valuable addition to the promotional 'mix' where the general public is the audience, chiefly because of the permanency of the message.

What was bad news for independent television proved to be the salvation of Britain's poster industry. The ban on television advertising of cigarettes in 1965 meant that many millions of pounds were suddenly released from promotional budgets. This avalanche of cash first flowed into publications and then overflowed on to Britain's poster sites.

Together, tobacco, spirits and beer advertising is estimated to account for 63% of the poster ('outdoor') market and this in turn disposes of the majority of the 55–60% of sites that are let on a permanent basis.

Poster advertising is now big business in the UK. With a land area of 93,026 square miles, the UK has the same number of poster sites — around 230,000 16-sheet units, as has the USA with a land area of 3,536,855 square miles. And whereas only 50% of US poster sites are let at any one time, the comparable figure for Britain is 80%.

In space expenditure, posters account for around £40m a year and since 1970 the cost of poster sites has risen at twice the rate of press and television advertising.

All is not rosy, however, for the site owners, three of whom control more than 60% of the space available.

Already controlled by Town and Country Planning Regulations 1969 to 1974, the industry now faces two investigations which might further restrict its activities.

The Monopolies and Mergers Commission, which began an inquiry into the business in October 1978, reported in July 1981, and the Office of Fair Trading, is now examining the industry's standard conditions of trading. The Monopolies and Mergers Commission calls for British Posters, a joint marketing company co-owned by the leading poster contractors, to be scrapped.

Half-a-dozen medium-sized agencies specialize in the logistics of poster publicity, creative work normally being handled by the client's own agency. Poster advertising's selling proposition is based on opportunities to see (OTS). The good sites, which can give 80% coverage of a community and therefore offer a high OTS, are marketed at premium rates.

A four-sheet (60in × 40in upright) might cost between £20 and £75 a month, whereas a 48-sheet (20ft × 10ft high) can range from £100 to £650 a month. 'Specials' — either particularly large sizes or particularly valuable sites, or a combination of both — can exceed £1,000 a month.

Ironically, a 16-sheet poster (6ft 8in × 10ft high) which is the basic 'module' of the poster business is often marketed at the same price — from £20 to £75 a month — as a four-sheet. The anomaly is the four-sheeter which is dear, and not the sixteen-sheeter which is in line with prevailing rates.

As the majority of prime sites tend to be let on a permanent or long-term basis companies contemplating an in-and-out campaign of, say, two months, normally accept a mix of one or two prime sites, plus numerous lesser ones. Provided the OTS figures available are accurate, the desired penetration can be achieved on this basis.

Advertising on buses, underground stations, and sports grounds, forms part of the outdoor advertising option, although prices vary widely from region to region.

The electronic written word

Word processing, Prestel and internal viewdata, electronic message systems and computerized news are different facets of the incursion of electronics into the traditional mix of media. Although developments in these areas are relatively recent, there is already a growing degree of convergence among them that emphasises their relevance and requires the communicator's attention and understanding.

The word processor was the earliest of the developments. Over the past fifteen years it has reached a stage of sophistication that is compatible with the newer technologies of computerized news and Prestel.

Its implications were not immediately apparent to the public relations profession. Rightly regarded as an evolution from the electric typewriter with the added ability to store and retrieve words, it offered an editing facility that made it useful for drafting articles and speeches and it has also been widely used for the repetitive typing of 'original' letters of invitation to press conferences and other presentations. Its potential reaches far beyond these simple practices.

The principal elements of a word processor are the keyboard which has control keys for the editing function as well as the standard alphanumeric set; the screen (increasingly common, but not standard) on which work is displayed; the print unit, commonly with a golf-ball or daisy-wheel (three times faster than the golf-ball) type head; storage — commonly floppy disc or diskette with capacities from 70,000 to 500,000 characters; and logic — that part which stores and provides the various functions and controls all the components of the system. The logic element can be shared between several word processors.

The latest word processors have moved closer to the data processing area and joint W.P./D.P. systems are now available. This means that word processing systems can now be linked to computers to provide the processing facilities and can also be used as terminals for most data processing applications. This gives the word processing system far greater scope and an integrated information system approach is now available. The system provides:

1 Massive storage facilities (380 megabytes and above — or 160,000 pages of A4 text).
2 Information storage and retrieval facility with easy access.
3 Communications via word processors and/or visual display units.
4 Technical computing facility.
5 Mainframe access.
6 Future international links.

These developments are of great relevance to the communicators: the word processor's ability to store internal and external data, such as mailing lists, accessible under a multiplicity of headings, e.g. topics dealt with by specific publications, correspondents by name, circulation, advertising rates, mechanical data, and so on; and the word processor's ability to communicate with other word processors, such as those used by computerized newspaper offices.

Although the introduction of new technology by Britain's newspapers trails behind many parts of the world — the USA's 1,800 newspapers have almost 2,000 computers — there is an inevitability about its advance.

What accounts for the pace of this advance?

'Quite simply, apart from the necessary speed and production efficiency which it engenders, the computer brings order to chaos in the newsroom. As modern communications techniques shrink the globe, the torrent of information flooding editorial offices has all but drowned the staff. Electronic processing makes the floodtide manageable. Editors conveniently and quickly know what stories they have on hand and can determine and find what they wish to use in the next edition.'[7]

What is foreshadowed here for the UK is the electronic press release: typed and edited on the word processor, stored while necessary approvals are obtained, and finally amended and distributed electronically to the newspapers' editorial computers.

Once there it will appear as a single-line entry when the relevant editor reviews the data bank on his visual display unit. He will also be able to call up the first paragraph to gauge the strength of the story before deciding whether to call up the whole story or to wipe it from the computer's memory.

The implications for the journalist are more far-reaching and extend into the realms of page layout, on-page ('stone') subbing, and ease of up-dating running stories through several editions.

Prestel

Just as the electronic newsroom is compatible with industry's word processors so, in due course, will be the Post Office's Prestel service which became generally available in 1979.

Unlike Ceefax and Oracle, the 'one-way' teletext services operated by the BBC and ITV, Prestel is interactive: it can be fed with information by the provider for subsequent access by all users of the service, or by designated categories of user.

Using Prestel, any organization may contract to make information available via the Post Office Prestel computer. Customers of Prestel, who may include private individuals, then have access to this information usually for a small fee (around 10p per page) through modified television sets connected to the computer by telephone.

Prestel is a two-way system using telephone lines which gives users the opportunity to conduct a 'conversation' with the Prestel computer and eventually with other Prestel users. As well as being able to select from a very wide range of information, Prestel customers may for example be able to

[7] Steinberg, D. President, PR Newswrite, New York, speaking at the Eighth PR World Congress, London, 1979

instruct the computer to send them goods and pay by credit card. Potential i
also seen for using the system for transmitting messages which ma
additionally be recorded in the absence of the recipient.

Prestel is also expected to become international, giving access to informa
tion stored on computers in other countries.

Businesses may be 'information providers', supplying information on thei
products and services, telling customers about stocks, or undertakin
corporate advertising.

Information providers may also become 'closed users' which means that th
information they store on the Post Office computer may be retrieved only b
the business itself or by those to whom it allows access. Possible uses includ
dissemination of company information to geographically diverse locations an
the provision of information to a particular profession. Additionally, Preste
will make some benefits of computers available to small businesses previousl
unable to afford them.

A very wide range of information is already available, but the depth o
information which will be provided — and the extent to which depth will b
governed by other more conventional and economical media such as printe
matter — is not yet clear.

There are currently over 500 information providers supplying abou
180,000 'pages' of information and additional capacity is available. The Pos
Office expects 2·6 million receivers to be in use by 1985/86 and 10 million in th
early 1990s.

Prestel is expected to do a number of things well, but it seems unlikely that i
will make great inroads into information currently supplied in, say, hard cop
form, for a number of years.

Facsimile transmission

One more means of distributing the written word electronically merits
mention, and that is facsimile transmission, also known as remote copying and
telecopying.

The technique of transmitting newspaper photographs by radio and by
telephone line has existed for many years and there are at present some 10,000
facsimile units in use by industry in the UK which employ the same
technology.

The Rank Xerox 400 Telecopier, at a rental of around £400 p.a., is widely
used in the UK, Europe and the USA.

Now the Post Office has launched Intelpost which puts the service at the
disposal of all: letters handed in at a city post office can be transmitted within
the UK, or to and from the USA, in a handover-to-delivery period of around
2½ hours. The cost is £4 for the first page and £2 for each succeeding page.

The advantage over Telex lies in the elimination of operator error and in the ability to transmit diagrams and pictures.

Visual and Audio-visual Aids

Visual aids are those media whose messages are directed at the eye, e.g. slides, overhead projector transparencies. They also include graphics and three-dimensional models, whether these are featured directly or in the form of photographs or slides.

Audio-visual aids are those media through which messages are directed simultaneously at the ear and the eye, e.g. film, video tape recordings incorporating sound tracks. While not in itself an audio-visual aid, the tape recorder is one means of providing the 'audio' element.

In considering the preparation of audio-visual programmes, the ground rules for public speaking outlined earlier in this chapter should be borne in mind. The visual aids available should then be deployed with a view to conveying the message as effectively as possible. They should not be used simply because they are available.

The effectiveness of visual aids may depend on the extent to which they help perception and 'memorization' physiologically, or their influence on an audience may be at an emotional level. Investigations have been conducted which examine their effect in two ways: by working outwards from the structure and function of the human eye and brain towards the stimulus being perceived; by following the 'chaining effect' of external stimuli from the start of the presentation, through what are called identification, internalization and memorization of the stimulus information.[8]

It has been stated that 'the human brain remembers 10% of what it reads, 20% of what it hears, but recalls over 60% of information seen and heard at the same time'[9], although no research source for the conclusion is offered. Research undertaken for National Panasonic is reported to show that after three days an oral communication was remembered by 15%, a written version of the same communication was remembered by 40%, and an audio-visual version by 75%.

While research in these areas is extensive, it is not yet conclusive. A useful discipline is therefore to examine the 'scale' of communications technology until the level is reached that promises to meet the communications objective most effectively.

[8] Klima, G. *Multi-media and human perception*, Meridan Press, Elmira, New York.
[9] 'Audio-visual is not just another toy', *Sales Engineering*, February 1978.

Thus, if the ascending scale of communications technology is as follows:

Recorded word, with video/film
↑
Spoken word — live, with video/film
↑
Spoken word — live, with static illustration
↑
Spoken word — live
↑
Illustrated written word
↑
Written word
↑
Ideograms

it is possible, at planning stage, to escalate through the scale until the appropriate level is reached.

Assuming that locational difficulties, the complexity of the message, and cost or other considerations indicate that video or film offers the best solution, it is then advisable to backtrack through the scale to decide which, if any, of the lower technology aids would complement the presentation.

Written material, for instance, especially if it uses the same graphics as the audio-visual programme, is an almost indispensable reinforcement to such programmes.

The following examples describe the main visual and audio-visual aids. Before using these techniques for the first time, advice should be sought about the relative merits of the competing models available and the possibility of hiring equipment should also be considered.

Flip charts

Flip charts are a basic aid to communication. They are simply large pads of plain cartridge or lower-quality paper, perforated for ease of tear-off, which can be desk- or tripod-mounted.

In effect they are a mobile 'blackboard', with the refinement that the information they are required to impart can be written or drawn on them in advance, using felt-tipped pens, each succeeding piece of information being revealed as the preceding page is folded back or discarded.

Where an air of spontaneity is required, the information can be faintly sketched-in in pencil, so that the presenter has only to follow the lines with a felt-tipped pen. This technique is also useful when the presenter wishes to build up gradually to the totality of information on a single sheet, especially if the graphics are complex.

Overhead projectors (OHP)

Originally introduced as a lecturing aid, the OHP has a simplicity and a versatility which have made it one of the most enduring visual aids.

It uses acetate transparencies, 8½in × 10½in (216 × 267 mm) up to 8¼in × 11¾in (201 × 297 mm), taped to a cardboard mount.

Transparencies can be prepared by colour photography, colour or black and white photo- or heat-copying, by hand — using OHP spirit pens, or by a combination of these techniques.

Information can be built up on transparencies during a presentation in the form of overlays, or can be revealed by the removal of 'masks'. The speakers can add to them using spirit pens.

The OHP is designed so that it can be operated at table-top height by a seated speaker. No blackout is needed although direct lighting on the screen reduces contrast.

Portable models are available which, though less robust than the standard models, are highly practical for the public relations man who needs to be mobile.

Film

Film has been around since the end of the last century. It is familiar, well-established, and the technology is highly developed and widely understood.

It occurs in three main forms, identified by the width of the film stock:

1 *35 mm* Used by professionals in the commercial cinema world. Very expensive and being ousted in smaller cinemas by 16 mm.
2 *16 mm* The professional and semi-professional format (newsmen, documentaries, industrial films, schools and universities). 16 mm is expensive but the ready availability of expertise, equipment, and distribution makes it attractive.
3 *8 mm* The old standard 8 mm and the new Super 8 (mm) which replaced it — Super 8 uses more of the existing frame area to produce a larger image area — are principally aimed at the amateur film-maker. They are of limited quality for professional use and share the generic problems of 16 mm and 35 mm film. Super 8 can be used in continuous cassette form with desk top projectors, such as the Fairchild 70 (£400 approximately). Programmes of

20 minutes' duration can be accommodated and the machines are widely used by salesforces and for exhibition work. A stop-frame option is available.

Film is high in sound and picture quality, but appears to be losing some ground to video tape production and distribution on the public relations front. All film requires mechanised, rather than electronic, production and projection systems and mechanised systems are incapable of being reduced dramatically in size.

Its chief advantages, ironically, derive from the protracted nature of the editing stages which allow a degree of refinement in the end-product, denied to its competitors, which is one of the beauties of film. It is still pre-eminent as an international distribution medium, because of the almost universal availability of 16 mm projectors.

A number of options are available to those who wish to venture into film without going to the extent of commissioning and overseeing the whole venture, and without incurring the costs of from less than £1,000 to more than £3,000 a minute for a specially produced product.

One such scheme is the National Coal Board 'Review', a ten-minute feature film produced by the NCB and distributed to commercial cinema circuits at monthly intervals.

The films are intended to be of general interest and regularly deal with topics with an industrial or technical content but are distinct from advertising.

It is normally necessary to sponsor the whole of the ten-minute film at a cost of £20,000 and the sponsor works through a director nominated by the N.C.B.

The Central Office of Information produces documentary films for showing overseas and also acquires films from corporate sponsors for dubbing and subsequent overseas distribution.

An alternative scheme exists whereby an independent producer will make a film about a company with a view to selling the film commercially in the UK and overseas. The sponsor subscribes half the agreed production cost, the other half being provided by the producers, who recover their contribution and retain any profit from cinema and television rentals and sales.

Before agreeing to take part in such schemes it is important that the sponsor should make every effort to validate the claims made by the producers, bearing in mind that distribution and revenue can never be guaranteed in advance.

'Architectural Newsreel' is a unique service directed towards the construction industry. It presents a thirty-minute film of four- and six-minute sequences dealing with products and other matters of interest to architects.

The film is presented during working hours on the premises of 1,000 architects' offices when supporting literature is distributed.

The distribution cost is £5,100 for films up to four minutes in length and

£7,200 for sequences up to six minutes. Production costs vary between £2,000 and £6,000-plus.

Sound tape
Sound tape is usually found in three formats.

Quarter-inch Open Reel Recorded at 15 ips (38·19 cm/sec); 3¾ ips (9·5 cm/sec); and 1⅞ ips (4·75 cm/sec): the higher the speed of recording, the greater the quality of recording and ease of editing.

Editing of sound tape is usually done by physically cutting and splicing, using non-magnetic equipment.

Reel-to-reel tape recorders are often stereophonic. This allows high quality playback in stereo or, when used in mono, a spare track which can be pulsed to operate projection equipment. Some recorders are modified to play stereophonically and include a pulsed track.

Audio-cassettes
Unlike video cassettes these generally exist in only one standard format, but care should be taken that the heads of the recorder match the tape coating (e.g. chromium oxide).

Like open reel recorders, cassettes can be recorded mono or stereophonically. They can be edited by cueing and erasing — but not by physically cutting — though a narrow tape and low playing speeds make this difficult.

The best results are achieved by producing cassette copies from a master edited ¼in open reel tape.

Sound cassettes can be used as a cheap store for micro computer programmes.

Sound cartridges
These recorded cartridges of ¼in tape normally produce sound of a higher quality than cassettes. They are usually stereophonic. Like all cartridges they have a limited application because they are continuous and cannot be wound backwards.

Slides

Slides taken on 35 mm or 2¼in sq film, black and white or colour, give a high quality static image which will stand considerable enlargement.

35 mm is the standard format and is usually projected in conjunction with Carousel projectors with a capacity of 80 slides (e.g. the Kodak Carousel SAV 2020; £395 approximately).

Slides can be used simply to illustrate a talk, or in conjunction with a tape recorder and pulse unit to provide an automatic slide/tape programme.

The use of two projectors with a dissolve unit, sometimes known as crossfade slide/tape, allows mixing and cuts from one slide to the next, controlled by a pre-recorded series of pulses on a sound tape. This avoids the harshness of a blank screen between slides.

The technique is now highly developed, so that professional displays using 200 or more slide projectors and a multiplicity of screens, controlled by computerised programming, can produce dramatic impact.

Crossfade and multi-screen slide/tape have the disadvantage of complex replay equipment and non-compatibility between different manufacturers' equipment.

Filmstrip

Slide/tape programmes can be transferred to filmstrip on which the 'slides' appear sequentially on a single strip of 35 mm or 16 mm film. There is also the 110 system, which employs 16 mm film horizontally.

Playback is through pulsed tape projectors which may be front-projected, back-projected, or both. There is a wide variety of equipment available in console and desk top form. For 16 mm systems the cost is £300–£380; for the 110 system around £400; and for 35 mm around £350–£450. The 110 system has the exclusive feature of allowing synchronized fast-forward and fast-reverse of the filmstrip and sound tape.

The advantages of filmstrip over individual slides are that the pictures remain in sequence and the strip itself is relatively lower in cost to duplicate and simpler to distribute than slides.

The disadvantage is the loss of the flexibility to up-date the slide programme cheaply and easily and non-compatibility between various makes of replay equipment.

Closed circuit television (CCTV)

CCTV involves transmitting live television, usually by cable, from one place to television 'monitors' (not ordinary domestic television sets) in nearby locations. It is valuable for relaying ceremonial occasions and small or intimate demonstrations to audiences who would not otherwise be able to be present or who would be unable to see detail.

Video tape recorders (VTR)

Video tape recorders are tape recorders (open reel) which store sound and picture information on magnetic tape.

The tape can be replayed and, if required, erased and re-recorded. It may be of various sizes, but in most cases may only be replayed on a machine of the specification upon which it was originally recorded. The Electronic Industries Association of Japan standard used by many Japanese manufacturers gives compatibility between EIAJ systems.

Information on video tape includes a synchronizing pulse which controls speed and stability, a black and white signal, a colour signal, and one or more sound tracks.

The width of the tape varies:

2in tape — professional use

1in tape ⎱
¾in tape ⎰ professional/higher education use

½in tape — industrial users and schools

Video cassette recorders

Developments in this area are so rapid that, as one commentator recently remarked, many proceed directly from the drawing board to the Science Museum.

Video cassette recorders employ the same principle as VTRs but the tape is housed in a cassette. Most non-broadcast video users use this equipment, although there is no single world cassette standard. The systems are of two types:

Professional: U-matic Standard (Sony/JVC/National/NTC)

This is a ¾in colour cassette standard used mainly by professional producers/ industry/higher education.

Machines must be matched to the appropriate TV system of the country, e.g. PAL (phase alternate line), SECAM (sequence and memory) and NTSC (National Television Standards Committee). Western Europe, except France, is PAL: France and East Europe are SECAM; and America and Japan are NTSC.

Full back-up technology exists for this type of machine and most software manufacturers produce on U-matic as a standard.

Semi-professional/domestic

The other half of the video cassette market is the semi-professional/schools/ domestic market which is not produced to a unified standard. Four main systems are evident. The primary use of all these machines is 'off air' recording. Most have built-in timing devices and are designed to play through the aerial input of a domestic TV set.

| 1 Philips N1500 (Philips and licensees) | Now discontinued. Cassettes: 30, 45 and 60 minute playing times. Colour ½in tape. |

2	Philips N1702 (Philips and licensees)	Superseded 1500 series; uses same cassette but plays 60, 90 and 180 minutes.
3	Philips V2000	Eight hours' playing time on one cassette.
4	VHS (JVC and licensees)	Flat format colour cassette, three hour playing time. Heavy penetration of domestic and rental market.
5	Sony Betamax (Sony and licensees)	Half-inch flat format colour cassette. Latest to enter UK market. Three hour playing time.

The domestic market is in a state of rapid development with constant changes in costs, playing times and licensed manufacturers.

Video/cartridge player (VCP)

Solely playback machines. Tape is recorded on open reel recorders then threaded into cartridges for ease of playback.

Lack of recording capability limits the use of video/cartridge machines which are therefore rarely encountered.

Video disc

The concept of video discs, which unlike cassettes are not re-usable, is that programmes may be stored on a cheap, mass-produced disc, similar to an LP record, which may be played through a domestic TV receiver. Though no recording facility exists on these machines, low cost, high quality, and large libraries of software could make the system highly competitive.

Among its advantages are ease of single-frame recall and display.

Since the mid-70s, video discs have been developed by many large companies, but problems in launching such a system — technical, financial and marketing — have prevented the system from taking off.

The growing market penetration of low cost video cassettes with increased quality and availability of small colour cameras is challenging the disc before it has reached the mass market at which it is aimed, although it is making inroads in the educational and industrial markets in the USA.

The video disc is only likely to be cost-effective against video cassette on duplication orders of 500 or more, because of the high origination cost for the disc master.

Video projection

Video projection has existed in various forms since the 1950s but has been of poor quality, high cost, and required total blackout.

Seen by the Japanese video giants as one of the main reasons inhibiting video from replacing film, great efforts are now being put into low cost, medium/small video projection units. Success may come, though possibly through some form of video screen rather than through an optical projection system which invariably demands expensive units.

The newer video projectors, and there are many systems available, are of much improved quality.

Combined uses

The distinctions between the technologies of film and video do not mean that they are mutually exclusive media: programmes that are 'encoded' on film are often transferred to video for use, or 'decoding', and *vice versa*.

To understand these interrelationships and their advantages it is necessary to distinguish between the encoding and decoding functions which are as follows:

Encoding:	Film 35 mm/16 mm	Video-tape 2 in, 1 in, ¾ in	Slide/tape 35 mm
Decoding	35 mm or 16 mm reel-to-reel *or* 8 mm film cassette *or* Video-cassette (transfer from film costing about £40–45/min)	Video cassette *or* 16 or 8 mm film (transfer from video to make negative costing about £40/min)	Twin Carousel with cross-fade *or* 35 mm or 16 mm film strip *or* 16 mm or 8 mm film *or* Video-cassette

Thus the means by which a programme is encoded does not dictate the way in which it will be decoded.

For example, a requirement might be for great precision and refinement at the editing stage and for low-cost duplication. This could be met by encoding on film and transferring to — re-usable — cassettes for decoding.

Commissioning audio-visual programmes

Assuming a decision to use an audio-visual programme has been taken, the next step is to prepare a brief for the producer, writer and director to work on. Often the production company will assist in production of the brief. In film and video the producer and director have reverse responsibilities from those that the titles imply in radio and television: the producer brings together the client, finance, and the production team, whilst the director controls the filming and post-production stages.

The brief should establish:

1 Precise marketing or other objectives to be met.
2 The nature of the audiences and their probable or known attitudes to the subject.
3 The preferred distribution system.
4 The nature of the message to be conveyed.
5 Supporting literature, e.g. promotional, required.
6 Budget.

The writer or writer/director will then create a treatment for a fee which will depend on the work involved. The treatment will indicate the creative and 'editorial' content and the preferred production medium.

Following discussions with the client, the treatment is then developed into a script following which the programme can be commissioned.

Two-dimensional Graphics

Two-dimensional graphics — photography and hand-prepared artwork — are a means of augmenting information provided by the written and spoken word. As such they feature not only in print (including posters), but in films and audio-visual presentations.

The public relations role in bringing together graphics with the printed or spoken word involves:

1 Assessing the need for a communications exercise.
2 Defining the message to be conveyed.
3 Choosing the media to be used.
4 Discussing with designers in the case of print, or producers in the case of film, the way in which graphics can be used to help interpret or complement the message.

The public relations practitioner must therefore be familiar with the techniques of illustration available, so that he can discuss them constructively and with a knowledge of their respective costs and effectiveness. It is not expected that he should have more than an intelligent appreciation of photographic techniques and an equally intelligent perception as to what constitutes a well-composed photograph or a suitably elaborative diagram.

Photography

Black and white and colour photography are traditionally the chief graphics components of public relations activities. Photography impinges on exhibitions, press relations, corporate advertising, and internal and external publications.

Mr Alan Hare, Chairman of the *Financial Times*, describes photography as 'the most immediate of all forms of communication' in his foreword to *Industry in Focus*[10] by former *Financial Times* Pictures Editor, Michael Colmer. The book is dedicated to, among others, 'colleagues in . . . press relations and management'.

Colmer argues that efforts to reflect industrial processes and activities through photography so as to create better understanding have not moved at the same pace as 'creative' photography. An implication of this is that those companies that are prepared to spend time and money on first-class photography will have little difficulty in placing the end-product in the editorial columns of the Press.

Having appeared in the Press, the utility of a good photograph is not exhausted: there remains the opportunity for using it in internal journals, advertising, sales publicity material, and in exhibitions. The procedure may in fact be reversed so that a photograph originated for, say, an exhibition will first be exploited through the Press.

The COI will assume responsibility for circulating suitable photographs to the press in 100 countries where 'blanket' coverage is sought, acting as an extension of the company's own Press Office.

An essential requirement is a means of co-ordinating the commissioning of photographs so that all involved are aware of the total activity in this area.

Where topical photographs are concerned, V.I.P. visits, retirements and so on, it must be remembered that these are of little or no interest to the daily newspaper unless delivered by hand, either as exposed film (by prior arrangement) or print, to the newspaper office immediately after the event. The alternative, if the event is sufficiently significant, is to invite the newspapers' staff photographers to attend a photo-call.

Sending captioned, allegedly topical photographs by post to daily newspapers is an irritant that tends to destroy the credibility of the public relations profession with the pictures editor.

Apart from the composition and quality of pictures, and the question of immediacy for pictures with intended topicality, there are a number of practical considerations to bear in mind when producing photographs for use inside or outside the company:

[10] Colmer, M. *Industry in Focus*, Business Books, 1974

1 Black and white prints for newspaper reproduction should be 10in × 8in glossies.
2 Photographs for colour reproduction in the technical Press are acceptable in a variety of forms and the requirements of each publication should be established in advance.
3 Photographs for television should be 10in × 8in matt, preferably in colour. Transparencies are acceptable from 35 mm upwards.
4 Copyright in photographs specifically commissioned from a photographer belongs to the client.
5 Copyright in photographs taken by a photographer and subsequently offered to and accepted by a client remains that of the photographer.
6 Unless otherwise negotiated, negatives are normally retained by the photographer.
7 When using live models, ensure that they complete the 'standard form for signature by models', devised by the Institute of Incorporated Photographers and the Institute of Practitioners in Advertising.

Costs of photography vary enormously. An in-house photographic unit is a practical proposition for large companies, but even those with their own staff tend to employ specialist photographers for occasions where a particular expertise is required.

Travel costs are a major expense when commissioning outside photographers, and it is important that the need for a particular style or quality of photograph should be weighed against the costs involved in having the 'ideal' photographer travel the length of the country to record it on film.

A photographer operating nearer the location may represent a better financial proposition without unduly sacrificing quality. With photographers' day rates of around £250–£300 for, say, ten black and white or eight colour shots, the possibility is usually worth examining.

There also exist, chiefly in London, a number of photographic libraries, whose services are available to industry as well as to the newspaper world. These can supply prints and transparencies of topical or historical subjects where exclusivity is not a requirement.

Storing and indexing of negatives and prints is too specialized a topic to treat at length here, but those responsible for handling an organization's photographic requirements will require reference and retrieval systems giving optimum accessibility.

Usually subject-based, the systems should indicate:

1 The location of the negative.
2 The form in which the negative is held, e.g. 35 mm black and white.
3 The copyright holder.

4 The date the photograph was taken.
5 Brief caption details.
6 Any restrictions governing publication, e.g. the need for acknowledgements.

Hand-prepared artwork

Charts, diagrams, drawings and paintings can be divided into two categories
of illustration: the interpretative (charts, diagrams), and the representational
(drawings and paintings), although the division is not an absolute one as the
example cited will demonstrate.

Their relevance is not confined to print but extends into the field of visual
aids where they can be animated or, through the use of more than one
transparency on an overhead projector, for instance, can be made to
demonstrate an evolving theme.

Graphics are being increasingly used in attempts by companies to simplify
the presentation of financial information to employees. The difficulties in
explaining value added statements or cash flow in terms of pie charts and bar
charts have led to numerous ingenious attempts to surmount the problem.
'Cash in', for instance, has been shown as liquid in a jug, improbably
segmented into coloured bands representing trading profit, depreciation and
replacements, and income from associates and investments; while 'Cash out'
has been represented by numerous tumblers — purchase of fixed assets and
investments, tax paid, dividends, increase in working capital, and interest on
loans, into which the contents of the jug are decanted.

Clarity is occasionally sacrificed to ingenuity on these occasions, and it is
well worth-while trying out 'roughs' of such graphics on a sample of the
intended audience before commissioning finished artwork.

A basic rule of public relations, of particular relevance in the context of
graphics, might be stated as:

$$simplicity + clarity = explicitness$$

Once more, costs cannot be stated with accuracy. Two 1979 examples give
some idea of possible costs, but the bold statement of costs ignores the
complexities involved in each job.

Job	*Design cost*
12-page tabloid financial report to em-ployees, original artwork on all pages	£6,200
48-page report and accounts: layout and print specification, no original artwork	£2,400

Three-dimensional Media

Signs, displays and models extend the basic media into the third dimension.
Each is normally an ancillary element in an activity having broader
implications:

1 Signs, where their form is not legislatively prescribed, fall within a
  company's house-style or its exhibitions design philosophy.
2 Displays are usually, though not invariably, associated with specific events,
  e.g. conferences, whose overall style they must complement.
3 Models are a 'tool' for exhibitions, photography and film.

As constituents of broader activities, the relevance of each of these will be
heightened or lessened according to its role. The form in which it is represented
will be governed by the nature and style of the activity of which it forms part.

Signs

It would be impractical to attempt to define what, other than clarity of purpose
and message, constitutes a good sign or good use of signs, but there are a
number of general considerations to be borne in mind when planning sign
usage. There is also a major legislative development ahead that will have its
effect on sign usage in the UK from 1981.

Signs can offer information and give warnings and instructions. They are
also one of the principal means through which we orientate ourselves in
unfamiliar surroundings. Their use in exhibitions and at conferences will
usually reflect a company's design philosophy and style, while observing any
constraints imposed by the organizer's: at 'joint' exhibitions, such as those
organized by the British Overseas Trade Board, it is customary for a standard
style to be observed by all exhibitors.

To an increasing extent signs are being required to bridge language barriers
and the use of ideographs — e.g. the male and female silhouettes to indicate
toilets — is achieving a large degree of standardization throughout the world.

Signs take on quite a different significance where they relate to safety
activities within premises where the Health and Safety at Work, etc., Act 1974
applies (with the exception of coal mines and certain transport activities).
Safety Sign Regulations 1980 Statutory Instrument No 1471 (available from
HMSO) became effective for all new safety signs from 1 January 1981.
Existing safety signs will have to be brought into line with the new regulations
by the end of 1986.

Signs command greater attention if they are illuminated, particularly when used indoors, e.g., at road, rail and air terminals (see Figure 6). Illumination also ensures that signs retain their usefulness after dusk.

Illuminated signs fall into four broad categories:

1 Identification (garage, café).
2 Point of sale.
3 Directional.
4 General, including advertising, Piccadilly Circus being the best known example.

Costs depend on the type of illumination: interior fluorescent, neon, overhead, as well as on the size and prominence of the site.

Members of the British Sign Association will advise on this aspect, as well as on the implications of the Town and Country Planning (Control of Advertisements) Regulations 1969.

Displays

Displays are exhibitions, and through usage the term has come to mean a small exhibition, usually in support of a broader activity.

It is customary at annual general meetings, for instance, for the company's activities and products to be represented in display form.

The 'hardware' of the display world is becoming highly specialized and increasingly modular in line with developments in the exhibitions world, and it is not proposed to deal with the relative merits of the competing systems.

Displays can, however, be broadly divided into two types:

1 Displays using existing, modular components.
2 Purpose-built displays.

The demountable quality inherent in modular systems can also be designed into purpose-built displays to achieve a mobility that permits the display to be transferred between sites.

The facility to use a display more than once has obvious cost advantages and, provided that safe storage is available between uses, it is often worth building demountable qualities into displays designed for specific occasions, but which have the potential for further use.

At their simplest, displays are conventionally of the 'storyboard' type with two-dimensional graphics and captions. At their most sophisticated, they can involve audio-visual techniques and working models, often push-button operated by the viewer.

The graphic content in either case can be tied in to that of the event at which the display is being used, if it has an overall design style, or it can reflect the thematic style chosen by the company for the occasion, or it can follow house-style.

Practical applications of and sites for displays include:

1 Receptions.
2 Product launches.
3 Conferences.
4 Presentations — to colleagues, customers, pressure groups, et cetera.
5 Office and works reception areas.
6 Office and works corridors having heavy pedestrian traffic.
7 Groundfloor windows of prestige offices.
8 Canteens — to tell employees the story behind new developments.
9 Customers' premises.
10 Job centres.
11 School dining and recreational areas.
12 Sports and recreational club premises.
13 Cinema and theatre foyers.
14 Libraries, museums and art galleries.

The list is not exhaustive. Building societies and banks, for instance, are often prepared to make some of their window or floor space available for displays where the purpose is to explain or entertain, rather than to advertise.

Models

As the costs of models are high they tend to be used sparingly, but there are numerous uses to which they can be put, including:

1 Presentation of building plans to local authorities.
2 Explaining the environmental impact of building plans to local communities.
3 Revealing the inner workings of machinery and plant at exhibitions.
4 Planning the layout of exhibition stands and displays and of offices and factories.
5 For photographic, film and video representation of theoretical concepts.

While model-making as a recreational activity is within the scope of most, the services of professional model-makers are required where the models are to be used for public exhibition.

There are a number of specialists in this type of work and their customers for the most part tend to come from the architectural profession and from the film and television industries.

Many companies who train craftsmen apprentices have an untapped resource of model-making skills which, with adequate supervision, can be diverted to highly cost-effective work by the engineering, planning and communications functions.

Models tend to be of relatively simple design if their role is conceptual or experimental, for instance in planning the layout of a factory. If, however, they have an explanatory or selling job to do, perhaps in explaining the environmental impact of a proposed building to civic authorities and the local community, then the key elements in the model — the proposed development and its immediate surroundings — will need to be presented with considerable realism.

Where it is intended to film the model (see Figure 7) then the wealth of detail required in order to achieve verisimilitude will be considerable, with a resulting impact on cost.

The chief advantage of models, whether used as an exhibition aid or for filming, is their three-dimensionality. They can be walked around, mechanized, illuminated, cutaway and generally be made an analogue of the real thing. Insofar as they reduce the demand for interpretation from the viewer, they reduce the risk of misinterpretation.

Composite Media

Composite media are combinations of basic media brought together for a specific occasion, the nature of which will dictate the way in which they are deployed. On most occasions there will be additional elements to be considered with which the basic media must mesh.

Special Events

Special events is a catch-all expression that embraces established categories of activity such as conferences, presentations and facility visits, as well as events that are difficult to categorize. They can range from an open day for employees' relatives to a royal visit, and from the opening of a new factory to a film *première*.

In each case the newsworthy element(s) should be identified and exploited; the positive qualities of the subject of the event should be emphasized; and the nature of the programme should be strictly relevant to the subject.

The following checklist derives from the Institute of Public Relations' Recommended Practice Paper No. 2 — 'Planning Special Events':

1 Fix the date — after checking with news agencies and other sources that there is no clash with events already arranged. Decide times of arrival and departure.

2 If a conference or symposium, decide the theme and list of guest speakers.

3 Prepare and issue guest invitations — including, where relevant, national and local dignitaries, ministers, M.P.s, mayors, educational leaders, major customers, suppliers, trade associations, shareholders (and husbands or wives).

4 Prepare and issue press invitations — considering whether the invitation should be by card, personal letter, or otherwise. Invitations will carry more weight if V.I.P.s are mentioned, but their acceptance must be cleared before precise times, venues, dress, and other details can be given.

5 Make hotel reservations and other bookings as necessary.

6 For special printed matter, early priority should be given to invitation cards, programmes, handbooks, guides and/or maps, histories, catalogues, film synopses.

7 Speeches: writing and clearance may well be the responsibility of the P.R.O. Welcome by chief host; introductions and briefing of guests (with model or plan?). Microphones and loudspeakers. Closed-circuit television for 'overflow' audiences. Name cards on platform. Recording facilities: shorthand, tape, videotape.

8 Arrange protocol of presentation of senior staff, long-service employees, and others.

9 Arrange bouquets, visitors' book, and similar details.

10 Brief tour guides, provide lapel badges, tour itineraries; rehearse exact timing of visit, check level of noise and screen off any sections not to be included in tour.

11 *Décor*: appearance of conference hall, banqueting room, and other facilities. Ensure staff are wearing clean uniforms or overalls; special clothing or headgear for visitors; clean vehicles; internal direction signs; appropriate flags and banners.

12 Transport to the event, during it, and on return journey. Booking of, and arrangements for, special train, aircraft, coaches, cars; special signs for the occasion (including AA or RAC); parking facilities; advise police and other public services.

13 Catering: for luncheons, dinner, tea, coffee — including service on special transport. Obtain and agree estimates. Top-table seating (protocol); place cards; press table arrangements; menus; MC/toastmaster; music; table decorations; marquees; toilet and cloakroom facilities — ladies and gentlemen; gratuities.

14 Wet weather programme: umbrellas, duckboards, insurance.

15 Press arrangements: notify Press radio, T.V., film units, photo agencies;

preparation of press kits; issue of press releases (including to those not represented); establishment of temporary Press Office and allied facilities.

16 Other media: prepare any associated advertising copy; posters, films, exhibits, historical and/or product displays or unveiling, other visual aids, (personnel involved, power-points or services required?).

17 Commissioned photography: both before and at the event—for the Press, record purposes and/or presentation; possibly album or prints to special guests. Brief photographer to consider significant 'backdrop' wherever possible, as well as subject in foreground.

18 Souvenirs — to special guests, or to all, on departure.

19 Overseas events or visits by foreigners: employ interpreters; arrange translations of literature, press material, and other print, including exhibition and/or display captions.

20 Final plan: obtain agreement to final plan, double-checking exact timing. Notify all concerned well in advance, emphasising that it is essential to adhere to agreed timing since the whole success of the event may depend on it.

21 Budget: produce detailed budget — including an allowance for contingencies, and obtain approval for each item before expense is incurred.

22 As soon as possible after the event — while impressions are still sharp — review every aspect of the occasion, and make a note of any weaknesses to be remedied in the future.

Press conferences

Bowman and Ellis[11] distinguish between news conference, press briefing and press reception, ascribing the following characteristics:

News conference — called when there is 'hard' news to give, e.g. discovery of a major new oilfield, signing of a trade treaty, announcement of a project that will create employment. Hard news conferences usually compress the time available for making the preparations outlined below.

Press briefing — generally called to put an event or development into context for those who need to write about it, thus helping them in their interpretation; more selectively, when a handful of specialist writers are taken into the confidence of, say, a government minister or chairman.

Press reception — for 'soft' news items, such as product launches (unless the product is sufficiently radical to merit a news conference), 'getting-to-know-you' occasions where the Press meet new executives, and so on.

[11] Bowman, P., Ellis, N. *Manual of Public Relations*, Heinemann

The following checklist is a guideline only and will need elaboration according to the nature of the event. It should be considered in conjunction with the special events checklist reproduced above.

1 *Timing*

If the timing is governed by external factors, e.g. publication of financial results, this will dictate the extent to which the considerations outlined below can be encompassed.

If the timing is entirely discretionary, the need to complete the following activities can be the principal consideration in setting the date.

In practice, there are normally external factors circumscribing this freedom: marketing plans may indicate a particular week, or even day, for the event, or there may be a risk of the story breaking in an uncontrolled way that has to be forestalled.

Other factors affecting timing are:

a The notice required by the Press (three weeks unless for a hard news story).
b The need to produce press packs, display material and visual aids.
c Availability of key company personnel.
d Availability of a suitable venue.
e Press dates of important publications.

2 *Invitees*

Most stories have angles that are not immediately apparent, so that as the primary invitation list is being drawn up it is necessary to examine the story for the less apparent angles.

Opening of a new prestige office may be relevant not only to the architectural, building and business Press but to catering Press (kitchens and dining areas), medical Press (surgery and welfare facilities), telecommunications Press (internal communications network), and many others.

The question of whether the additional media should be invited to the main conference, to separate ones, or should simply receive a specially tailored press pack will depend on the strength of the stories.

Photographers often receive less than their due consideration when invitation lists are drawn up, and reference to their requirements is made under item 4 (Invitations).

3 *Location/Venue*

Events for the regional Press rarely present a problem so far as venue is concerned, but events directed at the national Press can be more problematical. Manchester-based daily journalists, for instance, might reasonably expect stories emanating from their region to be directed to them, especially if the story is general news rather than specialist in nature.

However, as a general rule, where the story is likely to be relevant to the London editions of the dailies, or where it is aimed at the periodical Press, a London location is to be preferred.

While London hotels and head offices are often chosen for press conferences there are many less conventional venues available, e.g. livery halls, Thames boats. Access to rapid communications for the journalists, if a factor, makes it advisable to use a venue that is experienced in handling such events.

4 *Invitations*

Invitations to press conferences have been printed on vellum, leather, glass and doubtless many other materials, although the information given usually follows a conventional form:

a The name of the person or organization extending the invitation.
b The nature of the event.
c The time, place and date.
d The availability of refreshments.
e The name and address to which replies should be sent.

A detachable reply-paid card is an additional refinement, as is a street map on the reverse of the invitation, if the venue is other than easily located.

It is often advisable to include a covering letter elaborating on the nature of the event and pointing out whether special facilities will be available for photographers, television and radio. This might include details of private rooms for recording interviews, telephone and telex arrangements, the availability of models for filming and photography, and the anticipated duration of the conference, if this is not stated on the invitation.

For invitations that are sent to personally-known press contacts a covering letter or telephone call is mandatory.

As invitations begin to be returned a system should be established for:

a Telephoning those who have not replied within forty-eight hours of the scheduled date.
b Mailing press packs to those who decline the invitation.

5 *Chairman and speakers*

Decisions must be made at an early stage about who should speak at the conference, who should introduce the speakers, and who should be responsible for the smooth flow of operations on the day.

Failure to notify people sufficiently in advance of the timing of a conference can undermine it from the outset.

The requirement for a guest speaker should be established at this stage and his services secured, bearing in mind the need to distinguish between the guest speaker who will lend credibility to the proceedings and the 'celebrity' who, offered merely as window dressing, signals to the Press that the story is weak.

The speeches themselves should be checked, if not written, by the public relations adviser with responsibility for press relations.

He should also ensure that each speaker is given a set of probable questions and 'textbook' answers for reference at the conference.

6 Information (press packs)
Whether press information is presented in an elaborately silk-screened plastic pouch or a printed folder is of little importance, provided the overall effect is smart. Infinitely more important is the content of the press pack.

A press pack may contain basic factual press releases and photographs, or it may be more elaborate.

Contents may include:

a Programme of events.
b The main press release describing the topic/product that is the reason for the event.
c A background piece putting the topic into a wider context.
d A piece about the organization sponsoring the event.
e Biographies of speakers.
f Captioned photographs/diagrams (these should, where practicable, be reproductions of illustrations used in any audio-visual presentation).
g Copies of speeches (marked: 'Check against delivery'). Some speakers prefer to delay handing out copies of their speeches until after they have been delivered, a preference the Press does not endorse.
h Samples/souvenirs.
i Note pads/pens.

7 Visual aids
The use of the following should be considered:
a Displays.
b Trade or other literature relevant to the topic.
c Demonstrations.
d Audio-visual aids.

8 Reception and arrangements
Organizing arrangements at the conference venue is a distinct aspect of the planning process, involving some or all of the following:

a Provision of a raised table for speakers, plus lectern if required.
b Water jugs and glasses.
c Name cards for speakers.
d Seating for guests.
e Ashtrays.
f Sound and audio-visual equipment.
g Displays.
h Demonstration materials.
i Sets of additional captioned photographs.
j Reception desk(s).
k Receptionist.
l Secretarial assistance: for recording questions and answers.
m Visitors' book.
n Name badges — coded by shape, size or colour to distinguish guests from hosts.
o Decorative (e.g. floral) arrangements.
p Telephones.
q Telex.
r Toilet facilities.
s Drinks.
t Catering.

Special points to watch are:
a Speakers should, if possible, conduct their final rehearsal at the venue.
b Responsibility for operating visual aids should be clearly assigned, and all a.v. and demonstration equipment checked before the conference starts.
c Guests should be welcomed on arrival and there should be sufficient company personnel available to look after guests before and after the formal proceedings.
d The visitors' book will reveal any discrepancies between acceptances and attendances, so that press packs can be mailed to non-attenders.
e Timing: forty-five minutes should be adequate for presentations and questions and answers, unless the topic is particularly difficult to put across.

Sales presentations

A sales presentation is designed to:

1 Introduce a product to an audience.
2 Explain the product's benefits and selling points.
3 Outline the marketing programme, e.g. timing, advertising schedule, promotional aids.
4 Enthuse the audience who may be the company's own salesforce or dealers.

Among the most experienced and successful exponents of the sales presentation are the motor manufacturers who, co-ordinating or complementing what may be a simultaneous international product launch, have devised tried and successful techniques that much of industry emulates.

The success of Ford particularly in this area stems from advanced planning which, from the earliest practicable stage, involves all those who will have a part to play as the product moves off the drawing board and into the car showroom.

The programme for the launch to the Press, which is handled by the Public Affairs function, is integrated from the outset with Marketing's plans for the launch to dealers and consumers.

Sales presentations involve all the considerations already outlined under Special Events and Press Conferences with the exception that the contents of the information packs will differ.

Starting from a market research base, the product is evolved to the point at which a 'platform' — the points Ford wishes to make about the product — can be decided. This could be two years ahead of the launch for a new model, or one year ahead for a facelifted existing model.

The object at this stage is to identify as many plus points as can be deduced, and there may be more than a hundred of these, then to distill them into the most potent platform for presentations, advertising and public relations purposes.

Co-ordinating the launch is a committee on which the functions represented can find parallels throughout industry: sales, parts, service, merchandising, and public affairs.

A typical presentation might cover two days:

Day 1: Dealers' principals and sales directors.
Day 2: Parts managers; service managers; retail dealers; fleet customers.

The presenters and presentation materials are tailored to each audience and the two-day event is followed by regional presentations to salesmen.

Assuming a 10.30 a.m. start to the sales presentation, a normal programme would be as follows:

10.30
    Assemble; coffee.
10.50
    Move in to presentation area.
11.00/
11.20
    'State of the trade' presentation by the Chairman.

11.20/
11.40
      Sales potential presentation by Marketing Director.

11.40/
12.10
      The product story — marketing presentation, including availability of postal franking blocks, window dress-up kit, vehicle dress-up kit, modular display kit, mobiles and premium gifts.

12.10/
12.20
      Public affairs presentations — how the new model will be promoted through the Press.

12.20/
12.30
      Winding up session by sales director.

12.30/
13.00
      Drinks.

13.00
14.30
      Lunch.

Films and video are used throughout where they are capable of elaborating the message, in line with Ford's longstanding commitment to audio-visual aids.

Facility visits

Facility visits involve showing production plant or other facilities to an organization's publics. Conventionally seen in terms of press facility visits, they can also be organized for any sector of the public whose understanding or co-operation achieves heightened importance: local authorities, customers, educationalists and others.

While the Special Events checklist will again be useful, the degree of elaboration will vary according to the nature of the visitors. Many companies offer facility visits routinely, and the following schedule explains how arrangements are made by one company for regular factory visits by science stream students:

1 On receipt of visit request, check against visits diary.
2 If the date is free:
  a Confirm to the organizing teacher, sending teacher's notes which will form the basis for a lesson, plus 'how to find us' map for coach driver.

b Notify works management.
c Notify works guides.
d Book cinema.
e Decide level of catering and book facilities.
f Organize work book, safety spectacles, viewing cards.
g Two weeks before the projected visit, re-confirm the date with the organizing teacher.
3 If the date is not available, agree an alternative date and carry out actions 2a–g.

The above is a simplified version, omitting much domestic detail, but it embraces four elements demonstrating the attention paid to detail which in turn underlines the fact that if facility visits are to achieve a useful objective, then they must be planned down to the finest detail.

The first element is the provision of teachers' notes. As can be seen, these are provided to the teacher in advance of the visit and they provide information that will enable him to base a forty-five minute teaching period on the works visit.

Second is the provision of a work book which invites students to answer questions and complete sketches on the basis of information gleaned during the visit.

Third is the provision of viewing cards. These are a small gatefold publication incorporating a blue acetate viewing window which allows the students to look inside furnaces. The viewing card also shows a flow diagram of the process and gives a brief outline of the process and the company's other activities.

Fourth is the availability of a cinema for the showing of an introductory film. A specially produced audio-visual programme could replace this in a VIP programme.

The works guides referred to are all pensioners with practical experience of the process who have been trained to explain it clearly and succinctly.

Exhibitions

Exhibitions provide a temporary and potentially powerful focus for a product or service *in support of* an overall marketing plan. Only by assigning a specific role to each aspect of the plan does the success or failure of each part become responsive to subsequent analysis and evaluation.

The distinction between exhibitions and displays is somewhat arbitrary. In practice, the term 'exhibition' is generally used to describe the larger public event, e.g. the Motor Show; or trade show, e.g. the Mailing Efficiency

Exhibition. In each, stands from a variety of companies are brought together under a generic title.

A display (*see* Three-dimensional media p. 61) has come to mean a small exhibition staged in support of a broader activity, which may be a specific yet integral part of an exhibition stand.

The cost of taking part in an exhibition can range from a few thousand pounds for a small trade exhibition to high six-figure sums for the larger public and trade shows. Exhibiting overseas inflates these figures, although costs can be contained by participating in the joint venture exhibitions organised by the Central Office of Information and the British Overseas Trade Board.

The effectiveness of an exhibition is susceptible to measurement in qualitative and quantitative terms, but if it is to be allowed to perform satisfactorily against the chosen criteria it must be planned in the finest detail.

There is considerable literature on exhibition organisation and evaluation, including *Guide for Exhibitors* and *Value analysis in advertising: measure of the effectiveness of exhibitions and trade receptions*, both available from the Incorporated Society of British Advertisers (ISBA).

The principal objectives of the exhibitors who go through the meticulous process of staging an exhibition can be summarized as follows:

1 To publicize the company.
2 To meet existing customers and raise their interest in the products.
3 To meet potential customers and identify new sales areas/outlets.
4 To introduce new products/services.
5 To prepare the ground for further sales by inviting the appropriate authorities, associations and ministries to the stand for talks.
6 To support and/or evaluate the effectiveness of the local agent.
7 To assess the performance of competitors in terms of product, service, and presentation.
8 To give lectures/meet top technicians.
9 To aid market research and long-range planning.
10 To take orders.

Having decided to exhibit for one or more of the above reasons, and with the objectives clearly in mind at all stages, the following actions will need to be taken:

1 Select the exhibition where the visitor profile, if available, promises to deliver your target audience (see Figure 9).
2 Agree budget.
3 Negotiate the stand site, avoiding second-rate positions, e.g. subsidiary aisles, toilet and refreshment areas.

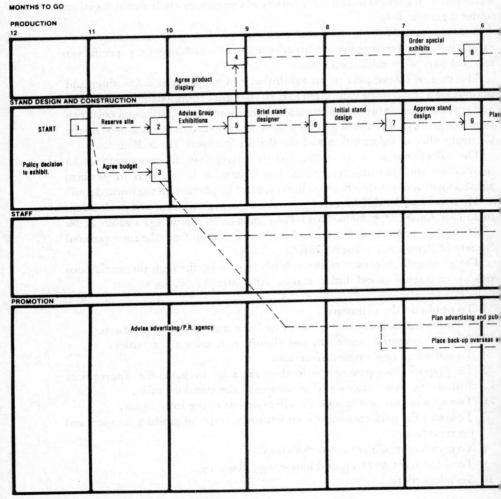

MONTHS TO GO

Figure 8   Planning for an exhibition.

4 Prepare a stand brief and progress schedule for the designer. State the objectives, products to be displayed/demonstrated, facilities required, e.g. lounge, office, cloakroom, audio-visual, entertainment. State whether house-style or a thematic style is to be used.

5 Appoint a stand manager. Brief him and his staff on the outline objectives of the stand and consult them about design aspects.

6 Prepare print, photographs and other illustrations for press packs, trade press and other advertising, and for use on stand.

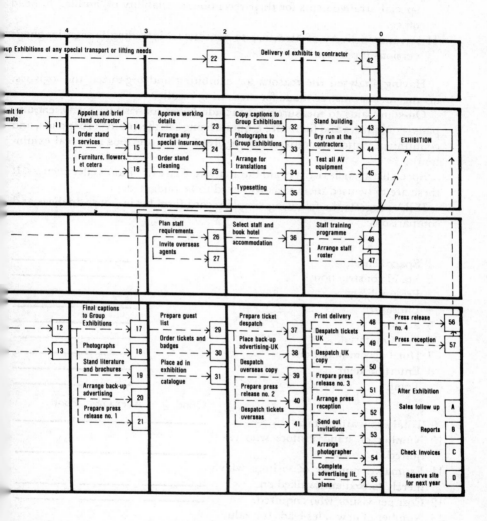

7 Write contractors' tenders on the basis of the design, specifying completion twenty-four hours before opening.

8 Prepare staff rota; engage receptionists; arrange telephones, catering, and staff/receptionist accommodation.

9 Provide editorial and/or advertisement for exhibition catalogue; order copies of catalogue and obtain exhibitors' complimentary tickets.

10 Give detailed briefing to stand manager and staff, including availability of literature, names of those the company particularly wishes to attract and

special arrangements for their reception, availability of 'hotline' to head office.

11 Arrange delivery of literature to contractor, including foreign language versions if relevant.

Having analysed the reasons for exhibiting and organized the logistics, arrangements must be made for measuring results.

On-stand aids to measurement include boxes for visiting cards, enquiry pads — enquiries and literature requests being satisfied daily, order pads, and counting of visitors (compare with figures for the previous identical exhibition).

Specialist agencies exist to aid the analysis of an exhibition's effectiveness. If these are to be used their costs will need to be budgeted.

ISBA suggests the following simple record form for in-house analysis and comparisons:

1 Space rental. ————————
2 Stand construction. ————————
3 Pre-publicity. ————————
4 Literature. ————————
5 Staffing. ————————
6 Press material. ————————
7 Hotel accommodation. ————————
8 Entertainment. ————————
   Total. ————————

	Good	Average	Poor
9 Total show attendance.	————	————	————
10 Number of stand visitors who enquired.	————	————	————
11 Estimated number of visitors who merely looked and walked on.	————	————	————
12 Cost per visitor who enquired.	————	————	————
13 Number of new sales leads (or value of orders where applicable).	————	————	————
14 Evaluation of exhibition and visitors to stand by own staff.	————	————	————
15 Evaluation of your stand and staff by reps.	————	————	————
16 Evaluation of exhibition by comparison with competitors.	————	————	————

Exploitation of the company's stand can be through direct mail, editorial and advertising.

The day prior to the public opening, or the first part of the opening day, is normally reserved for the Press and VIPs.

Press relations activities should precede the opening with a mail-out of press packs and invitations. Liaison with the exhibition press office will ensure that advantage can be taken of its facilities.

Where stand photographs are required for press, company newspaper or record purposes, it is possible to use the services of an exhibition's official photographers, although an exhibitor is usually free to engage the photographer of his choice.

Companies wishing to stage overseas exhibitions are advised to contact the British Overseas Trade Board (BOTB). Set up in 1972 to aid exporters, the BOTB's range of services has a Fairs and Promotions branch which offers three categories of exhibition participation to users. These are:

1 *The joint venture scheme*: a collective presentation of UK goods and/or services at a specialized trade fair overseas under the sponsorship of an approved trade association, Chamber of Commerce, or other appropriate non-profit-making body. The minimum number of firms acceptable is normally ten. Participation on inside space in 1981/82 cost £15/m^2 for first-time participants at that event, £20/m^2 for second-time participants, and £30/m^2 for all others. Outside space is charged at 50% of these rates.

Where the cost to the BOTB is £120/m^2 or more, charges were determined individually, with the aim of recovering 50% of estimated direct costs.

2 *The British Pavilion Scheme*: the BOTB organizes British Pavilions at certain international trade fairs overseas, usually outside Western Europe. The fairs are presented in national sections and the charge in 1980 was £50/m^2 (£25/m^2 outside) inclusive of display facilities and essential services.

3 *All-British exhibitions*: in overseas markets which are considered to be actually or potentially of special importance, but where there are no suitable international trade fairs the BOTB may organize special all-British exhibitions.

All-British exhibitions may be specialized, in which case the appropriate industry's representative body has an important part to play; or they may be of a general industrial nature, when Fairs and Promotions branch will be directly responsible for the recruitment of participants, sometimes through the agency of a British trade fair organizer.

There is no common fee for all-British exhibitions overseas and the charge to participants is announced at the same time as the event.

The BOTB also offers financial assistance for freight and travel costs.

The Central Office of Information and the BOTB publicity unit provide extensive publicity for exhibitions organized by the BOTB.

Export promotions

In a management consultancy survey of 256 vice-presidents of major US companies conducted in 1979, the UK was judged to be the world's fourth worst major industrialized nation when it comes to promoting exports. Worst of all was the USA, then the USSR and the People's Republic of China.

Why should this be? Provided the goods are readily available and have adequate price, performance and delivery characteristics, success should be assured — or should it? The missing ingredient is customer awareness: if the customer is unaware of the ·product's availability, or if it is promoted tentatively in an aggressive marketing environment, the product can still fail.

Public relations activities alone cannot promote exports. They must be part of an integrated marketing effort with all of the following characteristics:

1 Market research.
2 Awareness of tariff and non-tariff barriers.
3 Export intelligence.
4 Enthusiastic selling agencies in the target countries.
5 Satisfactory distribution and service networks.
6 Adequate command of the relevant language *or* the services of first-class translators.

Many of these requirements are matched by services available from the BOTB.

These include:

1 Financial aid for export marketing research.
2 Advice on tariffs and non-tariff barriers.
3 An export intelligence service that connects available goods and services with known overseas requirements.
4 A market entry guarantee scheme which provides financial aid for well-planned export promotions in new overseas markets.
5 Aid for companies taking part in overseas seminars and symposia bringing British products and services to the attention of buyers, users and technologists.
6 An import agency finding service.
7 Travel and other assistance for outward sales missions by British companies and for inward missions by overseas businessmen, journalists and others who can affect British exports.

Assistance through the Overseas Projects Group for large capital projects. An Exports to Japan Unit.

For companies who wish to make their own way in export markets, whether through sales visits, seminars, conferences, or by other means, an essential initial point of contact in each country should be the commercial attaché at the British Embassy.

The commercial attaché's advice will take account of national nuances that might otherwise be unobserved, and he can be particularly helpful in securing the interest of journalists and, where practicable and desirable, the participation of government and other national figures from the host country.

Sponsorship

Sponsorship is an activity undertaken by industry and other organizations in order to:

Increase sales
and/or
To alter the *way* in which the sponsor is perceived, or the *extent* to which he is perceived, by the publics to whose attention the sponsorship is directed.

Objectives for sponsorship can be set, but it is advisable to state an objective as, for example: '*To help increase awareness and favourability of the brand name*' rather than, '*To increase awareness and favourability of the brand name*'.

This is because sponsorship rarely takes place in a communications vacuum and its contribution is difficult to isolate from that of other media. The existence of corporate and/or manufacturers' consumer advertising in the same environment, for instance, will obscure the contribution of sponsorship to the achievement of a marketing objective.

Direct measurement becomes practicable only when sponsorship is the predominant tool in a promotional activity: the powerful but publicly little-known Cornhill Insurance Company sponsored the 1979 Test Series and raised public awareness of the company from 2 to 16%.

It should nevertheless be recognised that in the majority of cases the onus on sponsorship is to offer a *reasonable expectation* that it will complement other activities in a positive manner rather than that it should produce a *measurable* contribution.

The difficulties of analysing the effectiveness of sponsorship extend to attempts to estimate the size of the total sponsorship purse.

Sports sponsorship is believed to be running at a level of £30,000,000 a year in the UK ('The Persuaders', BBC 1, 23 August 1979). The arts, principally as music and theatre, account for about £3,000,000. Almost all of the money is thought to be provided by Britain's commercial and industrial institutions.

If the rewards are so intangible, why do they do it?

Historically, sponsors are fulfilling a role that was originally assumed by royalty and the great families who would offer their unselfish support of a person or activity in return for nothing more than reflected glory.

Patronage passed from the ruling classes as their wealth declined: first to the newly moneyed and leisured classes created by the industrial revolution and, as their wealth and influence also declined, the responsibility came to rest with the sole remaining centres of wealth, the corporate organizations.

Characteristic of the transfer of responsibility has been the increasing expectation that the costs should produce benefits; or more realistically that sponsorship objectives should be set which are in alignment with and in support of the objectives of other activities.

The message that this encompasses may sound churlish, but it is a practical one. The would-be sponsor must ask himself: 'What is my objective?' or, more bluntly, 'What's in it for my company?'. If there is little or no prospect of a benefit he is talking not about sponsorship, but about patronage.

There are many areas where the right type of sponsorship can be helpful. It can be used simply as an extension of existing publicity campaigns: as a complement to broad-spectrum public relations, advertising, direct mail, point of sale, and all the other marketing aids.

It can be used to help project or change a parent company, operating company, or brand image, including logos and symbols.

Having decided to enter sponsorship there are three major considerations:

1 The nature of the sponsored event.
2 The cost of promoting the sponsorship.
3 The sponsorship agreement.

Choosing the event to sponsor is a fine art and will depend upon a number of factors:

1 Which type of audience does the sponsor wish to reach?
2 Is he trying to — market a product?
              — change his reputation?
3 What funds are available?
4 With what type of activity would he like to link his product or reputation?
   a Something that will 'soften' the image of, say, a development company?
   b Something that will feminise the reputation, e.g. if Dunn & Co. wished to diversify into millinery.
   c Something that will masculinize the reputation, e.g. Yardley sponsor

motor racing when they entered the men's toiletries business with the Black Label range.

The permutations are limited only by the number of activities available for sponsorship.

The nature of the sponsored activity will dictate that of the promotional opportunities/obligations which may include:

1 Featuring the sponsorship in scheduled advertising.
2 Advertising the sponsorship to the primary audience, e.g. readers of the motoring Press.
3 Sending press packs to the relevant media, with a press conference if the story is strong enough.
4 A direct mail shot to relevant bodies, e.g. sports clubs and retail outlets, with colour posters, car stickers and window decals.
5 Receptions for Press, customers, and VIPs at the sponsored event.
6 Filming the event and placing copies with a film library.
7 Production of premium offer goods, e.g. tee-shirts.
8 Point-of-sale material.
9 Displays at the event.
10 Banners.
11 Prizes and trophies.
12 Provision of travel and accommodation assistance for competitors.
13 Post-event advertising, e.g. where a branded product has featured successfully in a competitive activity.

Costs of promoting a sponsorship can exceed the sum given to the sponsored organization. The costs of this aspect of the activity should therefore be calculated before any sponsorship agreement is signed.

The sponsorship agreement sets out the nature of the sponsor's financial commitment and defines what he will receive in return.

The sponsor will usually ensure that, among other points, the contract stipulates that:

1 The title of the event should include the corporate, company, or brand name.
2 The duration of the sponsorship and option(s) for renewal.
3 The sponsorship will not be shared.
4 The sponsor has a veto on competitive advertising at events.
5 Complimentary access to the event will be available for an agreed number of visitors.
6 Sponsor's receptions will be attended by, e.g., 'star' athletes from the sponsored event.

**Kodak Limited presents the first-ever
complete performance in Great Britain of**

The Haydn Oratorio

THE RETURN
OF TOBIAS

ROYAL
PHILHARMONIC
ORCHESTRA

Soloists:
Barbara Hendricks *Soprano*
Linda Zoghby *Mezzo*
Della Jones *Mezzo*
Philip Langridge *Tenor*
Benjamin Luxon *Bass*

Patron: Her Majesty Queen Elizabeth The Queen Mother
Leader: Barry Griffiths

**The Brighton
Festival Chorus**

Conductor:
ANTAL DORATI

Thursday, 13 December 1979, at 7·30pm

Greater London Council
Royal Festival Hall
Director: George Mann OBE

Tickets - Available from Box Office (Tel 01·928 3191) or
usual agents one month in advance of concert:
£1·40, £2·10, £3·00, £3·70, £4·40, £5·20 incl. 15% VAT
Performance will not end before 10·30pm.

This concert is presented by the
Royal Philharmonic Orchestra Ltd with financial
assistance from the **London Orchestral Concert
Board (representing the Arts Council of Great
Britain and the Greater London Council).**

Figure 10   Industrial companies' sponsorship of the arts can enhance their
standing with opinion leaders.

A number of organizations exist to match events with sponsors and/or *vice versa*. These include public relations consultancies, the Central Council of Physical Recreation's Sport Sponsorship Information Service, and the Association for Business Sponsorship of the Arts.

Support for the arts through patronage and sponsorship is an established activity among larger companies. Often undertaken on a long term basis, arts sponsorships demand more muted promotion than sports and recreational sponsorships and overt association may be confined to an announcement of the original contract and the appearance of the sponsoring organization's name on promotional material for the event being sponsored.

In supporting the arts the line between sponsorship and patronage becomes less distinct than elsewhere and an intended sponsorship can occasionally appear as patronage when viewed retrospectively.

Arts sponsorship opportunities — in music, theatre, and fine arts — continue to exceed the number of sponsors available to meet them. The situation has been aggravated by cutbacks in government funds available for the arts and there is little doubt that there is a wealth of goodwill to be earned by those willing to take advantage of the opportunities.

It is increasingly common for sponsorship 'brokers' to offer opportunities for shared sponsorship in the arts and in sport. Unless there are pressing reasons, and with the exception below it is difficult to envisage what these might be, shared sponsorship is to be avoided: the sponsorship message is invariably blurred and friction is almost inevitable.

The exception is sponsorship in association with the media, an example of which is the Langs Suprema *Times* Crossword Championship. Such an association ensures media coverage of the activity, but this must be weighed against the reluctance of other media to devote space to a rival's activities.

Educational Activities

It would be misleading to describe the antipathy of much of the teaching profession towards industry as a public relations problem. It is a problem for industry as a whole — from the Confederation of British Industry (CBI) in London and the regions, where the problem has been recognized, to the local sites of manufacturing companies.

Failure to overcome the antipathy will result in failure to improve the match between those leaving the educational system and the employment opportunities available.

The initial public relations role should be to alert employers to the opportunities available and to bring about the contacts that will lead to action. It is at local level that success will be achieved and where relationships between schools and industry yield results. The CBI and its Education and

Training Committee under the chairmanship of Lord Carr has strongly urged such initiatives as a matter of policy and this has led the CBI to establish the Understanding British Industry (UBI) project and to support and encourage the work of the Science and Technology Regional Organizations and other local bodies.

UBI and the Institution of Mechanical Engineers have inaugurated schemes which transfer teachers from the classroom to the factory for periods of up to a year. These operate at local, rather than national, levels and offer models for companies wishing to emulate them.

Once the gap between teachers and industry has been bridged, there are numerous initiatives that the public relations function can take, including:

1 Preparation of teaching kits on specific topics, e.g. energy conservation.
2 Programmes of office and works visits (see Facility Visits p.71).
3 One-day 'This is industry' courses for student teachers conducted half at college (theory), half at a factory or office.
4 Sponsored 'small businesses', where children raise funds by making and marketing products with 'loan capital' provided by parents. These events are normally competitive, the most successful at raising funds being the winner. Entrants are advised by their sponsoring industry.
5 Provision of wallcharts, 35 mm slide packs, films, and video cassette programmes on industrial/commercial topics.
6 Aid with school projects where local schools are competitively involved with regional or national schools or organizations.
7 Loan or gift of scientific equipment in good order.
8 Sponsoring of field trips.
9 Provision of raw material samples with supporting literature explaining their origin and use in the manufacturing process.
10 Loan of recreational and other facilities.

The difficult financial climate in which educationalists must operate means that corporate assistance is today not so much an opportunity as an obligation.

No company is too small, or too big, to start exploratory talks with schools in its area to see which type of assistance might be most helpful.

ACKNOWLEDGEMENTS

The author of this chapter on Media would like to acknowledge the help he received in its compilation from the following:
Adshel Ltd.
Audit Bureau of Circulations.

Britain's national newspaper editors.
British Direct Mail Advertisers Association.
British Direct Marketing Association.
British Industrial & Scientific Film Association.
British Overseas Trade Board.
Brown, Peter; Multimark.
Charles Barker City Ltd.
Charles Barker Lyons Ltd.
Chittock, John; the *Financial Times*.
Direct Mail Producers' Association.
EIBIS International.
Ford Motor Co. Ltd.
Gordon Audio Visual Ltd.
'Hi-fi for Pleasure'.
Hope, Christopher; World Wide Pictures Ltd.
Independent Television Authority.
Independent Television Companies Association.
Institute of Practitioners in Advertising.
Media Expenditure Analysis Ltd.
Chris Moore.
National Coal Board.
Pilkington Brothers Ltd.
Robophone Facilities Ltd.
The Incorporated Society of British Advertisers Ltd.
Universal News Services.

3

Timing and Handling of Material

Frank Jefkins

News — its nature and criteria

News consists of information which is of interest and value to the recipient who may be a reader, listener or viewer. Generally, the news media consist of the mass media of the Press, radio and television, but in public relations we also use media directed at small or selective audiences, such as house journals, newsletters, documentary films, closed circuit television, private radio stations, video and audio tapes, notice-boards, posters, handbills, brochures and personal letters.

We should not forget that in public relations we deal with many publics, and also with individuals. There are many occasions when *private* or sponsored media — as distinct from commercial or official media — have to be created, or when face-to-face communication may be necessary. In every case the criteria are, in the words of Ivy Ledbetter Lee in his statement to the American Press in 1906, that PR material should be of 'interest and value', *not to the sender but to the recipient*. The greatest fault with much public relations material is that it aims to please clients or employers, and lacks 'box office' appeal. This is often a very hard lesson to learn, but the status, integrity and success of the PR practitioner depends on his professional ability to please the 'box office', so that he ultimately pleases his client or employer.

Written PR material consists chiefly of news releases or news reports and feature articles. The expression 'handout' should never be used nor really should the expression 'press release' be used because radio and television are among the recipients. However, 'press relations' is still used although 'media relations' would seem to be more appropriate.

News releases and feature articles are totally different in their form and content, in their preparation and cost, and in their effectiveness. An article is not a long news release, and a news item is not a short article. Nor is either an advertisement. The PR writer should therefore understand which kind of material he is writing, if only that ideally whatever he writes should be publishable as it stands subject to editorial requirements. For instance, an editor may shorten a piece to fit the space, or insert sub-headings if he wants them, but he should not have to rewrite the piece. Some of the best examples of acceptable news releases are those to which the journalist has added his own by-line as if he has written it himself, or it may be attributed to a staff writer such as 'by our science correspondent'. Sometimes, however, journalists will insist on rewriting simply to assert their own creative independence, or to introduce a special house style. If the original is clearly and concisely written it should not matter if it is paraphrased. The important thing is to get the facts published correctly. The more simple the information, the less easily can it be distorted. This applies whether one is writing about custard powder or microelectronics.

Kinds of News

It may be thought that only 'hard' news (that is, news about current affairs and major events) is news, but news can be any information which is of interest and value to people. Some topics are in the news continuously, the Olympic games or solar energy, for instance, so that news is not always about something which has just happened. In an intellectual newspaper (which usually has a small circulation) the news may be about political, economic, financial and other 'serious' subjects, but in a popular paper (with a multi-million circulation) the kind of news will be very different. It is a fact of life that most people prefer to be entertained by their newspaper. It is important, therefore, that the PR practitioner understands the kind of news required by different newspapers, and it would be foolish to send the same story to 'all nationals'. One of the reasons for the love-hate relationship between editors and PROs is that the former receive so many irrelevant news releases.

In a women's magazine (or women's feature in a newspaper) the news may be mainly about fashion, beauty, homemaking, cookery and other feminine interests. A new cosmetic is news to a woman, a new motor-car is news to a motorist, a new policy is news to an insurance broker. The need is to address the right story to the right publication, feature editor or special correspondent. One does not send news about a new holiday attraction to 'the editor' of a daily newspaper, but to the travel editor, preferably by name.

The test of whether an item is news is whether there are readers who will benefit from having gained this information. No-one is likely to benefit from the announcement that the marketing manager has been renamed the marketing director, and yet far too many PR stories are as trivial as that. The editor acts as a referee between suppliers of information and his readers.

Subject to the limitations of space, he will select the best stories which will please his readers, bearing in mind that he may have to compete for readers by publishing different or better stories. Thus the PRO has not only to provide publishable releases, but news which is sufficiently important to compete with other good stories when space is limited. Consequently, even a very good release may not be published.

In those countries where bribery and corruption are a way of life, it may be normal practice to attach a banknote to a release or give money to reporters at press conferences; but this becomes a self-defeating farce because everybody does it and in the end the editor will print what he wants to print.

The PRO has no right to expect publication. He cannot bribe or pressurize the editor, and it is also foolish to include covering letters pleading for the editor's support. The story must seek publication on its own merits subject to editorial policy, preferences and decisions. Most editors receive far more news than they can possibly print, not just from PROs, but from regular, paid journalistic sources, such as reporters and news agencies.

This implies that:

1 Every PR story should be of publishable interest and standard.
2 It should be sent only to the *minimum* number of publications likely to print it.
3 The PRO should do his own 'copy-tasting' and resist sending out a story that is unlikely to interest a large number of readers of the journals on the selected mailing list.
4 The PRO should understand copy deadlines — the latest time, day, week and month when the editor must receive the story. This entails knowing whether the publication is printed by letterpress, lithography or photo-gravure. Magazines printed by photogravure (e.g. most British women's magazines) may require copy up to three months in advance. Newspapers and magazines printed by offset-litho may require copy hours or days sooner than ones printed by letterpress. Advertisement copy dates can be a useful guide, and these are published on rate cards and in reference books such as *British Rate and Data*. Many news releases fail to be published simply because they arrive too late. The copy date consideration also concerns dates, days of the week and time of day for press receptions. A helpful rule is that press receptions are often best held early in the day, early in the week and early in the month, however inconvenient to top management.

The above implications suggest that the essence of good press relations is appreciating how to service the Press. A very large number of releases received by editors — at least 50 per cent — do not obey the above constraints, and should never have been posted. That is why so many editors keep large plastic dustbins in which to deposit useless releases, many of which bear famous names. Undoubtedly, the news release is the worst produced piece of PR material.

It is therefore worth repeating that the PRO should aim to please the editor and the reader, in which case he will also please his employer or client. But if he merely pleases his employer or client, and fails to please the editor, he will please no-one. Too much PR is of this negative quality, which is rather like an architect agreeing with the client that the roof should be in the basement. This means that there may be times when the PR practitioner — whether house PRO or consultant — must exercise his advisory and professional capacity and explain why a release should be written in a certain way, and even why it should not be sent out at all. PROs who try to justify their existence by sending out as many releases as possible, and perhaps to a seemingly impressive large mailing list, are poor practitioners who are doing PR a disservice. They are annoying editors, wasting their own and other people's time and money, making it impossible to achieve cost-effective maximum coverage, and harming the prospects of getting really good stories published.

Basic Rules for News Releases

Content

1 The *subject* must be at the very beginning of the news release, ideally in the very first few words. If reports are examined in newspapers it will be seen that this is standard practice. The writer must be careful to decide what is the subject. It may not be the name of his organization (or client), although it is a common mistake to start releases with the name of the organization. It is journalistic practice to put the name at the end of the sentence, e.g. *A new route to Singapore will be flown by British Airways* rather than *British Airways will fly a new route to Singapore.* The new route is the subject.

   However, the subject may differ according to the media, and it may be unwise to issue only one version of a story. Thus, to take the above example, British Airways could be the subject for aviation journals, and the route for business journals, but for general newspapers the company name should be at the end of the sentence. The writer has to judge accordingly, and should not be persuaded to begin the story with a company name just because this pleases the vanity of management.

2 The *opening paragraph* should be a brief summary of the whole release. If only this paragraph is printed, the writer will then have succeeded in communicating his essential message. If newspapers are studied it will be apparent that if only the first paragraphs are read, the reader will have an excellent digest of all the news.

Sometimes newspapers have editions published at different times of the day or night. A PR story may occupy a lot of space in the early editions, but as more news comes in and new editions are printed, the original reports may be cut to accommodate fresh material. It is therefore a sound rule that a good news release should be capable of being cut from the bottom up.

3 The release should be as *short* as possible, and this can be helped by the use of short words, short sentences and short paragraphs. Most releases can be written on one sheet of paper — an A4 sheet will take about 300 words. Some can be written in one paragraph, or even one sentence, e.g. appointment stories for the business Press such as the *Financial Times*. Releases sent to news agencies such as the Press Association (UK distribution) or Reuters (overseas distribution) should not exceed 100 words, since very brief reports are put out on wire services.

4 *Puffery* must be avoided, however enthusiastic one feels about the subject. Eulogies kill stories. A news release is not an advertisement. It must present bare facts only, without self-praise, superlatives or comment. It is the editor's privilege to praise or criticize. Marketing, advertising and management people are apt to criticize drafts of news releases because they do not boost the organization or product. But the PRO is not writing advertisement copy or propaganda: he is writing *news* and the difference is immense. This requires the elimination or avoidance of superlatives and *clichés* such as 'renowned', 'brand leader', 'world famous', 'leading', 'foremost', 'unique' and other advertising expressions.

Similarly, sentences beginning 'We are proud to announce' have no place in a news release. In any case, pronouns such as 'we' and 'you' should not be used if the story is to be printed as if written in the editorial office. The writer is not sending a personal letter to the editor.

These faults are demonstrated in the following unpublishable version of the example quoted in 1 previously: *The renowned British Airways, the world's largest airline, is proud to announce that it will fly an exciting new route to Singapore.* Good advertisement copy though this may be, an editor would consider it an unusable puff.

5 *Initials and acronyms.* If the organization is known by its initials, e.g. IBM, ITT, BOC, ICI or IBA, the full name should be spelt out in the first reference, thus Independent Broadcasting Authority with subsequent references reduced to the initials IBA. This prevents confusion. For instance, what does AA mean? The Automobile Association, The Advertising Association or Alcoholics Anonymous? Certain organizations are fortunate in having sets of initials or abbreviations which make easily remembered words or acronyms, typical ones being Fiat, Sabena, Scats, Toshiba and CAM itself. It may be necessary to write 'Sabena, the Belgian national airline', or spell out CAM which is seldom understood and often

confused with Cambridge. There are even complete words like Elf which need to be associated with petrol to avoid confusion with the initials of, say, the Eritrean Liberation Front.

6 *Never generalize*. Advertisement copy can be emotive and unspecific, using expressions like 'six gorgeous colours', but in a news release the actual colours should be stated. A release must be cold-bloodedly factual, not fanciful. It must not refer vaguely to 'economical', 'money-saving', 'time-saving' or 'labour-saving'. Nor should there be meaningless remarks like 'exhaustive research', or unsubstantiated statements such as 'fastest', 'cheapest' or 'biggest'. Such things should be implied by given facts. Again, the editor should not have to ring up for essential facts which are not secret and should have been included. This may call for more detailed research before writing a release. 'Woolly' stories result from inadequate information. The writer must be sure of his facts, and also check them, not take it for granted that other people have given him correct information, no matter what their authority. Numbers can be treacherous, as can be the spelling of people's names. Because newspapers are produced very rapidly, mistakes are common, but there is no excuse for the PRO to supply inaccurate information, for he has the time and the means to check everything.

7 *Dates*. Be specific. How recent is recently? Never use this empty expression. It is dangerous to say that something has happened or will happen 'yesterday', 'today', 'tomorrow' or 'next month'. Give the actual date. Some journals are published daily, weekly, monthly or quarterly, and vague dates can be pointless to an editor looking at a release some time after the event. Again, editors prefer a story about something which has happened or about a product which is available now, rather than about something which is destined to occur in the future and might never happen. It is better to announce the introduction of a product which is in the shops now, rather than issue a release about a product which will be on sale next month, unless advance information is being given to the trade press or to a magazine printed by photogravure.

8 *Be consistent*. Decide whether you are going to prefix names with 'Mr' or not and adhere to that decision consistently. Don't mix styles such as one-and-a-half and 1½, Common Market and EEC, America and USA, motor bike and motor cycle, or Northern Ireland and Ulster. Some readers might think the two were different.

9 Watch your *spelling*. The most commonly misspelt words are: *Separate*, *questionnaire*, *personnel*, *past* (for *passed*), and *alright* for *all right*.

Presentation

A news release is a manuscript and it should follow printing requirements

which often differ from secretarial practice. PR secretaries need to be taught
how to type news releases, articles and other copy such as material for house
journals. When material has been amended and retyped by someone else (e.g.
the managing director's secretary) it is usually necessary to retype before
submission to an editor or printer in order to eliminate the non-printing and
publishing styles which have been introduced inadvertently. Editors respect
press material which is produced professionally.

It should go without saying that a release should be reproduced on one side
of the paper only. No-one — editor, typesetter or word processor — is going to
look on the back. There should be good margins on both sides, and the
material should be double-spaced, so that amendments and especially
printing instructions such as type mark-ups can be written in the available
space by the editor. Editors rarely have time to retype releases, and a well
written, well presented piece can be subbed, marked up and sent for setting as
original copy. Evidence of this can always be seen during a visit to a newspaper
print shop. This belies the false theory that long stories should be sent to
editors, so that they can cut out the bits they do not want. So it follows that the
fewer amendments the editor has to make, the less work he has to do in making
the story printable, let alone publishable.

1 *Press release heading* Flamboyant headings look like sales letters and can
  irritate editors who will be encouraged to expect the story to be a puff.
  These rules are worth following:

  a Identify the release as a release in contrast to a business letterheading by
    using words such as 'News' or 'Information', e.g. 'News from XYZ Ltd'.
  b Print the heading in one colour only, but by all means use the 'house'
    colour if there is one.
  c Use the organization's symbol, logo, badge, emblem, or coat-of-arms for
    quick identification.
  d Place the detailed name, address and telephone number *at the foot* of the
    sheet in modest, but legible, type.
  e Give as much space as possible to the story.
  f Don't use slogans, or any other sort of advertising device.

2 *Headline* Don't write a catchy headline. Identify the story briefly, e.g. *New
  Sausage from Walls*. It is unlikely that the headline will be used as editors write
  their own headlines to suit house-styles, to be original and to fit the space or
  suit the size of display face being used.
3 *Sub-headings* are usually unnecessary in a release. Editors may or may not use
  sub-headings for special effects, or as part of the typographical design of the

page. The writer of a release cannot foresee editorial intentions. However, a sub-heading may be used to separate details of, say, two models of a machine if this clarifies the story, but this is exceptional.

4 *Paragraphing* Book style is adopted by most publishers in contrast to the block paragraphs used for business letters. The first paragraph is not indented (this originating from illuminated handwritten bibles), and all subsequent paragraphs are indented. Some newspapers indent even the first paragraph, but it is best to adopt the book style described above, otherwise the editor has to mark up paragraph indents.

5 Never *underline* in a release as this is a printing instruction to set in italics. Italics can be indicated in this way in a feature article.

6 *Capital letters (Caps)* These should not be used indiscriminately or for purposes of emphasis. Normally, caps should be restricted to proper names of people or organisations and geographical place names, e.g. Smith or London. Certain of the highest dignitaries such as Her Majesty the Queen, Prime Minister, Rabbi, Archbishop and Field Marshal are given initial caps, but these are denied to lesser people such as chairmen, managing directors and others with job titles. Not even the *Financial Times* prints managing director with a cap M and D. It is pure puffery to put a company or brand name entirely in caps. Moreover, it is noticeable that acronyms are styled Fiat, not FIAT, Sabena, not SABENA in the Press, although pronounceable initials such as UNO, UNESCO and CAM are permitted full caps.

7 *Abbreviations* With the exception of *i.e.* and *e.g.* the Press do not use full stops or full points between initials representing names, and so ICI, IBM, CAM, IPR, BSc(Econ), DipCAM, MCAM and mpg should be typed as shown here.

8 *Figures and Signs* Figures in news releases are usually spelt out one to nine, and afterwards written as numbers until they become unwieldy and it is clearer to put thousands and millions into words. However, numbers are retained for dates, addresses, prices, specifications and so on. Sentences should not begin with a number. For example: 'Six delegates made two attempts to present a petition to 10 Downing Street on October 1.' The ampersand (&) is never used in sentences, and the percentage sign (%) is spelt out (per cent or percent).

9 *Dates* As shown in the preceding example, the month is given first and 'st', 'nd', 'th' and 'nd' endings are not used by the Press.

10 *For Immediate Release.* This is pointless, otherwise why send the story? 'Ends' is equally redundant, except in an editorial office where copy is being sent down for setting on separate and perhaps isolated pieces of paper and being set by different operators, so that it is important to identify the final piece of

copy. This does not apply to a news release, especially if it consists of a single sheet, and when the end of the story can be shown clearly by the name of the author, his telephone number and the date.

11 *Continuations.* If a story runs to a second or third page, 'more' should be typed in the bottom righthand corner. Succeeding pages should be numbered, and it is helpful to repeat the headline in the top lefthand corner, but clearly separated from the text.

12 *Embargoes* should not be used unless absolutely essential, and they should state the date and time when the story may be printed. An embargo should be a privilege, not an instruction, enabling the editor to have advance information of, say, a speech which is to be delivered on a future date, or about a report before it is published. Editors are not bound to obey embargoes and they will ignore those which are frivolous or which disadvantage them in relation to other media, such as radio or TV. However, when a Parliamentary Lobby Correspondent is given a White Paper twenty-four hours before publication he would lose his privileges if he disregarded that embargo. Other embargoes which are quickly accepted are those concerning Stock Exchange rules, or time differentials between different parts of the world. But Sunday newspapers defy embargoes on book reviews.

Feature Articles

Feature articles are usually longer than news releases and deal with their subjects in more detail and in a more creative style. They call for research, interviews and interpretation of information. They are more literary, and the writer can employ more stylistic and creative writing, make comments, use anecdotes and quotations, pose hypothetical questions, and generally embellish the piece with all the skills of authorship as distinct from objective factual reporting. A big distinction is the opening paragraph which must not give away the essence of the whole story, but must tempt the reader to read on.

The PRO can be in a splendid position to supply ideas for feature articles, provide facilities for staff journalists to write them, or write them himself. He often has access to article material which is unknown to editors, and can therefore be of genuine interest to them.

But the interest and value criteria should be strictly observed, and the organization, product, service or any other subject should not be plugged indiscriminately. Such references should occur only where their absence would be wrong. It is possible to write a PR article where the commercial references are restricted to the by-line or a picture caption. A good PR article should be worthy of acceptance as part of the authoritative literature on the subject.

Publication of Articles

Articles are distributed differently from news releases. The news release can be broadcast to any number of editors who may reject or rewrite it at their discretion, or seek more information and change or enlarge the story, or simply accept and print it as it stands. But a feature article is a single piece published by one journal. It should not be written and submitted speculatively. The best procedure is as follows:

1 Decide on the subject of the article.
2 Make sure that you have access to required information. Permission may be required to write about the subject and further permission to conduct interviews and take pictures — as when the article is about a customer's use of a product, e.g. a vehicle being used by a transport company.
3 Select the most suitable publication.
4 Write to or telephone the editor, setting out your proposition. Large circulation journals will probably wish to appoint a staff journalist to write the article. Other journals, especially trade and technical papers, may be more willing to let the PRO write (or supply) the article — 'supply' because the article could be written by the PRO himself, a member of his organization, or by a commissioned freelance writer, or perhaps by a PR consultant. Articles can be 'ghosted' in the name of a company personality whose authorship will give authority, but who is not himself a practised writer. In the case of the supplied article, the proposition should be set out in businesslike terms. The editor should be asked, if he accepts the idea, to state:
  a The number of words required.
  b Any special treatment required — technical, popular, human interest and so on.
  c Number and kind of illustrations required.
  d Proposed date of publication.
  e Deadline for supply of the article to the editor.

The editor may accept the offer 'subject to sight of the copy', which is fair enough. Provided the article is written to a publishable standard, the writer guarantees that his facts have been checked (copies of the draft having been approved or amended by all those who have provided information, and approved by those giving permission for the article to be written), and puffery has been avoided by keeping commercial references to a minimum, the article will be published as written. The editor may make minor amendments to make the article fit the space, or to comply with 'house style', but he will not rewrite it as he would be entitled to with a news release. The onus is on the writer to give the editor a professionally written publishable article.

If the article has been thoroughly researched the quality of the article can result from the author having so much information he has to write concisely in order to keep the piece down to the required number of words. This discipline of research, selection of information, and concise writing will help the author to produce an article that is factual, interesting and easy to read. The dull, wordy generalized article usually results from not having sufficient to write about. But the article which covers a lot of gound in the minimum number of words is one which carries the reader's interest along at a good pace and so makes good reading.

The production of a feature article is thus a practical exercise. The writer is doing the editor a favour in supplying material which the editor could not have obtained himself. It is an exclusive. The editor is not doing the PRO a favour in printing it. Consequently, the editor is commissioning the writer (generally without fee, although PR writers who are recognized authorities on their subject may be paid), and so it is unnecessary to entertain the editor. Wining and dining editors in order to get articles published can only suggest that the proposed article will not be good enough to achieve publication on its own merits.

Thousands of PR articles on scores of topics for many employers and clients have been published solely on the basis of a letter or telephone call making a proposition and the author receiving instructions as just described. A busy PRO who writes many articles simply does not have the time to entertain editors. It should not be necessary to buy advertisement space to support good feature articles, which are frequently in publications in which the organizations concerned never advertise.

Two things should be remembered about PR articles. They take time to negotiate, research, prepare and check, and publication dates may be weeks or months ahead. Feature article writing is seldom a quick job, and it is time-consuming, whereas it is possible to dictate a news release over the telephone. Therefore, article writing needs to be slotted into the overall PR programme for the period. And since time is the biggest cost factor in PR, the cost of producing PR articles needs to be carefully budgeted. For instance, it may pay to confine interviews and visits to within fifty miles of base, rather than incur travel and overnight stays. All in all, the total time involved in the production of an article (even if the actual writing time is only two or three hours) could be from three to five days, especially if the research and interviews involve travel. Against this cost can be held the many values resulting from publication. Its volume of space, prominence and importance in the publication, long life (which can be extended by having reprints), and general authority and prestige should show a profit on even a high cost. For example, a series of articles in the municipal Press resulted in a company establishing its reputation among the local authorities of Britain, the majority of whom are now its customers. The exclusive signed feature article can therefore be a very powerful form of PR communication.

Articles written by staff writers incur few costs beyond providing facilities such as escorting journalists, making advance arrangements for interviews and visits, and providing transportation and hospitality such as meals and hotel accommodation. If possible, the PRO should arrange to check the journalist's draft. However, journalists may be unwilling to submit drafts in case the PRO demands unreasonable amendments. The PRO should stipulate that he wishes only to check the accuracy of spellings, facts and figures in the journalist's own interest.

Syndicated Articles

The preceding section discussed the *exclusive* feature article, a one-off effort, but articles may be offered to more than one editor on the syndication principle that the same piece is not offered to editors of rival publications with competing circulations. There are about one hundred daily newspapers published outside London — chiefly evening newspapers — and it would be perfectly acceptable to offer the same article to papers published far enough apart — say, Bristol, Norwich, Manchester, Newcastle and Glasgow — to have exclusive readership. It would not be acceptable to offer the same article to national newspapers or magazines.

Syndicated articles should not be distributed like news releases, unless one is using an international service like that of EIBIS which translates articles and mails them to appropriate publications overseas. Even then, EIBIS applies the same rule, country by country, avoiding duplication.

The method is to send a synopsis of a free-of-fee article to selected editors, stating that it is not being offered to rivals but on a first refusal basis, and editors are invited to request the article either for consideration or for definite publication. Illustrations can be offered in the same way, perhaps with a sheet of miniatures. This method can be very effective; it has been known for identical articles to be published in seventy newspapers in the same week. Such articles are usually fairly short, from 750 to 1000 words, which makes them both more acceptable and less likely to be cut. It also helps if the author is a well-known authority on the subject, and professional authors may be commissioned for the purpose.

Working with the Printer

As we have seen, the production of press relations material requires at least some elementary understanding of printing processes and requirements and of the ways of the publishing world. It is also necessary to understand the characteristics of the media, so that blanket mailings are avoided and media lists are tailor-made for each story. This calls for familiarity with the media lists of PIMS or EMA (Editorial Media Analysis), or with directories such as *Benn's Press Directory, Willing's Press Guide*, and the *PR-Planner*.

There will also be many occasions when the PR practitioner will be dealing directly with the printer. This applies to the production of house journals, brochures, leaflets, manuals, sponsored books and other print. Now he has to be his own editor. He also has to be capable of managing the job from getting print quotations, writing and designing the job, to following it through to the delivery date.

The more he knows about printing processes, kinds of paper, typefaces, methods of binding, preparation of copy and artwork, typesetting and word processing or photo-typesetting methods, and proof-reading, the more efficient he will be in his relations with the printer. All this cannot be gone into in this chapter, but is not as complicated as it sounds. It is very interesting and a good all-round knowledge will result in good print delivered on time at the most economical cost. An excellent, brief and extremely well illustrated guide is the little book *Pocket Pal*. Every PRO should have a copy.

Printers are craftsmen whose skill should be respected and advice listened to. However, most printers tend to specialize in particular classes of work as specified in the printing section of *Advertiser's Annual*. This also means that they will have the right machines for the job whether it be printing stationery, labels, books, newspapers, posters or postage stamps. Choosing an appropriate printer for the job is the first step.

Most printers are only too pleased to explain how they work, and what they need from the customer. One of the great attractions of public relations is that it is a perpetual education, and the good practitioner is one who is always ready to learn. An important part of the process of working with the printer is the willingness to find out.

Next, it is important to understand that one is not the only customer, and that one is dealing with men, machines and time, and that these resources have to be allocated to each stage of the job. Thus, it is necessary to create a time schedule which may look something like this:

D–90   Quotations invited based on dummy layout and estimation оι number of words and illustrations, together with details of quality, quantity, size, colours, etc.
D–80   Quotations received.
D–75   Quotation accepted.
D–75   Job written, artwork produced.
D–60   Layout and type mark-ups prepared.

D–55 Copy supplied to the printer.
D–35 Proofs received.
D–30 Corrected proofs returned to the printer.
D–day Finished print delivered.
(The D–figures can be replaced by actual dates agreed with the printer.)

In some cases there will be two or more proof stages, such as galley proofs, then page proofs, and finally machine proofs which will be checked at the printers. Galley proofs are long proofs of the text set solid with no display lines; page proofs resemble the finished job; and machine proofs are of corrected page proofs or of colour work. It is the responsibility of the customer to honour the timetable, otherwise overtime charges may be incurred, or the delivery date will have to be changed. The PRO must therefore agree a timetable which is feasible, bearing in mind that other people — employers or clients — can cause delays. Some people do not know what they want until they see it in print; ideally, the PRO has to try to get everything approved *before* it goes to the printer.

One of the most important aspects is the correction of proofs. It is extremely easy to miss errors, as can be seen by reading a daily newspaper which employs professional proof-readers. Proofs should be read slowly, syllable by syllable, and it pays to seek help in reading proofs. Strangers to the copy will often spot mistakes overlooked by the author who is too familiar with what he is reading. The most careless proof-readers are clients and others with authority to approve. Second and third readings will often reveal previously overlooked errors. For instance, the words 'of' and 'or' are frequently mistakenly set. It is easy to read what one expects to find. Special attention should be paid to the spelling of names: Nielsen, Neilsen, and Neilson have all been known to appear in the same paragraph!

Special attention is also required in checking figures and specification details, and it pays to go back to original sources in case the copy was wrong. New copy should not be introduced if at all possible. Changes should be made so that they are confined to the column or page, and not be allowed to disrupt succeeding pages or columns. This means that numbers, words or characters have to be counted to avoid an over-run onto the next column or page.

Apart from spelling errors it is essential to look out for the transposition of characters, wrong punctuation, wrong spacing, the emergence of characters from a different typeface (wrong fount), the rising of spaces (in letterpress) which produce black instead of white spaces, irregular lines caused by loose type and other defects. If the job has been photo-set the proof may be a photo-copy of a paste-up, and items may have been pasted-up incorrectly. Very curious things happen with photo-type-setting which may be produced by computer, and it is possible for the operator to depress the *italic* key and then forget to change it, so that instead of one word appearing in italics, a whole sentence or paragraph is italicized. One way and another, proof-reading is a detective job, and the reader must take nothing for granted. It won't be all right on the night unless the proof-reader gets it right before the presses roll.

The printing industry uses a standard set of proof correction symbols, and these can be learned as one handles more and more print. They are a kind of printer's shorthand. The main thing is to make all corrections absolutely clear to the printer, even if not every symbol is used. There is a simple method of keeping corrections tidy and legible. Divide the page or column with a vertical line down the middle. This can be done mentally or with a soft pencil. Then write all the corrections to the left of the 'line' in the left-hand margin, and all those to the right of the 'line' in the right-hand margin ensuring the order in which the corrections appear (from left to right) reflects their position in the line. Use the colours your printer recommends. Extensive amendments or additions should be typed as fresh copy, rather than scribbled on the proof, with an instruction to see the attached new copy and where it is to appear.

If there are many corrections it is sensible to call for a 'revised proof', when it can be surprising to see how many corrections have been overlooked by the printer.

There are particular symbols which are used repeatedly, such as those for delete (really a 'd' attached to an oblique), and the little 'y' inverted for insert, while the actual deletions should be made in the text by striking an oblique through the error. Never blot out or cross out with wriggly lines. The transposition and punctuation symbols (such as the dot in a circle for full point, and the acorn cup symbol for an apostrophe) are easy to remember. Gradually, the rest become familiar with practice as sensible ways of communicating with the printer.

With this introduction, the following is the standard set of proof correction symbols, reproduced by courtesy of the British Printing Industries Federation, and based on the recommendations of the British Standards Institution (BS 1219:1958).

Symbols for correcting proofs

The symbols for correcting proofs used in this booklet are taken from a British Standard BS 5261: *Part 2 1976 Copy preparation and proof correction – Specification for typographic requirements, marks for copy preparation and proof correction, proofing procedure.* It was prepared by the British Standards Institution following discussions on an international standard for proof correction symbols to replace the former British Standard which used several English words or initial letters unacceptable internationally.

Extracts from the new Standard are given below and all authors, printers, and publishers are recommended to adopt the new correction symbols.

Instruction	Textual Mark	Marginal Mark
Correction is concluded	None	/
Leave unchanged	– – – – – – under character to remain	✓ (circled)
Push down risen spacing material	Encircle blemish	⊥
Insert in text the matter indicated in the margin	⋏	New matter followed by ⋏
Insert additional matter identified by a letter in a diamond	⋏	⋏ Followed by for example ◇A
Delete	/ through character(s) or ├───┤ through word(s) to be deleted	♂

Instruction	Textual Mark	Marginal Mark
Delete and close up	⌒ through character or ⊢━━━⊣ through character e.g. chara⌒cter chara⌒⌒cter	♂
Substitute character or substitute part of one or more word(s)	/ through character or ⊢━━━⊣ through word(s)	New character or new word(s)
Wrong fount. Replace by character(s) of correct fount	Encircle character(s) to be changed	⊗
Change damaged character(s)	Encircle character(s) to be changed	✕
Set in or change to italic	___ under character(s) to be set or changed	⊔
Set in or change to capital letters	≡ under character(s) to be set or changed	≡
Set in or change to small capital letters	≡ under character(s) to be set or changed	=
Set in or change to capital letters for initial letters and small capital letters for the rest of the words	≡ under initial letters and ≡ under rest of word(s)	≊
Set in or change to bold type	∿∿∿ ·under character(s) to be set or changed	∿
Change capital letters to lower case letters	Encircle character(s) to be changed	≢
Change italic to upright type	Encircle character(s) to be changed	⊔⌐

Instruction	Textual Mark	Marginal Mark
Invert type	Encircle character to be inverted	↻
Substitute or insert full stop or decimal point	/ through character or ⋏ where required	⊙
Substitute or insert semi-colon	/ through character or ⋏ where required	;
Substitute or insert comma	/ through character or ⋏ where required	,
Start new paragraph	⌐_	⌐_
Run on (no new paragraph)	͜⟩	͜⟩
Centre	[enclosing matter to be centred]	[ ]
Indent	⊏	⊏
Cancel indent	←⊏	⊏
Move matter specified distance to the right	⌐enclosing matter to be moved to the right→	⊏

Instruction	Textual Mark	Marginal Mark
Take over character(s), word(s) or line to next line, column or page		
Take back character(s), word(s) or line to previous line, column or page		
Raise matter	over matter to be raised under matter to be raised	
Lower matter	over matter to be lowered under matter to be lowered	
Correct horizontal alignment	Single line above and below misaligned matter e.g. mi_{sa}li_{gn}ed	
Close up. Delete space between characters or words	linking characters	
Insert space between characters	between characters affected	
Insert space between words	between words affected	
Reduce space between characters	between characters affected	
Reduce space between words	between words affected	
Make space appear equal between characters or words	between characters or words affected	

4

Public Relations in a Large Industrial Company

David Morgan Rees

The outside world intrudes increasingly upon the conduct of a company's affairs, questioning motives and judging performance from levels of understanding which may vary from the expert and informed, to the cynical, ignorant or prejudiced. Financial analyst, politician, government official, consumerist, environmentalist, or trade union official can all scrutinize a particular company and demand information or action. This is quite apart from the proper interest of institutional or private shareholder, employee, supplier and customer.

Perhaps with more urgency today than ever before, at a time when many are questioning the competence of individual companies and many the ability of the whole private enterprise system to respond to and satisfy the present and future needs and aspirations of modern society, it is vital for everyone, at different levels, to play their part in explaining with sincerity and conviction to a wide variety of people the relevance and achievement of their own company in the total industrial scene and the importance of its continuing prosperity. An industrial company's efficiency as an organization must increasingly be matched by an awareness and acceptance of its social responsibilities: as a good employer, a considerate member of the local community and upholder of high standards of business ethics, efficient production and technical performance.

This involves considerable subtleties of attitudes and opinions, but the end product of any public relations programme in our increasingly 'open' society, which itself demands and legislates for greater disclosure of information, must ultimately be related to a company's reputation: to the creation of understanding and, as a result, the achievement of goodwill towards the organization and its activities. This is a challenge to all who are responsible for the public relations initiative of a company making a product or providing a service. For goodwill, that invisible, intangible asset, is still the most highly-valued public relations 'prize' from which all else follows in seeking to change attitudes and opinions favourably as the only satisfactory means of achieving a company's corporate objectives. And is not the most succinct definition of public relations 'good performance, publicly acknowledged'?

The larger the company the greater its communication responsibilities, the wider its public relations objectives and the effort needed to achieve and sustain these. In a small or medium-sized company, operating in one country or market only, such objectives and practices tend to be related to narrower, more precise needs which can be more easily measured: the launch of a new product, the obtaining of a larger market share, or the recruitment of more skilled labour. Also, some companies, by the nature of their products and services, inevitably have a high public 'profile' and a greater need to communicate: a food manufacturer must ensure a wider awareness of its activities than, say, a specialist supplier to the computer industry. A manufacturing organization will in turn have a different 'profile' from a bank or insurance company.

A multinational industrial company has very significant and complex public relations responsibilities today. With widely decentralized manufacturing and distribution activities, often carried out in financial partnership with a variety of local business interests, it has to plan and monitor its public relations policies and practices across geographical, political and cultural frontiers. The communication problems are considerable because a multinational company today tends to be type-cast by critics (who are only too happy to generalize) in the role of an international villain, arrogantly flouting national authority.

Much more work though has been done in the 'seventies by various bodies to formalize suggested codes of conduct for multinationals, including the Organization for Economic Co-operation and Development (OECD), whose Declaration and Decisions on International Investment and Multinational Enterprises, described as 'a pioneering approach in a highly complex and widely debated subject', was promulgated in 1976 and aimed at 'improving the international investment climate through joint undertakings by the governments of Member countries which should strengthen confidence between multinational enterprises and States; they aim further at encouraging the positive contributions of multinational enterprises to economic and social progress and minimizing or resolving difficulties that may result from their activities, through internationally-agreed guidelines, inter-governmental consultations and review mechanisms.'

In 1977 the International Labour Organization published the Tripartite Declaration of Principles concerning Multinational Enterprises and Social Policy (endorsed in the UK by the Minister of Employment, Director-General of the CBI and Secretary of the TUC) which aimed 'to encourage the positive contribution which multinational enterprises can make to economic and social progress and to minimize and resolve the difficulties to which their various operations may give rise' by setting out guiding principles on employment, training, conditions of work and life, and industrial relations 'which government, employers' and workers' organizations and multinational enterprises are recommended to observe on a voluntary basis.'

The public relations responsibilities of a multinational have to be discharged with special care where a company has investments in particularly sensitive areas which are subject to the pressures of world-wide political opinion, for example, a manufacturing organization in South Africa or Chile, however well-established, commercially and morally justified such activities may be. Such a company has to be concerned about its public reputation, not only in its country of origin, but also in the estimation of businessmen many thousands of miles away from corporate headquarters. A negligent or indifferent public relations attitude at such a distance could jeopardize future investment, sour relationships with political and business leaders and create an unfavourable local employee relations climate. This is particularly important where a multinational company has investments in economies at varying stages of development: what is right, in a public relations approach, for Europe will not necessarily be appropriate for West Africa or Indonesia.

This places a premium on well-conceived corporate public relations objectives and policy which are scrupulously communicated and maintained throughout the whole organization of a large industrial company with subsidiaries and associates at work in many countries. Inspiration, for example, aided by simple and clear guidelines, may come from the centre, but enthusiasm and willing co-operation are vitally necessary from the operating companies, so that there is a reasonably consistent approach and achievement, which takes account of both group policy and local initiative.

Having stressed the scale of the public relations function in a large industrial company (whether multinational or not), it is important not to overlook certain simple and fundamental principles which apply to good public relations practice in industry today. Some pundits are in danger of clouding the issue by choosing different terminology such as 'corporate affairs' or 'public affairs', implying that different standards and parameters are involved where large companies operate. Perhaps it is merely necessary to say that PR is PR in a large company, only more so!

Although seemingly an abstraction arising only from its corporate documents, a company is like an individual (and no two companies are exactly alike): it acts and reacts, has a 'character' or 'personality', is admired or disliked according to what people have personally experienced or heard about it. These people form the various 'publics' which must be considered in the way a large industrial company safeguards or actively promotes its reputation and achieves its corporate objectives as a business. Every company has to consider the effects of its policies and actions on many different publics:

1 Customers.
2 Employees.
3 Trade Unions.
4 Shareholders and 'the City' (this will also include overseas financial audiences).
5 Suppliers.
6 Politicians and Government departments (UK and overseas).
7 Opinion formers and specialist groups.
8 The Media.
9 Local authorities.
10 Local communities.
11 Educational bodies.

These must each be considered carefully in terms of particular language cultural or political needs when a multinational is appraising its relationship.

Remembering that the creation and maintenance of goodwill towards an organization is the desirable overall result of public relations activity, creating the climate which aids achievement of its corporate objectives, a company is closely concerned with its own image. 'Image' is a word which is much used and often misunderstood. It must not be confused with 'identity'. 'Image' is the impression which various publics have of a particular company. Its 'identity' is its personality or character composed by its range of activities and its corporate philosophy and management style. But does a company's 'image' as a manufacturer or service organization bear any relationship to its actual 'identity', or is there a credibility gap? This is a recurrent preoccupation of public relations practitioners, which can only be resolved by specialized and often costly research. It may well be that, having carried out this research, the results are highly disconcerting to the sponsoring company because the credibility gap between 'image' and 'identity' is so wide. This presents management with a real challenge to bridge the gap by a public relations programme to ensure that the company is seen by others in a way which is accurate and does justice to the company's true character.

How the company chooses to project itself will depend greatly on its business and marketing strategy. Some companies like ICI, Dunlop, Nestlé and Shell market their products and services clearly under the umbrella of their group name. Others like Unilever, Procter & Gamble or the Imperial Group prefer to use subsidiary companies or brand names without any involvement of the group's identity. The TI Group is an example, however, of a company which has changed its approach from the second to the first, to a close identification with the parent company. The commercial value of a corporate identity is difficult to quantify, but is of great significance to the total public relations approach. Building or reinforcing an image of quality and reliability in the customer's mind may make him aware that he is buying from a company which is well established, invests in research and is a responsible corporate citizen.

There is a public relations angle to every aspect of business today. Therefore, fully effective public relations activities involve many individuals in an organization and are only as good as the company's management and resulting corporate behaviour. Often a company's own employees are the most convincing public relations agents. If employees speak well of the product, the after-sales service, the working environment, as well as the quality of the management, this counts for a great deal, as a support for the specialized communication techniques which are used to ensure that the full 'identity' of the company is projected most effectively to the chosen 'target' audiences. Rumour and suspicion about the integrity of a company's fortunes or the quality of its industrial relations travel fast in the financial and business world. The collective eyes and ears of the London Stock Exchange are finely attuned to signals of impending disaster. Competitors are quick to take advantage of any malaise in the market place and suppliers need reassurance. Good news, unfortunately, is much harder to spread than bad or undesirable stories about a company. No company should overlook or underestimate the importance of employee help in endorsing and aiding the public relations effort. Similarly, poor employee relations can wreck the work of the public relations team, however skilled and dedicated.

A company must have thought deeply enough about its own character to decide exactly what sort of company it is and how it wants to be perceived by its various 'target' audiences. The public relations effort must operate against the background of corporate 'touch-stones' which are held and actively practised by the organization. This corporate responsibility, together with a sensitive awareness of public relations, is a very powerful expression of the social conscience which industrial companies of any size must strive to develop.

Some of the broad precepts held by a large industrial company with many subsidiaries and activities around the world might include the following aims:

1 To carry out its operations throughout the world according to the highest standards of conduct and ethics, striving in all things to build and safeguard a strong corporate 'reputation'.
2 To make every possible effort to develop and maintain an efficient, loyal, productive and contented organization of employees who believe in their work, the company and the contribution which both make to the well-being of society.

3 To consider, in making decisions affecting the conduct of the company's affairs as far as is reasonably possible, what is best and right, not only for the company, but for a wider society, so that the company can be seen to be responsible and conscious of its wider obligations.
4 To make every reasonable effort to create and maintain a good working relationship between the company, its employees and the communities in which they operate.
5 To support and enhance the best beliefs and practices of the private enterprise system.
6 To be consistent and persistent in the application of the company's policies to each and every situation, rather than adopting what may be expedient in dealing with a particular problem or situation.

But is it enough just to have noble thoughts? A company operates in a tough and rapidly changing world. It has products to manufacture and sell which must satisfy definite customer needs. This commercial hurly-burly is a stern test of a company's entrepreneurial ability (as well as its sense of public relations) to maintain high standards of corporate responsibility *and* produce healthy profits with a plentiful cash flow for future investment. A company today must not only be successful and honourable in all its dealings, but must be seen to be so.

Within a framework of simple and clearly expressed objectives, public relations activity in a large industrial company must be energetic and versatile in its operation. It relies on a communications programme which is designed carefully to arouse interest, inform and impress people whose goodwill is necessary for the company's reputation and survival. Although many people play their part in a programme which enhances the total corporate reputation, the prime responsibility for public relations in any company must rest with the chairman or the chief executive on behalf of the company's main board. As with every other kind of management function, it is a question of leadership. The man at the top must have the conviction that good public relations is important for his company and the dedicated concern to see that its policies and practices are effectively and efficiently carried out by the full management team, according to the highest standards. He must ensure that these are communicated expertly, both internally and externally.

The successful management of a corporate public relations activity is delegated via a close and trusted link to the corporate public relations executive. Because of the swiftly changing nature of the pressures and demands on the public relations function, as well as the close interaction of external events and internal company developments, it is essential that the public relations executive reports directly to the chairman if he is an executive chairman or, otherwise, to the chief executive, to ensure that the link with top management thinking and the leader of the company is as close as possible. Unless the public relations adviser is tuned in to top management decision-making, then he or she will work in a vacuum and be unable to advise on or help to achieve the company's public relations objectives.

Usually the public relations objectives of an industrial company or group of companies can be expressed very briefly. If this is not the case then the thinking behind them has not been sufficiently crystallized. Underlying any statement of corporate public relations policy is the company's recognition of the value and importance of the favourable interest in its affairs by many different people. As a means of ensuring that this interest is as favourable and well-informed as possible, a company must communicate regularly and accurately about its activities. A large company may want its experience, market coverage and technological leadership to be acknowledged by present and future customers, its excellent training schemes and career prospects and good working environment to be known to potential employees and the local communities where it operates, its financial control and investment policies to be clear to the City and to shareholders, actual and potential.

The job of planning and executing this full-scale communication pro-gramme for a large company will be an exciting and demanding challenge for the public relations executive. The corporate public relations function of a large industrial company is unlikely to be concerned in detail with any form of product or technical public relations activity. These usually are the responsi-bility of the operating subsidiaries, unless any specific problems arise which are likely to affect the company's reputation as a whole. It is concerned with the company's corporate public relations objectives and only with those of subsidiaries in an advisory capacity. Therefore the corporate public relations responsibilities must include the following:

1 Helping to establish and maintain the reputation of the whole group of companies in accordance with its corporate objectives by contact with key opinion formers, including the City and Management Press, and through any necessary corporate publicity programme, such as institutional adver-tising, films and audio-visual programmes.
2 Establishment and supervision of an agreed budget for total public relations activity.
3 Identifying and advising on long-term public relations needs.
4 Interpreting to top management current or anticipated attitudes by key publics towards the company's affairs, including monitoring of the media coverage.
5 Liaison with public relations functions in the operating subsidiary com-panies and advice on individual needs as requested or required, and establishment of guidelines (what to say, what not to say — and by whom).

6 Advising on latest communication ideas and techniques, in liaison with the top personnel management function, for employee communication programmes, and for industrial relations and training needs.
7 Advice on contact with specialized opinion-forming groups, including international, national and local politicians, consumer or other groups likely to have a special interest in the company's conduct.
8 Publication of corporate literature designed to give comprehensive information about the company's activities and resources.
9 Advising on corporate design matters to ensure an appropriate presentation of corporate identity.

Financial public relations are one of the most important and interesting aspects of a corporate public relations executive's work. Where a public quoted company is involved, the discipline imposed by the London Stock Exchange is strong and precise, contained in the pages of *Admission of Securities to Listing*, the famous 'yellow book' which decrees what information must be disclosed to the Stock Exchange and to shareholders: that is, 'any information necessary to enable the shareholders and the public to appraise the position of the company and to avoid the establishment of a false market in its securities'. Each development materially affecting the company's assets and its financial performance must be disclosed at the earliest opportunity. This is 'price sensitive' information, which influences the stock market's valuation. A company must be scrupulous in its observance of this, even to the issuing of instructions which are understood by line managers at local level. An indiscreet remark made out of context and at the wrong time on a key issue could affect the company's share price either up or down. The Stock Exchange does not like 'surprises'. Financial journalists, of course, thrive on them as 'news'.

Attitudes towards financial public relations by various companies can differ. Some like to maintain very close links with financial journalists. Their reason for doing so is that if a company's affairs are well understood then its financial performance, when published for the whole or half year, is likely to be commented on more accurately. Others feel that over-close contact with financial journalists can be a two-edged weapon. There are some companies who appear to love the limelight. Yet a too eager pursuit of financial coverage may lead to journalists' boredom or cynicism.

The correct course for the average industrial company is probably a judicious mixture of being responsive yet restrained. Financial journalists have to cover a wide range and number of companies. Few can hope to be experts in depth for more than a handful of the most interesting companies quoted on the Stock Exchange. It is up to the public relations adviser to know who really matters amongst financial journalists and to ensure that contact with them is on the right basis, with something of real interest and value for them to write about.

The full range of corporate financial public relations activity is likely to include, in liaison with the top executive and his financial director, the following elements:

1 Financial publications (the annual report and accounts, and interim statements to shareholders).
2 Handling the major statutory financial announcements by the company — the preliminary and interim results — and assistance with answering journalists' and stockbrokers' enquiries.
3 Organizing financial press briefings as well as maintaining on-going links with financial journalists — and special meetings for investment analysts and stockbrokers.
4 Organizing press visits to plants for financial journalists and others with specialized interests, such as commodities.
5 Initiation of feature articles about the company in City pages of newspapers and magazines.
6 Answering press enquiries.

One of the most demanding and difficult aspects of financial public relations is if the company is in the situation of being bid for in a take-over deal, or is in process of acquiring another company itself. This is a time when contact with top management and with all the company's other specialist advisers is crucial. A plan and a detailed programme of information has to be worked out and adhered to with military precision. There are a number of examples where a bid, which the board of directors has considered not to be in the best interest of shareholders, has been fought off with courage, determination and skilled public relations. The classic case is where Courtaulds resisted and beat off a bid approach from ICI, realizing at an almost-too-late stage the value of effective public relations. There is a great deal to be said for establishing a contingency plan for acute situations such as these. Being prepared could mean the difference between winning or losing.

Another tense situation involving the need for impeccable financial relations activity is when a large public company turns in poor half-year or year-end figures, particularly if these are unexpected. Disappointment within the organization and scepticism outside are rife. It is very much a question of morale, confidence and credibility. Top management is suddenly 'on trial' and a variety of different 'publics' now come into sharp focus. Understandably a first reaction is for the company to keep its head down while the storm of comment rages and get on with the urgent job of putting matters right. But under such unfortunate circumstances the need is to be ready with answers to questions which explain and clarify the bad news, when approached by brokers, analysts and anxious shareholders, as well as inquisitive financial journalists. It is a time when key top management spokesmen cannot afford to take refuge in evasion or blandness. Although the company must not duck such questions, there is one vital principle which must be remembered by all who talk to the Press and other key audiences at this time. Answers and comments must be restricted to what has already been said to shareholders. Nothing can be added which has not already been published, except by way of clarification. Otherwise the company would be in danger of passing additional 'price sensitive' information to others which is not necessarily available directly to shareholders, who are legally entitled to hear it first, or to employees who are also morally (where not legally) entitled to it. Every word by the company needs to be checked and weighed by the top management team for accuracy and correct emphasis.

As well as being in tune with top management thinking, the corporate public relations function must be lean and active. The staffing will be small, but with wide and versatile skills, together with experience of the worlds of finance, business and the media. In a large, decentralized group of companies, much of the routine public relations activity geared to marketing and technical plans takes place at subsidiary company level. Similarly, important work in communication programmes for employees, which needs to be carried out with increasing frequency and depth today, will tend in a large company to be initiated at more local levels where such programmes can be designed to match the employees' horizon of interest and concern. Broad policies will be established at corporate level, but rarely is it possible — or desirable — to dictate or control these local communications in detail: this may have the effect of damping down all initiative. But the corporate public relations adviser must be well aware of what is going on around the organization and have some shrewd, but not restrictive, form of monitoring, regularly receiving all policy statements or press releases issued by subsidiary companies, with a full feed-back of all press comment.

Therefore, a very personal kind of effort is required by the corporate public relations function which is not dependent on formal organizational patterns. Often the informal method of keeping an eye on things, aided by shrewd inspiration of ideas and persuasion, is the more effective, with approachability and knowledge of local operating conditions and problems affecting each subsidiary, gained from personal experience and observation by regular visits, being the ideal. A helpful aid to such an approach is the establishment of some brief but clear guidelines which delineate local authority and responsibility for public relations. This gives the right framework for local initiative.

Such guidelines in a large organization become particularly important where financial information is provided for employees. With legislation either enacted or talked about by successive governments in the UK on information disclosure, it must remain very much the care and concern of individual companies to implement this. A policy should be evolved by top management and guidelines established on what can or should be said — and what cannot be said without express top management approval. Similarly, where industrial relations problems arise, which need local press initiative, such as redundancies, factory closures, accidents and product liability situations, the public relations people in the subsidiary must be fully aware of their responsibility for briefing and consulting with the corporate public relations executive. Such a working relationship should not be difficult to sustain with the right calibre of public relations team, together with sympathetic and interested support from local management.

The procedures which make liaison with the centre by the operating subsidiary companies in a large group a simple and logical routine, could be as follows:

1 To assist the Corporate Public Relations Executive, copies of all publications produced by individual companies, including brochures, catalogues, press releases and newsletters/bulletins should be sent to the Corporate Public Relations Office as soon as possible *after* publication. This includes all Group companies in Europe and overseas.
2 The Corporate Public Relations Office should always be consulted *before* any PR action is taken in the following cases by individual companies in UK and Europe:
  a Release of any financial or commercial information (acquisitions, disposals, market-share situations, new distributorships) to the Press.
  b Press conference, interviews and briefing of individual journalists, or press releases on major industrial relations matters (disputes, closures, new methods of working, management techniques), or major commercial development likely to affect the group as a whole (including any legal problems regarding a contract, product or service), or senior management appointment.
  c Participation by senior management as speaker on company affairs on TV, radio, film or major conference.
3 Details should be given as soon as possible in advance of any major organizational change, marketing development or programme planned by individual companies which may have a bearing on the group as a whole.
4 The appointment by individual companies in the UK and Europe of outside advertising and/or PR design consultants or agencies should be discussed with the Corporate Public Relations executive *before* any contract is signed.
5 Copies of all corporate publications, press releases, briefs and bulletins prepared by the Corporate Public Relations Office will be sent to the

managing directors of individual group companies in the UK and abroad *before* these are released outside the group.

What is the exact role of the top public relations executive in a large industrial company? Inevitably this must be a curious mixture of planner, watch-dog, catalyst, communicator, *savant*, stimulant, advisor and *confidant*. He or she must have a strong awareness of the company's 'identity', its management philosophy and style, its employee policies and the significance of the organizational structure. Such awareness and knowledge builds the respect and co-operation of other members of the management team.

The ability to be objective is a considerable asset in many situations which can become tense with conflicting management politics and loyalties. This is a particularly helpful aid to effective decision-making. Often where top management has become so engrossed in the complexities of a problem that it can only consider the need to make an important decision based on carefully sifted and studied facts, the public relations executive must get his or her management colleagues to consider fully the effects of that decision and how best it can be communicated within the company and to the outside world. This might seem obvious. But the difficulty management sometimes faces is that the process of decision-making today can be so fraught and complex, against a background of rapidly changing international events, that once the decision is made at top level it can be regarded, in a curious way, as an end in itself and not the beginning of a sequence of events which may have far-reaching effects for the company and many people associated with it. It needs someone with objectivity (and courage?) at the appropriate stage to ask a number of pertinent questions such as 'Do you realize that if you do that . . ?' or 'What exactly do you mean by this . . ?' or 'How will this be interpreted by . . ?' By asking pertinent questions, making the intelligent suggestion and offering the imaginative idea, the public relations executive can help to turn a complex piece of management reasoning, obvious to the immediate participants, into more effective action for the greater benefit of the company. Today it is more important than ever for management decisions not only to be right, but to be seen to be so by all who are affected.

As well as acting as a catalyst, the corporate public relations executive must have a strong intuitive sense of when to act as a stimulant. This requires an ability to listen, to observe the significance of many kinds of signals both within the company and outside amongst its various 'publics' and an infinite reserve of diplomacy and resilience to remind people of their public relations obligations as managers and to prod them into action. From time to time the public relations executive may have to 'sell' the essential nature of his or her services. For example, in a hectic industrial relations situation, personnel management may need a tactful reminder that the most effective way of getting a sympathetic and fair press reaction is to involve the public relations executive at an initial stage rather than at the last minute.

It is important for the public relations executive at corporate level to see the connections between one set of circumstances and another. In a surprising number of cases a pattern can be glimpsed in apparently separate and disparate elements. With this need to see connections and perceive patterns where at first none seem to exist, a good memory is as invaluable as an analytical mind. A new set of circumstances may seem self-contained and simple, yet the public relations executive may well remember other factors from a previous situation which if considered and linked to the present one may produce a better compound result — or avoid a serious and costly communications mistake.

Does this emphasis on the need for a top public relations executive to be as creative and versatile as possible imply that he or she must at all times be self-sufficient? Certainly he or she must know at least a little about a great many things which affect a large industrial company — and yet be a specialist in the skills of the public relations profession. But part of the responsibility of the top public relations job must be to know when to call in and make the best use of an outside adviser, the public relations consultant, who can bring an extra dimension or fresh point of view to the solving of a difficult communications problem or the maximizing of a public relations opportunity.

The exceedingly tough business conditions in world trading, the increasing complexity of global politics, the growing responsibility for preserving our environment as well as the new exigencies of industrial relations have convinced industrialists of the necessity and value of having skilled and experienced public relations advisers in the top management team. However skilled a communicator the chief executive may be he will, if he is wise, have the support of someone at his elbow on whose public relations sensitivity, experience and knowledge he can draw to the fullest extent — someone who is not only a contributor of ideas but a watch-dog observing the ways in which the company is perceived both within and outside the organization, as well as social changes which may assist or hinder the company's activities.

In corporate public relations today the variety of the unexpected — be it unwelcome take-over bids, 'U' turns of politicians, kidnappings of senior executives, the activities of pressure groups, the closure of an old-established plant in an area of high unemployment, or the need to reschedule a 'rights' issue on the Stock Market — is both a challenge and a reward. But perhaps the greatest satisfaction for the corporate public relations executive is wholeheartedly accepting the responsibility for playing a vital part in the ways in which a large company relates to its key audiences. Results of his or her work will usually be cumulative and long-term. Goodwill towards a company is an asset which needs to be painstakingly built up and jealously guarded. Only the highest standards are ultimately acceptable in public relations. Just as a company has its corporate responsibilities, so the public relations executive has a duty to be loyal to the company and true to the principles of the public relations profession. Today, as never before, integrity and sensitivity are vital factors in public relations, whether in the multinational corporation, or the small specialist manufacturer.

5

Public Relations in Marketing

Graham Kemp

The real problem is to decide where marketing ends and public relations begins. Many people still profess to find marketing a somewhat arcane profession. Others see little difference between marketing and selling. Everybody, of course, understands what advertising is all about and where it fits! Or do they?

Our obsession with compartments and specialized activities in life often gets in the way of common sense. We try to pretend that only we in our special compartment really understand what our little trade is all about, and what it contributes; forgetting that in the end the only thing that matters is what works for the organization as a whole.

Conventional definitions of PR are of little help in marketing strategy. Supplying information is all very well, but who needs it? Do our target audiences want knowledge for its own sake or because it will help them make a profit? *What is it all for?*

Consider the case of the company trying to get a new brand of pasta on to the supermarket shelves. The buyer knows about pasta, especially spaghetti and ravioli, but get him on to lasagne, tagliatelli or fetuccini and he's in trouble. Ask him to stock the *whole* pasta range and his own confusion will probably dictate a conservative buying policy — to stock spaghetti and preferably on the bottom shelf where nobody can see it and from which nobody will pick it up.

That is a real problem, a PR problem; but it is also a marketing problem. The pasta industry has simply not yet managed to find a way of getting its benefits and its story across to customers. Who needs pasta?

Conventional publicity at this stage is probably wasteful. Consumers are unaware of the pleasures of pasta, and the role it can fill in the diet, and are possibly even suspicious of what it does to their figures. Recipes and cookery leaflets will simply pile up unused.

In publicity terms, they probably want to see pasta associated with people

119

they admire and whose tastes they are probably trying to emulate. They also want to see the product on the shelf, to be able to read the label, compare prices, try one pack at a time. But the only packet on the shelf is spaghetti. The salesman's story about fetuccini has fallen on deaf ears.

The real PR task at this stage in the marketing process is, or ought to be, to convince the retailer that there really could be a market for a wider range of pastas, and that means a lot of hard work building up the story, the data, experience from overseas, the merchandising arguments; all the familiar patter between buyers and sellers in retailing.

All of this is 'communication'; all of it is within the competence of professional PR men. But the marketing director has just called in the advertising agency and the PR man only comes in when the agency recommends some trade press publicity.

Fortunately, a great many people in the PR profession *can* produce examples of their effectiveness in co-ordinating advertising, sales promotion and other publicity techniques. The problem is that too many people dispute between themselves the right to present and delineate communications strategy. The marketing director regards it as his province; advertising agencies believe that they are the real experts and they have the power because they command large budgets. The PR or 'public affairs' director too often plays a negative role, stopping campaigns in their tracks for good and sensitive reasons, but rarely contributing to the *formulation* of a marketing communications strategy.

The ground rules in this power game have been laid down for a great many years, but now I suggest is the time to begin to move the pitch somewhere else, or at least to move the goal-posts.

At its very best, public relations can be the discipline that really determines the content of the messages companies aim at their customers and target audiences. Most of the other disciplines are used by people with too many axes to grind for particular techniques. Very few communications problems can be solved by advertising.

PR techniques can be fitted into a marketing strategy at several points. In the development of a totally new product concept, for example, a lot of work has got to be done to identify the latent consumer needs which have compelled the company to develop that product in the first place. If the product has emerged out of technology pure and simple, then it may fail merely because there was no consumer need that it actually fitted at that particular time.

Take the emerging video revolution. For some ten years now we have been bombarded with publicity about different types of video systems, and there have been a great many editorials suggesting that the video player in the home was far too expensive to become a normal consumer purchase. Yet this is now becoming one of the fastest-moving markets since the arrival of television itself, and all because of the very obvious consumer needs that video fills.

Three television channels may seem enough for anyone, but most people like to be continuously entertained. If the channels have closed down, or if they are repeating old films, or running programmes which are of no particular interest, then there is a need for some alternative entertainment.

You do not have to be a marketing genius to recognize that people in those circumstances will respond very readily to opportunities to play their own films on television; or to replay old films, or old programmes and that moreover they would be prepared to spend quite a lot of money to have this facility.

After all, the same thing happened with audio tapes. Record companies may not like what it has done to their market, but the audio tape has filled a real consumer need in making it possible for enthusiasts to record their own music from records or from radio programmes. It was bound to be popular; it was bound to fill a consumer need; and it is inevitable that the same thing will happen to video tapes.

The role of publicity and communications in this market is to home in on the real need and explain in well-researched material — for journalists, for advertisers *and* for the trade — the benefits of the different systems and the home entertainment opportunities they provide. Additionally, publicity can help consumers to come to terms with the equipment itself by explaining simply how it is all used.

Later, in the development of a market, there comes a point when saturation is reached and then the only way through for the manufacturer is by some form of product improvement or by expanding the size of the market itself.

Take the case of the budgerigar. The Budgerigar Information Council back in the 'sixties was born out of one of the most inspired PR briefs, or, more precisely, one of the most inspired marketing briefs. Back to the compartments again. It was the Petfoods division of Mars that initiated the Council at a time when the birdseed market had come to an apparent standstill.

The market had either to become a battle of brands and diminishing returns, or the industry had to go in some other direction. History does not record who it was that came up with the simple brief: 'to expand the budgerigar population'. But once stated, the PR task became straightforward — endless publicity and promotions about the pleasure to be found in keeping budgerigars.

There were endless budgerigar clubs and shows, pamphlets, articles, Press conferences, books — a real orchestration of activity designed to start a budgerigar craze. It worked. The publicity was interminable. The result: an increase in the budgerigar population and a natural growth in the market for birdseed.

That seems to me, still, to be a practical and creative use for publicity — not hidden away in a separate compartment from advertising, promotion and

marketing, but positioned slightly ahead of these techniques and introduced a
the point at which markets are being created. On its own it can create
awareness and visibility; positioned at the right point in the marketing process
it can be the catalyst that creates opportunities.

It also helps me to make the point that in putting together a publicity
strategy, the tools (even then) included:

1 Pamphlets.
2 Meetings.
3 Corporate advertising.
4 Press conferences.
5 Films.
6 Special reports.
7 Sponsored books.

To which you could add today:

8 Video tapes.
9 Radio tapes.

The real problem for companies is that too many of these special techniques
are promoted singly by the entrepreneurs concerned as all-purpose panaceas.
It is sometimes argued, for example, that the solution to all employee
communications problems lies in newspapers or in video, or in briefing group
training, depending on the technique you happen to be promoting.

What really matters in the end, though, is the intellectual effort brought to
bear on the problems, on the capacity to think through each problem or
understand each issue, company by company, plant by plant.

Understanding the psychology of management is difficult enough, let alone
the psychology of the workforce, but understanding the psychology of *any* key
target audience is certainly what this business is all about. If we don't
understand them, they won't understand us.

Twenty years ago, the problem for frozen food manufacturers was to provide
low temperature storage facilities in the shops and in the home. You cannot sell
frozen foods, clearly, without a chain of low-temperature distribution from the
factory to the home. It fell to Birds Eye in those early years to shoulder the
burden of education and publicity in this industry, and it did so with
considerable panache.

Trying to convince retailers that they should invest in refrigeration when
volume was clearly not all that profitable called for creative skills and the kind
of resources that one prays for at critical times like the present.

At the start of the 'sixties, only 10,000 retailers owned cabinets; by 1975 the
number had risen to 113,000. Publicity and education played a huge part in

this exercise. There were profitability studies, publicity exercises based on retail case histories and new types of refrigeration, attempts to persuade retailers to set up frozen food 'shops within shops' (all of which led to the development of freezer centres).

The next task was to encourage housewives to buy refrigerators with frozen food compartments or, better still, home freezers.

The weapons used included:

1 Seminars.
2 Cookery books.
3 Press conferences.
4 Schools demonstrations.
5 A magazine.

Today, almost half the population owns a freezer and more than half the frozen foods eaten are bought by home freezer owners.

The point of this example is to show where and at what point PR comes into its own; not in a separate compartment, but as an integral part of the marketing effort, perhaps even slightly ahead of it, but conceived as part of the same long-term strategy.

Unfortunately, far too many marketing men seem incapable of writing long-term strategy which is why so many of them conceive PR as a substitute for advertising. How often are PR executives asked to provide 'free publicity'? How often also are PR executives asked to provide 'visibility' for brand names?

'Visibility' is the curse of the PR profession — a substitute for thought and based largely on the principle that if you can't make your case heard (because there really isn't one) then at least you can make a lot of noise.

The Campaign for Real Ale, or CAMRA, was conceived in the early 'seventies in response to what its originators thought was the disappearance of good old English ale as the keg beer and lager revolution got under way. Keg beer and lager are taken very much for granted today, forgetting, perhaps, that they, in their time, were a response by the brewers to the problems of transporting cask-conditioned beer over anything but a short distance.

The campaign was started by a group of journalists and now publishes its own monthly newspaper, called *What's Brewing*. It holds meetings all over the country; it runs press conferences; provides evidence for government committees and has generally made itself a most effective nuisance to the brewers. It has even bought its own pubs and set up a limited company in its own right. It also publishes the *Good Beer Guide*.

Now this was not a marketing-led activity. If anything, the market was, and is, going in a fundamentally different direction, and mainly towards lager. But it does illustrate the point about publicity *influencing* markets. If CAMRA had not existed, it is unlikely that marketing directors would have revised their basic strategies. Now, most of the majors have reintroduced local brews and local brand names; so you could say in this case that PR, in its widest sense, has been effective in making a case heard by a lot of people and did actually influence marketing strategy.

If companies and organizations used similar techniques with as much panache as CAMRA, then I believe they could achieve their objectives much more readily.

In some of the work my own company has done for the brewing industry, specifically for Whitbread, we addressed ourselves to the problem of selling more wine across the bar. The problem here to a great extent was the attitudes of licensees, untrained in the finer arts of winemanship and not helped to any great extent by lack of facilities for keeping wine at the right temperature and getting the right measures into the glass and so forth.

The approach was not simply one of communication. It was necessary first to develop and answer some of the practical merchandising problems experienced by licensees in selling wine.

The answer was simple, inexpensive, but effective; a display unit that had the dual purpose of keeping white wines at the correct temperature and advertising the fact that wine was for sale. Over 3,000 Whitbread pubs now have similar units to this one.

The merchandising unit was supported by a whole range of display material, designed to make customers forcibly aware of wine as one of their options in the pub. Clear pricing was another area which experience and research established was crucial to a licensee in developing sales of wine.

Finally, it was necessary to give licensees the information and advice necessary to run a simple wine operation in a public house. This was accomplished by means of a simple wine manual guiding licensees on all aspects of selling, storing, promoting and serving wine for increased profitability.

Supplemented by a simple guide to the wines available from their local depot, Whitbread licensees participating in the scheme are now well placed to compete against wine bars and other more recent alcoholic drink outlets.

The results of this 'communication in action' were soon evident in sales statistics. Many licensees achieved wine sales increases of 200 per cent and more and a volume increase of 50 per cent in the main brand of wine used by Stowells, the Whitbread wine and spirit subsidiary, in these promotions.

Many industrial marketing problems present similar challenges, especially when marketing techniques have not been taken to an advanced level. In companies where engineers and scientists are in the ascendance, sheer obsession with technology often blinds them to the realities of the marketplace, where more salesmen and journalists have to deal with people who do not understand technology at all.

There was once even a problem in selling aluminium. One of Britain's leading aluminium suppliers worked very closely with shop fitters and fabricators to persuade shopkeepers to modernize their shop fronts with aluminium. The market (and the profit) belonged to the fabricators and shop fitters, but the resistance of the shopkeeper had to be overcome by generic campaigns underlining the durability and appearance of aluminium. Advertising product by product would have been impossibly expensive and less effective in breaking down the general resistance.

Once the difference between publicity and communication has been defined in this way, the disciplines can be stated more easily:

1 *What is the problem?* Is it lack of awareness, misconception, wilful misunderstanding, or just inadequate communication?
2 *Who is the target group?* Whom are you trying to reach and how much do you know about them? Research should produce an audience profile.
3 *What is the objective?* To inform, persuade, convert, correct, change attitudes towards the brand or product or product type?
4 *Media* — Should you use films, video, pamphlets, speeches, conferences, leaflets, press campaigns, film strips, advertising?
5 *Cost* — What funds are available and how should they be allocated?
6 *Evaluation* — How do you know if the money has been well spent? By measuring attitude and opinion against the stated objectives when the campaign has been completed? Or by newspaper exposure?

Newspaper exposure of a brand name can undoubtedly be enormously valuable at a particular stage of the evolution of a product strategy. Early in 1979, General Motors took the decision to introduce a range of spare parts for the growing DIY car maintenance market. Unipart and others had made some impact previously, and the market was growing steadily, but General Motors' brand, A C Delco, was virtually unknown. It was completely unknown to the general Press and not particularly visible even to the specialist Press.

The solution my company provided was a special and authoritative report on the European component parts market under the Delco imprint. It set out to establish the size and value of the market, where A C Delco was positioned in it, and what prospects there were for those who decided to stock car components in supermarkets, garage forecourts, and elsewhere.

The report received widespread publicity and was also used extensively in presentations to the retail trade, who at that time were unaware of the growth of this market and therefore sceptical of the claims made by the company's salesmen on their calls.

The campaign was subsequently developed, and extended into dealer newspapers, consumer presentations, and a general plethora of publicity designed to stimulate car maintenance interest among the general public.

At another stage in the development of industrial markets, and not only industrial markets, sheer misunderstanding by the public can sometimes lead to impossible situations and to consumer resistance.

This sort of problem was experienced by the gas industry, at the time it introduced North Sea gas and sought to convert gas cookers in Britain's homes to North Sea gas installations. Conversion was unsought and unwanted by most of the industry's customers. It was decided upon with little consultation and necessitated intrusion into millions of homes, demanding physical and mental adjustment in every gas kitchen. The PR task was to convince customers that it was necessary and that the benefits would outweigh some short-lived inconvenience.

An essential factor in the communications programme was the training and instruction of the industry's own employees.

The industry's domestic, commercial and industrial customers had to be helped to understand the reasons for conversion, what would be involved and what was being asked of them in the way of co-operation and patience. There had to be no concealment of difficulties, no false promises; and above all, honesty.

To get the PR programme across, the industry enlisted the help of national and local media, Press, radio, and television. A volume of specialized literature in the form of letters, brochures, and other direct mail material was prepared and delivered individually to more than thirteen million customers.

It was also necessary to involve and convince leaders of public opinion of the industry's thinking and intentions, so that when the inevitable criticism erupted, they might be expected to bring to bear an informed mind and hopefully a sympathetic ear. This called for the fullest possible briefing of members of Parliament, local authorities, consumers' organizations, and the countless officials of many societies and clubs that actually interest themselves in public affairs. To reinforce this facet of the PR programme, special talks and films were prepared.

All of this activity had to take place against the shifting backcloth of the conversion exercise itself. Good intentions were frequently put in doubt by unavoidable mistakes and calamities, arising mainly from initial inexperience. After a hesitant start, the operation ran into a barrier of complaints which resulted in a standstill being imposed in certain regions to allow the backlog of complaints to be cleared.

Gradually, a combination of patient competence and the rising cost of competitive fuels began to demonstrate the benefits promised by the industry, not only to its own customers but to the nation. A public relations operation that had begun as an exercise to combat ignorance and suspicion gradually became, with proper modesty, a proven success and came to be acknowledged as such in Parliament.

Informing the customer, though, was a high priority. It involved explaining to thirteen million people, not all of whom understood English, in clear everyday terms why conversion was necessary, how it would affect them, how it would help to minimize the inconvenience, and the benefits they might expect.

Information about natural gas, its source under the North Sea, its qualities, how it differed from manufactured gas, why it was in the national interest to make the change, its discovery, drilling and the life of the gas fields, fell within the purview of the British Gas Headquarters.

A leaflet (*Natural High Speed Gas*) was among the first of the publications produced. It told briefly of the impending arrival of natural gas, outlined how it differed from town gas, and discussed in very general terms what conversion involved and the effect of natural gas on new appliances.

This was followed by a fuller account of North Sea discoveries (*Natural Gas from the North Sea*), which described the formation and nature of the gas; the geological strata and areas of the North Sea in which it was found; the discovery of natural gas in the Netherlands; the search for favourable structures in the North Sea, and the distribution of gas within Britain; the effect of the discoveries on British industry; the conversion of the town gas system and all gas appliances, and the advantages North Sea gas would bring.

A third brochure (*Investment in Natural Gas*) gave an outline of the industry's plans and prospects based on natural gas. It touched on the current and projected demand for gas and gas appliances; offered estimates of availability; and gave details of the finance required to introduce natural gas from the North Sea.

A simpler publication called *Natural Gas and what it means to You* was produced for every gas householder. It explained in clear and simple language such things as getting used to natural gas; lighting the gas; using cookers, water heaters, refrigerators, central heating. And it drew attention to the cheaper tariffs introduced by the regions at the time of conversion.

All of which helps to make the case that PR really comes into its own when it is securely based on trading and business imperatives. There is a huge job to be done also in persuading the business's own employees that the company is leading them in the right direction, but that presupposes that managements are clear about where they are going in their own marketplaces.

Recognition of that is going to call for a much stronger awareness of business problems among journalists, communicators, advertising and PR men. The trade Press in particular has a considerable role to play in this process, but the trade Press is not always clear about its role or about the story it has to tell to potential advertisers.

In 1978 Benn Brothers, one of Britain's largest trade Press companies, was enlightened enough to recognize that advertising agencies and other space buyers were unaware of, or unconvinced by, the case for the trade Press as a vehicle of trade communications. As a response to this need, they commissioned a research study among users and published the first real examination of the trade Press in this country. It was called *The Trade Press in Britain.*

The research revealed that:

1 British businessmen rely heavily on the trade Press for information about their industries.
2 Nearly nine out of ten chief executives described the trade Press as the most authoritative source of information on their industry.
3 The majority read as many as five different trade journals, yet much less value was placed on their importance for advertising.
4 The trade Press accounts for a larger share of total advertising expenditure than consumer magazines and overall circulation is increasing.

Benn Bros was able to put these facts to advertising agencies at presentations, in leaflets and in considerable press publicity.

Later, the company published an even more interesting study called *How Retailers Buy*, and the findings from this report have a considerable bearing on the case I am trying to argue for the role of PR in marketing.

A number of significant messages emerged:

1 A product's perceived market potential is by far the most important single factor in deciding to stock a product for the first time.
2 The trade Press and well-informed sales representatives are key channels of communications between suppliers and retailers.
3 Retailers are more receptive to suppliers, their products, and their representatives when they have been advertising in the trade Press.

When asked to list the factors taken into account when deciding to stock an offered product, chemists named the following:

1 Product potential.   58%
2 Selling price.   56%
3 Level and type of advertising.   39%
4 Company's reputation.   29%
5 Trade margin.   27%

And where did chemists get their information?

The research as a whole confirmed the value of well-informed representatives and the trade Press for respondents' information needs. But the chemists gave first place to the trade Press for four out of the seven subjects named, and almost equal placing with representatives for a fifth subject:

	Trade Press	Representatives
1 Market trends.	51%	29%
2 Brand share.	53%	33%
3 Prices and margins.	54%	34%
4 Supplier's performance.	36%	31%
5 Product details.	48%	51%

For market trends, brand share, and suppliers' performance, the multiples rated the trade Press even higher than this. It was clearly shown to have a vital role in shaping retailers' decision-making. Response to the 'usefulness of the trade Press' question showed 93% of chemist retailers found the trade Press very useful or quite useful.

So, our conclusion was that the trade Press had a major role to play in convincing the trade of the viability of markets.

This kind of activity is the true province of the PR professional, acting as catalyst and communicator in new markets. It calls for knowledge, creativity and a command of all of the tools of the trade.

In a sense, the old concept of the publicity manager is being revived; the all-purpose expert responsible for all forms of publicity including advertising, sales promotion and the organization of special events. The difference, though, is that today he has also got to be Master of the Arts of behavioural psychology, publishing, conference management, training, marketing, print, video and audio-visual techniques, industrial relations and the emergence of the new information processing techniques as well.

That may seem a tall order, but I believe that PR is demonstrating its relevance to business objectives and the changing business environment.

Recession is going to make every business manager question his publicity expenditure and business managers will want to know what that expenditure delivers, either in sales or in profits.

If better internal communications can be shown to improve productivity, they will continue to command investment; so, too, will communications strategies that help to break down sales resistance.

Publicity stunts and exercises designed to win exposure on television, or a few column inches in the wrong part of the newspaper, are doomed, except among those too careless to define their business objectives or too stupid to realize that they are being conned.

6

PR Consultancy — Background and Definition

Michael Morley

Public relations consultancy (or counselling as it is known in the USA) was one of the fastest-growing businesses of the 'seventies. There is every prospect that this growth will continue in the last two decades of this century. The description 'consultancy', as applied to the majority of firms, individuals, partnerships and companies that established themselves in practice in the early years following World War II, was less than accurate; at that stage the larger part of the services offered to clients consisted of practical implementation of public relations programmes and there was less emphasis on the analysis of problems and the supply of advice alone, than is the case nowadays. Because several of the early post-war practitioners had a background in journalism — although by no means all of them — the element of consultancy and advice grew out of their special knowledge of the working of the media, the correct way to present a story for publication and a feeling for the way in which the public might react to publicity in the media.

The majority of budgets were within the control of the marketing departments of business organizations and, given that they were generally a tiny percentage of the advertising budgets, it was natural that these PR or publicity programmes were entrusted to the advertising agency; the agency after all was staffed with skilled communicators who could do the job required. Moreover, because they controlled the larger advertising budget it was often assumed, if not said aloud, that they exercised considerable leverage over the media which would ensure the desired level of 'editorial' publicity.

The advertising agencies took on staff as the demand for PR services increased and established special departments which in due course grew into separate subsidiary companies engaged exclusively in public relations, so that the proper fees and costings could be established for the services which had grown too great to be given 'free' as a service to large advertisers. Because they were in such close contact with client organizations, combined with the fact

130

that they had resources of finance and the ancillary services involved in all branches of communications (design, production, printing) the PR divisions, or subsidiary companies of the large advertising agencies, established themselves as the largest 'consultancies' in the United Kingdom.

While these developments were taking place a number of independent PR consultancies had established themselves and were gaining in reputation. Some specialized in a specific branch, others were generalist. But they had one great strength outside their skills as PR practitioners; they *had* to survive on what they could earn by providing PR advice and services. This meant they had to establish themselves as viable businesses charging realistic fees which covered all their costs and left profits for investment. Unless they managed this, they would cease to exist. Many not only managed to exist — they flourished, and took over the leadership from the advertising agency offshoots, which nevertheless still form a substantial and important element of the total provision of consultancy services. Indeed, in the early 'eighties no less than three large, international consultancies were acquired by advertising agencies conscious to re-establish themselves in public relations.

The description 'public relations consultancy' today is suitable, but still less than accurate, for the majority of firms. While there are a number of people practising as consultants only (they do not engage in the practical implementation of the advice and strategies they recommend) the majority of public relations companies are both *consultants* and *agents*. This is the reason why, together with the origins of ad. agency PR divisions, the PR consultancy is often referred to in casual conversation as 'the agency'.

For the majority of consultancies there are two clearly defined roles:

1 The provision of expert and objective advice to clients based on a knowledge of the mechanisms that will affect the opinion of key publics, allied to a good knowledge of those clients' organizations, their industries and markets. In this the consultant will draw on experience gained from previous assignments of a similar nature.

2 To act as the PR agent of the client, assuming responsibility for *executing* agreed programmes on the client's behalf. This might involve, for example, the establishment of an information office for the client and the provision of PR personnel and the various production services called for.

Often one consultancy will fulfil both roles with the senior staff (partners or directors) providing the consultancy service and then involving other executive staff in the agency function. It is not unusual, however, for an organization to retain the services of more than one consultancy to meet its needs for advice on the one hand — often specialist in nature — and agency-type services on the other.

Types of Consultancy

A large proportion of the consultancies in the 'top 15' in the UK could describe themselves as 'full service', in that they have staffs with a blend of experience that enables them to offer both consulting and agency services across the different 'specialities' within public relations — media relations, technical communications, governmental relations, employee communications, international communications, etc. Even if the full range of highly qualified specialist advice is not available within the consultancy, the 'full service' firm will in most instances be able to co-opt the necessary qualified person into their team as a part-time adviser.

The 'seventies saw the rapid development of a number of strictly specialist consultancies. The description 'specialist' can be applied in a number of ways.

There are consultancies which specialize in particular branches of industry; examples are firms which operate exclusively in the field of medicine, or those which confine themselves to clients involved in travel, tourism and related activities, and yet more which concentrate on fashion and beauty.

More generally, however, specialization means that the firm restricts itself to one of the sub-specializations of public relations. Probably the most highly developed 'genre' is that of financial PR, perhaps more properly called Investor Relations, which supports a significant number of large consultancies as well as several individual consultants. In this speciality the public relations consultancy not only has the responsibility for the client's PR, but also for its financial advertising and the production of the annual report and accounts.

Another speciality that has developed in step with the increasing tide of industrial and commercial legislation during the 'sixties and 'seventies is that of governmental relations. Some firms concentrate exclusively on monitoring political developments and proposed legislation or regulations and in advising and assisting clients to present their views to government. They deal with elected representatives and influential paid officials at local, national and international (viz. EEC) level. Many of the founders and executives in such consultancies have been — or are — active in political life.

Along with governmental and investor relations, other specialities can be mentioned: employee relations, sponsorship in sport and culture and community relations.

There is a further method of specialization — by communications technique. Firms in this category would not class themselves as PR consultants — even specialist ones as just described.

In fact, they are usually consultants and agents to PR consultancies, or the PR departments of organizations. Described in another way they are sub-contractors offering highly specialized technical services in constant use by the larger, full service consultancies. They cover media and speech training, press release distribution, design, artwork, opinion research, photography, film, scripting, AV presentations and production, events organization, writing, translation, and printing. It is an essential requirement of every PR consultancy to have established a full range of such services and for the quality of work and its cost to be kept under constant review. In this respect the consultancy is acting as the client's agent, in the legal sense, with all the accountability that it entails.

PR Consultancy Structures

The majority of PR consultancies are privately owned limited companies. It is perhaps surprising that with aspirations to professional status this form of corporate structure for PR firms should be the norm, rather than the partnership structure to be found in the accountancy and legal professions. In many instances the senior members of the staff are board directors and it is not unusual for them to be shareholders as well. Most PR companies have some method of profit-sharing to enable at least senior staff to participate in the success of the enterprise.

Because of the origins of many PR companies being linked with advertising agencies it is common, but an error, to compare structures and costings between these two branches of communications. In this respect PR consultancies are closer, in many ways, to firms of solicitors or chartered accountants. They charge fees related to the time spent on client work and although several consultancies charge an additional commission on production costs, this mainly helps to reflect the changing volume of work without constant fee adjustment and is seldom a major source of income.

There are two main kinds of operational structure within PR consultancies as related to client service. Here the examples chosen relate to typical full service, rather than to specialist consultancies.

The first, and less usual nowadays, is the *functional* structure. This has an obvious relation to the usual advertising agency structure. The primary consultant and programme supervisor is usually entitled the account director. His job is to advise the client, agree the strategy, budget and method of operation for the programme and then mobilize the resources of the consultancy/agency and its sub-contractors. In a functionally structured consultancy the other staff are specialists in one aspect of PR work and invariably work on all the consultancy's clients under the supervision of the account director. So if the programme agreed with the client is extensive and demands a wide range of actions, such as an intensive Press relations campaign, a strong effort with local radio stations, a briefing for MPs and an audio-visual presentation for general use, he will brief: the head of the consultancy press office, the specialist whose sole task is working with radio and TV, the public affairs specialist and an executive from the audio-visual and film section. The merits of the functional system are clear to see. The disadvantages only become obvious in practice. Too many people are involved, those responsible for the actual execution do not have close enough contact with the client and in general the costings mean that the time of the account director and the functional executives is spread across too wide a range of projects for the correct degree of commitment and attention to be given to each. Another problem is that the person aspiring to a broad career in PR can easily get trapped in a single functional department.

The more usual structure now is that of the account group in which the account director and one or more executives are responsible for a group of clients whose interests are in some way related.

Many consultancies form their account groups by PR speciality (rather than *functional* speciality) and will have, for example, account groups for clients whose needs are in investor relations, and others for government relations, technical and industrial PR, consumer marketing PR, and so on. The heads of these groups might have started as specialists but they will have been trained and have developed over time as competent all-round consultants and executives. Alternatively, they may have started as all-rounders, but then developed a specialist skill. In such a consultancy, the top management will have discussed fully with the client his needs. If the work is largely, say, public affairs, the client will be served by the government relations group. The head of this group will himself offer consulting services and will also undertake or supervise directly much of the practical work of the programme. If the client is large and his programme involves intensive activity in, say, government relations, investor relations and marketing PR the work will be divided into three programmes undertaken by three different groups with a management co-ordinator appointed to oversee the quality of service to the client. Such account groups are, in effect, mini-consultancies, and in many cases are managed as profit centres. Because of this they provide not only the chance to work well as a team, but also as a training for senior management positions.

PR Consultancy Costs

Consultancies are in business to make a profit for the shareholders and a good living for their staff, as well as to offer service to clients. In general they seek to make an overall profit from income of between 10% and 20% before tax. From this overall profit must be paid dividends to shareholders and profit-sharing to staff. The balance will go to finance the growth of the consultancy and provide it with the necessary reserves to ensure stability. Thus a consultancy with an income of £1,000,000 *per annum* should expect to make a pre-tax profit of £100,000. Part of that — say £20,000 — might be allocated for profit-sharing, or an annual bonus. A prudent board might also have invested say £20,000 in new equipment as the likely profit became known. Of the remaining balance of £60,000, half will go in taxes leaving say £30,000 to cover dividends and cash to be retained in the business.

To achieve that profit, however, will have required good management and a policy which is adhered to. The policy might dictate that the consultancy charges its clients in one of a number of ways. Whichever way is chosen will not affect one thing: that is that staff salaries will be the largest single cost of the consultancy. The surveys of members of the Public Relations Consultants Association (PRCA) show that in nearly all consultancies staff salaries are always around 50% of income. So the £1,000,000 consultancy will have an annual wages bill of £500,000. The second largest single cost (about 10%) is for rent. Then come all the other costs such as telephone, travel, entertaining, staff employment, training, and so on, which must not amount to more than a further 30% if the minimum 10% profit is to be made.

When a consultancy discusses its costs in this way with clients, it seldom has difficulties in agreeing the fees appropriate for the task — whichever system is chosen.

These are the main fee systems in operation at the moment.

Fixed Fee negotiated annually with the client based on historical experience of the volume of work (time) involved, or estimated based on experience against a detailed agreed programme. This is usually paid monthly in twelve equal parts.

Retainer Fee and Hourly or Per Diem *Charges*. In this system the client pays a very modest retainer fee which means he can draw on the consultancy service when needed, but the retainer does not 'buy' any service and is payable even when no work is done. When service is needed, an agreed hourly rate is charged to the client. This might be broken down by the hours put in by individuals, e.g. one rate for a senior consultant, another for a secretary, and shown as such to the client on the invoice. But it is more usual for a uniform 'team' time rate to be established which reflects the average of the combined time of consultant, executives and secretary. In certain countries, but not in the UK, hourly rates are established and recommended by the national PR institutes.

Minimum Fee and Hourly Charges. Often confused with the retainer system because of similarities, but with significant differences. The minimum fee is invariably more substantial than the retainer and reflects the fact that the consultancy has calculated that it is likely to spend that amount of time each month working for the client and has assigned the staff to do so. The hourly charge comes into operation when the basic time has been used up. Thus, when a client pays a minimum fee of £1,500 per month for say fifty hours wor at £30 per hour, and the actual time expended in the month is sixty hours, hi bill for that month will be £1,800. In a month when only forty hours work ar done the minimum fee of £1,500 is still payable. Sometimes there is a quarterl 'equalization' system built in to reflect the ups and downs that are inevitable

Nowadays it is normal for consultancies to charge disbursements an production costs extra to the fee. These are charges for travel, telephone postage, printing, photography, etc., and a commission is sometimes added t these expenditures.

The various methods of charging and consultancy/client agreements ar fully described in a document produced by the Public Relations Consultant Association.

Working with the Client

In the majority of respects the working day and practical duties of the PI consultancy executive are similar to those of his equivalent in the PI department of an industrial concern or government department and need no be repeated here. In fact, the likelihood nowadays is that he will find himsel working in close co-operation with a PR professional or at least an experience communicator within the client organization. Until the mid 'sixties it wa normal for clients embarking on PR programmes to make a decision either t retain an external consultancy/agency or to employ a PR executive internally Now it is relatively common for the larger, forward-looking organizations t have established internal PR departments and for these to retain additionall the services of a consultancy.

In the case of well-staffed departments, the prime need is for objectiv external consultancy; in other cases where the internal staff is small, but ther is a need for a heavy time input for a defined period, it makes sense to retain consultancy's 'agency' services.

In this context it is possible to highlight the special qualities, over and abov those needed by all PR practitioners, that are required of a consultanc executive:

1 He should observe the successes and failures of techniques used for othe consultancy clients and bring this experience to bear for the benefit of th clients he is serving.
2 He should achieve mastery and knowledge of the sub-contracting service available to the consultancy that will benefit his clients.
3 He should be able to use the resources and the expertise of othe professionals within the consultancy when faced with a complex problem

4 His regular contact with other professionals in the firm should sharpen his creative edge.

5 He should have strong powers of analysis, presentation and creativity because a consultancy has to *sell* its services in competition with other consultancies. In short, he has to win the right to practise PR.

6 He must develop an understanding of budgeting and business management. These are vital if he is to develop a career within a growing organization.

7 He should keep abreast with media developments, new communications techniques and the current mood of public opinion on a variety of issues if his advice is to be valued as objective and reliable.

8 He must manage his own time expertly, allocating it as appropriate between client contact, programme execution, monitoring results, reporting to client and maintaining direct contact with the media and other 'publics'. This can be most difficult if the right time blend is to be achieved. But it has to be since it is for a combination of expertise and time that the client pays the consultancy.

7

Public Relations in Central Government

John Cole-Morgan

The operation of a democracy is dependent upon a regular two-way flow of information between government and governed. How to communicate occupies the minds of government ministers and civil servants often as much as policy. There is little point in passing a law or providing a service if no one is made aware of it. And, for example, how does a government explain to a nation living beyond its means that at any one time the cake of national wealth is finite and that it has the choice of producing more or consuming less? Such problems faced governments long before the professional services of information specialists became an integral part of the government machine. This chapter therefore looks first at the traditional means of communication and then at the specialist services on which governments can now call for assistance.

The traditional contact between government and governed is through Parliament. When in debates the Minister speaks on subjects with which his Department is concerned — setting out policy, answering criticism and producing facts and arguments — the Government Department is making an effort to establish and maintain mutual understanding between itself and the people of the country, as much as when it issues a press notice. During Question Time the Minister has to stand up to criticism and justify the action of his department. Many of the questions are inspired by press reports or matters brought to MPs' notice by their constituents. Continuous exposure to Parliamentary Questions helps to keep departments abreast of the general tide of public opinion, or at least warns them when they are running contrary to it. Parliament of course is not the sole means of contact with the outside world for a Minister. A Minister has ready access to Press, radio and television and it is fairly certain that anything newsworthy he says to his constituents, or on a public platform, will be reported. But the Government does not have privileged access to the media; it is the importance and newsworthiness of Ministers' statements which are decisive.

Figure 1 (*above*) Internal Journals: tabloids are taking over from magazines.

Figure 4 Posters can help to make a company's public stop and think. This poster is addressed particularly to the

Cash flow

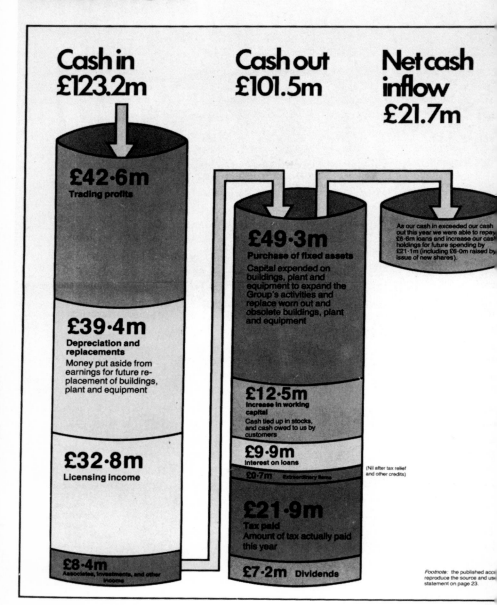

**Cash in
£123.2m**

**Cash out
£101.5m**

**Net cash
inflow
£21.7m**

£42·6m
Trading profits

£39·4m
Depreciation and
replacements
Money put aside from
earnings for future re-
placement of buildings,
plant and equipment

£32·8m
Licensing income

£8·4m
Associates, investments, and other
income

£49·3m
Purchase of fixed assets
Capital expended on
buildings, plant and
equipment to expand the
Group's activities and
replace worn out and
obsolete buildings, plant
and equipment

£12·5m
Increase in working
capital
Cash tied up in stocks,
and cash owed to us by
customers

£9·9m
Interest on loans

£0·7m   Extraordinary items

£21·9m
Tax paid
Amount of tax actually paid
this year

£7·2m   Dividends

As our cash in exceeded our cash
out this year we were able to repay
£6·6m loans and increase our cash
holdings for future spending by
£21·1m (including £6·0m raised by
issue of new shares).

(Nil after tax relief
and other credits)

Footnote: the published acco
reproduce the source and use
statement on page 23.

Figure 5   Good graphics help to put across complex messages.

From time to time the Minister will meet the Lobby correspondents. Every important British newspaper and agency has a Lobby correspondent and usually a deputy as well. Lobby correspondents have the special privilege of access to the Members Lobby just outside the Chamber of the House of Commons. They therefore have the opportunity of discussing with the Minister the political topics of the day. It is the code of Lobby correspondents not to reveal the source of information given to them and therefore Ministers can provide them with background information, or reveal the way in which they intend to deal with a particular subject. The existence of the Lobby greatly eases communication between Government Departments and the Press, especially as Lobby correspondents are so easily contacted. However, Ministers usually only go to the Lobby at the invitation of the Lobby Correspondents Association.

Ministers deal directly with a great number of people. They visit factories, hospitals, schools: they receive deputations and they correspond with members of the public, commercial companies, trade associations, local authorities, etc. In addition, they receive a great many letters from fellow MPs on behalf of constituents and as a result are well placed to assess public opinion and the likely public reaction to Government actions.

Ministers are not the only people to make public statements on Government matters. Some senior officials make public speeches on non-political subjects on behalf of their Ministers, and officials generally write to individual members of the public and appear before Parliamentary Committees and Royal Commissions, as well as maintaining special contact with particular groups on a day-to-day basis.

Each Government Department has its own special publics. The Department of Education and Science, for example, has four special publics — universities, local education authorities, teachers and parents. In some cases the responsibility for communication with the public is delegated onto *quasi*-governmental bodies, such as the British Council, the British Tourist Authority, the British Standards Institution and the British Overseas Trade Board.

A large number of papers are initiated by Government Departments and laid before Parliament, but there is in addition a great deal of information which comes from Government Departments which is not laid before Parliament. Much of it is statistical, such as the Monthly Digest of Statistics and most of it is printed through Her Majesty's Stationery Office.

The British Government Information Services

It is now over thirty years since, after false starts mainly stimulated by the needs of two world wars, Government finally established a recognized inter-departmental professional service to effect communication between Government and the various publics it serves. Previously, the status of Press Officers in Government Departments was uncertain, but the increasing and more detailed part played by Government in the daily lives of British citizens made it essential that a citizen be told of his new rights and of his responsibilities as soon as possible after Parliament has legislated. The increase in the number and complexity of social and economic measures affecting the life of the community and the change in Britain's relations with the world at large, coincided with the growth in technical means of disseminating information widely, and quickly made essential the establishment of organized information services, skilled in dealing with how to say what Departments wanted to say. At home, the Government information services can supplement news media in explaining legislation and other matters to the public in Britain. Overseas, information work supports the country's diplomatic, economic and commercial aims abroad.

Political Neutrality

The information services are staffed by civil servants whose duty it is, as for all civil servants, to explain and further the policies of the Government of the day, regardless of its political complexion. Therefore, it has been necessary to ensure that the information services are not used for party political, as distinct from governmental, purposes.

All Ministers have a dual position as Heads of their Departments and also as members of their own political party. The line between the two is not always clear. However, when Ministers make speeches, the rule is that the information services only operate on official occasions and publicize their speeches only by issuing a purely factual press statement. When a Minister speaks on a party platform, for example in a party political broadcast or on a party occasion, publicity will only be given through the party's channels.

During general elections, the official information services suspend most activity, from nomination day to polling, to avoid competing with parliamentary candidates for the public's attention.

At all times the issue of press notices and the selection of papers for press advertising is made on the basis of their effectiveness in reaching the public

Information officers are not allowed to discuss the merits of Government policy with the Press or public, although they may repeat to enquirers the declared objectives and ideas of their Ministers, e.g. quotes from speeches. The convention has grown up that the information services give the public, usually through the Press and broadcasting media, the background of facts against which proposed legislation can be set. Public money is not normally spent o

producing paid publicity about a subject still under parliamentary consideration.

Parliamentary Privilege

The contents of Parliamentary Bills, White Papers, and other matters which
are subject to parliamentary privilege, cannot be anticipated by Information
Officers, but they can, however, arrange for the Press to receive information
simultaneously with this information being given to Parliament.

Departmental Information Services

Each Departmental Minister is responsible to Parliament for the information
policy of his Department. There is an Information Division in every major
Department. The size, structure and title may vary from Department to
Department, but the objectives are similar and the Information Divisions have
similar functions and common problems.

In 1947 the objectives of Information Divisions were defined as follows:

1 To create and maintain informed opinion about the subjects with which
  each Department deals.
2 To use all methods of publicity, as suitable, to help the Department to
  achieve its purpose.
3 To assist and advise in all matters bearing on relations between the
  Department and its public.
4 To advise the Department on the public's reaction to the policies or actions
  of the Department.

The Information Officers who staff the home Departments usually have
relevant experience in journalism, publishing, advertising, photography,
films, broadcasting, exhibitions, etc. In the Foreign and Commonwealth
Office, however, information staff are non-specialist officers of the Diplomatic
Service.

Sir Harold Wilson, writing in the journal of the Institute of Public Relations,
said: 'The Information Officer's duty is to give facts, either on his own
initiative, or more frequently, in response to enquiries from the Press or the
public. It is not part of his duties to engage in political propaganda, still less to
build up the image of any of the Ministers of his Department.' The
Information Officer therefore provides a service not only to his Department
and to his Ministers, but to the media. The Minister makes his pronounce-
ments to 600 MPs, but they are intended to be understood by the whole nation.
The Press and broadcasting media act as middlemen, but they need the

information at a time and in a form they can use. From their needs has grow
the practice of issuing the embargoed press notice and advance circulation
publications.

The Role of the Chief Information Officer

The Chief Information Officer serves his Minister as an expert in publi
relations. With a status usually of Assistant Secretary (which is a senic
management post) or above, he has direct access to the Minister and th
Permanent Secretary (the chief executive of the Department) and attends
great number of policy-forming meetings held by Ministers and senior civ
servants. He is responsible for advising his Department on the public relatior
implications of their policies and also he is responsible for the quality of th
Press and public relations work done by his Division. He does not formula
policy, but in trying to put it over to others often finds himself contributing t
the shaping of policy. He has three kinds of duty towards the public:

1 To tell them what Government is doing on their behalf and with thei
  money.
2 To make them aware of their rights and obligations.
3 To persuade them to do something, e.g. to wear seat belts.

In some Departments the Information Division is expected to dra
Ministers' speeches. In others they may never see them until they are in th
final form. At press conferences a Minister will normally be accompanied b
his Chief Information Officer or a deputy, as well as other senior Departmenta
officials. Chief Information Officers meet weekly to exchange views and to so
out the diary of forthcoming events to avoid clashing of dates for importar
announcements.

Although the Information Division is there to serve the Minister, most of th
Chief Information Officer's time is spent advising Civil Service colleagues an
the Information Division exists as a service Division to the rest of th
Department in the same way as a public relations firm operates on behalf of it
clients. The Information Division therefore receives very large numbers c
internal papers from which it sifts matters which may be of interest to th
public and organizes the release of that information which can and should b
made public.

The Information Division is the main contact between the Department an
the Press, television and radio. If a Minister talks directly to the Press, he wil
normally tell the Information Division what he said. Most Departments hav
rules on how and when civil servants may talk to the media and civil servant

normally consult the Information Division or ask them to be present when they have any contact with the media.

Usually the Chief Information Officer sees more of his Minister than does any other civil servant, except the Permanent Secretary, in the Department and he is therefore required to make his judgments from his own knowledge and evaluation of the policy of the Department and the Minister's thinking. The Chief Information Officer through his Press Officers is expected to answer questions which the Press have a right to put to Government on matters of fact and to provide guidance on matters of interpretation. It is therefore important that the Press Officer is part of the communications scene and that he is known by journalists. In many Departments a Duty Press Officer is available around the clock to answer enquiries.

The Organization of the Information Division

Most Information Divisions have three sections, press, publicity and briefing. The Publicity Section deals with paid publicity — everything from press and television advertising to the production of books, posters and films. Publicity directly affects the work of the Department by making it easier to administer; for example, when the general public is called upon to take specific action at a certain time, or by making known the services and benefits available. From time to time, the duties of the Departmental information staff include the mounting of campaigns aimed directly at the public, for example the 'Save It' campaign mounted by the Department of Energy and the 'Clunk Click' campaign mounted by the Department of Transport. In such cases the Department would seek the assistance of the Central Office of Information which would advise the Department on advertising methods and brief the agency appointed to handle the campaign, but the responsibility for the campaign still rests with the Department's Chief Information Officer on behalf of his Minister. Judgment of how things should be told must be his. In most Departments the Briefing Section is concerned with the collection of information and the preparation of briefing and the writing of articles and speeches.

Central Office of Information

The Central Office of Information is a non–Ministerial common service Department which produces publicity material at the request of Ministerial Departments for use in the United Kingdom and overseas with a present staff of about 900, of which nearly half are in the Information Officer group, most of whom are specialists recruited from the private sector. The COI either creates material itself or arranges for commercial agencies to do so. Press and

television advertising campaigns are undertaken by advertising agencies an
films are made by film companies under contract.

The COI is headed by its Director-General assisted by the Deputy Directc
General. There are four Groups — three Production Groups covering hom
and overseas work, each headed by a Director and each sub-divided int
specialized services, and a Client Services Group.

Advertising

The Advertising Service handles Government advertising campaigns fc
most Departments. It advises Departments on advertising methods, recom
mends on the cost-effective deployment of funds available, briefs the agenc
appointed to handle the campaign and monitors the day-to-day worl
Recruitment advertising for the armed services, police, nurses, etc., accoun
for a large proportion of the total expenditure.

Home Publications

Home Publications writes, edits, designs and arranges distribution for a wid
range of booklets, leaflets and posters throughout the United Kingdon
explaining the effects of government policy and legislation to many differel
audiences. A substantial amount of printed recruitment material is produce
for the armed and public services.

Printing is arranged through Her Majesty's Stationery Office which als
acts as publisher for titles put on sale.

Up to 3,000 publications are produced annually.

Research Unit

Although much of the Research Unit's work relates to advertising, a wid
variety of projects concern other areas of government publicity includin
print (such as leaflets, information booklets and forms), exhibitions, an
films. The overall purpose is to enhance the cost-effectiveness of the COI
publicity output by means of independent market research. Projects includ
background research to help understand a target market as well as creativ
development research and 'evaluation research' to check specific campaigns

The purpose of evaluative research is often to help determine whether th
cost of the campaign was more than offset by the resulting savings, e.g. i
reduction in road accidents or fires in the home.

Viewdata

Co-ordination of government input to the viewdata system is linked with th design and implementation of viewdata data banks for a wide variety of purposes.

Photographic Services

A wide variety of photographic services is provided for government departments, other COI Services, overseas missions and foreign correspondents. A sales counter supplies Crown Copyright pictures to the general public on payment of standard fees. The Section has its own photographers, photo researchers, darkrooms, and a photographic library that contains a stock of some 300,000 black-and-white and colour photographs covering most aspects of British life and activities and well-known personalities in every sphere.

Exhibitions

The Exhibition Service plans, designs and supervises the construction of a large number of exhibitions and displays for government departments in the United Kingdom.

Overseas, it deals with exhibitions and displays funded by the Foreign and Commonwealth Office, ranging from modest displays to British participation, often co-ordinated with other EEC countries, in major trade fairs and world expositions.

Government support for participation by British companies in overseas trade fairs is the responsibility of the British Overseas Trade Board.

Films and Television

The Films and Television Service provides television programmes, films, video tape and audio-visual presentations for use in Britain and overseas. Most of them are produced or commissioned by the COI, but films are also acquired from other sources and distributed by the COI. Over thirty-five advertising commercials and twenty-five short public service television features for free transmission are produced each year. At any one time some thirty longer documentary films and video tape programmes are in production. Home departments brief the COI on their requirements and although it often commissions outside technical services, the COI maintains creative and financial control and is responsible for ensuring that the resulting product fulfils its purpose. It is responsible for a variety of television programmes and documentaries, which receive widespread transmission overseas. The COI is responsible for the provision of facilities for resident television correspondents and teams visiting from overseas.

Overseas Press

News items, feature articles, topical commentaries and press pictures are supplied daily by telex or airmail to British missions abroad, mainly for reproduction in local newspapers and periodicals. A special industrial service provides stories about new products, processes, and services and gives publicity support to British participation in exhibitions and trade fairs, at home and abroad. Supplements on particular industries are prepared and placed in leading overseas trade and technical magazines.

Overseas Publications and Foreign Languages

Books, pamphlets, folders and magazines are produced for overseas use and, depending on their destination, may contain material of general interest or specifically in support of exports. The reference services include the annual 'Britain' handbook, the monthly Survey of Current Affairs, and a range of titles on individual topics. Photographic display material — posters and captioned picture sets — are also provided. The translation services of the Foreign Language Sections are used by all COI's overseas services.

Radio

Radio items and programmes are supplied by direct line or on tape, for transmission by radio stations overseas, and by local radio stations in the United Kingdom. Overseas items are supplied in a total of five languages.

Overseas Visitors and Information Studies

Arrangements are made for some 2,000 visitors annually at the request of the Foreign and Commonwealth Office. Most of the visitors are officially invited to Britain as guests of the British Government, but help is also given to sponsored visitors who come at their own expense but need help in arranging a programme and making contacts. Visits vary in length from a few days to three to four weeks. Each is individually planned to take account of the needs and wishes of the visitor. Training courses for information officers to overseas governments, and introductory courses for Diplomatic Service commercial and information personnel, are provided by the Information Studies Unit.

Regional Organization

A regional information network is provided by seven COI regional offices in England, the Scottish Information Office, the Welsh Information Office and the Northern Ireland Information services. These offices, as well as providing a common Departmental information service in their regions, are responsible for collecting and supplying material from the regions to COI headquarters for use in the overseas information services and they assist with the arrangements for overseas visitors.

Overseas Information Services

Just over half of COI staff are employed on overseas services and export publicity accounts for over half of all overseas work. The objective of the official British information services overseas is to present the facts and Britain's point of view, so that people of other countries have every opportunity of understanding British ideas, policies and objectives. The objectives of commercial publicity are to support Britain's position as a nation dependent on trade (both visible and invisible) by convincing overseas opinion that Britain is a stable, skilled, forward-looking, technologically advanced industrial nation and a sound trading partner.

The methods used to meet the overseas publicity objectives vary with the development of policies, the requirements of overseas posts, the definition of target audiences and the available media; but overall the main elements of the COI's publicity output, not necessarily in order of priority, are:

1 Information about positive political, social, environmental and particularly economic developments.
2 Publicity for British exporters participating in BOTB-supported joint ventures, trade missions and other events overseas; and publicity for major UK trade fairs.
3 Publicity for new and improved products, processes and services which show in specific case history terms that British industry is producing the goods overseas which buyers want.
4 Extended publicity for products and services whose excellence is such that they reflect credit on British industry as a whole.
5 Publicity designed to show the achievement and reliability of sectors of British industry and commerce, e.g. aerospace, ceramics, chemicals, North Sea oil, the City of London.
6 Publicity for research and development which shows that British exporters are backed by scientific and technological initiative and follow through of a high order.

The British overseas information services were late to develop and evolved rather haphazardly. The Earl of Drogheda in a summary of a report of an enquiry into the services published in April 1954 said, 'They have always, moreover, been regarded as something of a Cinderella by a people who instinctively dislike the idea of self-advertisement'.

Overseas information policy is set by the Foreign and Commonwealth Office, guided in commercial matters by the Department of Trade and Industry and the British Overseas Trade Board. The effectiveness of the overseas information service depends in part on the efficiency of the Diplomatic Service officers who staff the information posts in our Embassies, High Commissions and Consulates overseas. These are non-specialists, but are often supported by locally engaged officers with information experience.

In general the British Government does not buy space in overseas media, so it is only possible to obtain press coverage or radio, or television time, if the material supplied is good enough and meets the publisher's criteria of topicality and relevance. As stated earlier, the COI is responsible for providing feature articles, news items and photographs for the Press, films and news material for television, plus line feeds, tapes and scripts for radio, reference documents for selective distribution, books and magazines for free distribution overseas. It is also responsible for staging exhibitions other than trade and cultural exhibitions which are the responsibility of the British Overseas Trade Board and the British Council respectively.

Britain's image overseas is also influenced by two other official elements — the BBC's external services and the British Council.

BBC External Services

The BBC through its External Services broadcasts all over the world in English and, at the time of going to press, thirty-six foreign language services for a total of some 727 hours a week. The main objectives are to give unbiased news, to reflect British opinion and to project British life and culture. News bulletins, current affairs programmes, political commentaries and topical magazine programmes form the main part of the output.

The languages in which the external services broadcast and the length of time each language is on the air are prescribed by the Government. Apart from this, the BBC has full responsibility and it is completely independent in determining the content of news and other programmes. The BBC World Service broadcasts for twenty-four hours a day in English and BBC news bulletins and other programmes are rebroadcast by the domestic radio services of many countries.

The British Council

The British Council is part of Britain's overseas representation. Its aim is to promote overseas an enduring understanding and appreciation of Britain through cultural, educational and technical co-operation. Although funded mainly by the British Government it is a non-political, independent organization with a Royal Charter. In most countries it works independently of the British Embassy, wherever possible in separate premises. Through its staff in about eighty countries it aims to establish lasting relationships by arranging training and study in Britain; sending British specialists overseas; recruiting British teachers for posts overseas; supplying information about Britain through its 100 or so libraries overseas; teaching the English language; presenting British arts overseas; arranging exchange programmes; and helping to develop links between educational and scientific institutions and twinnings between towns and regions.

ACKNOWLEDGEMENTS

In preparing this chapter I have drawn widely on a report of the Royal Institute of Public Administration entitled *The Government Explains — A Study of the Information Services*, written by Marjorie Ogilvy-Webb and published by Allen & Unwin in 1965. I was also guided by a Civil Service College lecture entitled *The Role of the Information Officer* given by Mr Henry James in 1975, when he was Director General of the Central Office of Information.

FURTHER READING

The student may find it helpful to consult the annual edition of the *Official Handbook on Britain* published by Her Majesty's Stationery Office, the COI reference sheet *British Government Information Services* and the COI booklet *Guide to Overseas Services*. The names and titles of those involved in Government information work in the UK are published twice yearly in a COI booklet *Public Relations, Information and Press Officers in Government Departments, Public Corporations, etc;*, the names of Information Officers in Britain's Embassies, Consulates and High Commissions overseas are available from the Diplomatic Service Overseas Reference List available from the Staff Records Section of the Foreign and Commonwealth Office.

Note. The views expressed by the author are his own and should not be interpreted as those of the Department of Trade or the British Council.

8

Public Relations in Local Government

Geoffrey Lewis

Government is Public Relations

The Institute's definition of public relations practice, the deliberate, planned and sustained effort to establish and maintain mutual understanding between an organization and its public, applies as much to local government as it does to any other operation: commercial, industrial or governmental. The basic tenets remain the same, only the application of those tenets may vary.

In a sense local government is, itself, a vast public relations exercise. Local government officers are employed by the public; their salaries are paid by the public; they work for the public and they are responsible to members elected by the public. In turn, these elected representatives are answerable to the public and at regular intervals they seek public approval for their policies and actions. If the public do not approve, then the ruling members are literally 'sacked' and new members with new policies take their place.

Thus the framework for establishing and maintaining mutual understanding between 'the organization' and 'the public' already exists and has done so for a very long time with the elected member as the focus of communication.

But things change. From yesterday's face-to-face meetings between member and public in the village hall, face-to-face meetings today are more likely to take place before television cameras or on radio with audiences of millions. Communication is instantaneous.

The member making a statement in committee at 4 pm may well be defending or explaining that statement on local radio by 4.15 pm and facing the television cameras at 6 pm. If radio facilities are permitted in the committee room, the statement may even be broadcast live.

With committee meetings now open to both Press and public; with the advent of local radio and television, the day of the leisurely created and much considered bulletin is over. Anticipation, speed, familiarity with his organiza-

150

tion and its policies, together with a knowledge of media requirements, are some of the essential ingredients that go to make up the modern local government public relations practitioner.

This situation has been made more complex by the fact that change of pace in communication has been accompanied by a vast increase in the *numbers* trying to communicate.

Local government, elected by the people to work for the people, has somehow to make its voice heard above all the others, if democracy is to have any meaning at all. It must shout as loudly, as skilfully and as subtly as all the others; it must compete for attention to gain interest in its actions, if it is to obtain that essential ingredient for local government success: mutual understanding.

It is for this reason that, while the elected representative must remain at all times the central and major communicator, many local authorities today make use of the skills of the professional public relations practitioner.

Where it Begins

Public relations activity in the Town Hall or Civic Centre begins, as do so many things in life, with the fundamental and often overlooked minor matters. It begins at the front door, on the telephone and with correspondence.

The pleasantly decorated entrance hall; the cheerful, helpful and polite receptionist and the courteous telephonist create at the outset an atmosphere which offers members and officers alike a chance of dealing on level terms with callers.

Letters which begin 'Dear Sir/Madam' when the name of the addressee is known enhance the feeling of bureaucracy, creating at once a barrier between writer and recipient.

Small matters indeed, but nonetheless important when multiplied by the numbers of letters written, telephone calls received or visitors seen. If every member of the public who wrote to, visited or called at the Town Hall felt that they had been well-treated and said so to their friends and relatives, there might be no need to employ public relations practitioners at all!

Duties and Objectives

Simply stated, the duties and objectives of a local authority public relations unit is to tell the public what is happening in the Town Hall and to tell the council, in turn, the attitude of the public to those events. The public relations practitioner should not be employed to convince the public that the council's policies are the only ones worthy of consideration, but he should be there to attempt to ensure that the public are given the facts unfettered by distortion.

He does not make policy, that is the job of the elected representative, but he does help to ensure that the policy when made is understood by the people the council serves. He will always advise the council on the way to present those policies publicly, particularly in news terms, bearing in mind that matters of importance are not always in themselves newsworthy. By his news sense he should be able to ensure that most items he is asked to handle are acceptable to the media, but when they are not he should have the courage to say so. As any public relations officer knows, nothing antagonizes journalists more than a series of news releases fit only for 'the spike', except, perhaps, press conferences held only to inflate someone's ego. The reputation of the council and the public relations practitioner will suffer as a result.

Since local government is itself a vast public relations operation, it would seem sensible for the public relations practitioner to have a place within the top management structure. Unfortunately, this is not always the case. However he should at least ensure that he has ready access to the Chief Executive, the Leader of the Council and the Chief Whip and that he establishes sufficient confidence with them to be advised of all policies under consideration (confidential or otherwise), so that he can plan in advance the best method for the public announcement. Every policy, every decision, poses the question how do we tell the public and what will the reaction be?

While ensuring that he has ready access to the Leader, Chief Whip and Chief Executive, the public relations officer will also establish close relationships with all committee chairmen, and chief officers, for it is only by such relationships that he can anticipate problems and act with speed.

PRO — Not Politician

One point should be made clear: the public relations officer works for the council. He does not work for a political party. The policies of the council are established by the current majority party and it is these policies, once they have entered the administrative machinery, and have become council policies, that the public relations officer handles. The political complexion of the majority party may change and the change may bring with it completely new policies. The public relations officer will explain those policies with the same expertise that he used under the previous majority party.

The official viewpoint is the view of the council and, while the press or public may not like that view, they will at least accept that it is being delivered by an impartial officer and not by someone with a political axe to grind.

Press, Radio and TV

As a method of communication the Press, from a local authority viewpoint, has a weakness. For one thing it has, within the laws of libel, the freedom to print what it chooses and sometimes what it chooses is not to the authority's liking. For another, it has limited space and does not always print the council's story in full.

Thus, the overwhelming desire to rush into print should be restrained even though the tendency of members may be to judge success by column inches.

More important probably is the long-term build up of good relations and trust with regular correspondents, not so much with the objective of getting more material published, but rather to ensure that what is published is accurate and a fair interpretation of the situation.

This is not to suggest that very few releases should be issued, but that those that are issued really contain news.

Good relationships with the Press, radio and TV are essential and this can best be established by offering them the facilities with which to do their job. The minimum offer is a press room, with phones, in which to write their copy. Larger and more sophisticated authorities offer rooms for use as radio studios, with live broadcasting facilities from council and committee chambers and closed circuit television from the council chamber to the press room, so that journalists can write their copy while keeping an eye on the council's proceedings.

Fundamental to this relationship is the supply of agendas and documents. It is unfair, to say the least, to expect any journalist to report council business without being supplied with the necessary background papers.

The public relations officer himself should attend as many committee meetings as possible, if only to keep himself briefed on Members' attitudes and to maintain his relationships with them. He must also be ready to answer Members' questions or to present proposals for consideration and speak to those proposals.

Press and public relations officers should not act as barriers between the council and the Press, although they should avoid passing journalists to other officers wherever possible. After all, it is part of the public relations officer's duty to save time for both sides and he fails if, in most cases, he cannot supply the answers to press questions himself.

Feature and in-depth articles are, of course, best done by face-to-face interviews and when such interviews are wanted the public relations officer should arrange the interview, making sure that the interviewee really does know his subject. He should brief the officer concerned on what the journalist wants and attend the interview himself, both for self-instruction and to ensure the officer is not tempted to stray from a subject on which he is an expert to one on which he is not. Officers, of course, can only be interviewed on fact, not policy. Policy must be a matter for the elected members.

GLC

public relations branch
news service

Greater London Council
The County Hall
London SE1 7PB

01-633 7700 or 6529 (Housing)
7866 or 3235 (Planning & Communications)
2032 or 7977 (Policy & Resources; Recreation
& Community Services)

July 23, 1979

No. 226

THE CHANGING FACE OF LEICESTER SQUARE

The western side of Leicester Square is to be closed to traffic, paved over and new trees planted.

The Greater London Council's Central Area Planning Committee has agreed that the necessary traffic orders should be made to close this part of the square and turn it into a pedestrian area, as has already been done with the north and south sides.

Mr Sandy Sandford, Chairman of the committee, said today: "This is the last stage of the pedestrianisation of the Square. It will be a focal point for tourists and Londoners and I hope they will find it an area of peace and enjoyment.

"We had planned to plant 18 trees, but the Pedestrians' Association and the Leicester Square and Coventry Street Association thought it was too many, so we revised the scheme to include six at each end, with an open space between.

"Talks have been held with Westminster City Council and the Leicester Square and Coventry Street Association on the maintenance of the area and the layout of the central gardens, and a subsequent report may come before my committee."

The scheme includes decorative paving and light clusters and is estimated to cost £78,655.

END

Press contact: Mary Matthews (01) 633 7866

Figure 11   A GLC press release which helps the journalist. Note the double spacing for sub-editorial changes and the name of the contact at the bottom of the page. (Reproduced courtesy of the Greater London Council.)

Reserved for the Leader

Certain topics of public interest will probably be reserved for the Leader of the Council and, where committee responsibilities overlap, committee chairmen should be given, through the political party machinery, firm boundaries in terms of press, radio and television interviews.

Essential to the whole functioning of a local authority press office is the creation of an efficient and fast method of checking. News releases must be checked with Departments for fact and with committee chairmen for accuracy of policy interpretation. Sometimes more than one chairman and Department are involved.

Tedious though it may be, checking is all important and speed can be achieved by sending copies of drafts simultaneously to all concerned. No local authority can afford to issue inaccurate statements about its own policies.

Local government news need not be dull. Indeed it can, quite frequently, be entertaining. It may be difficult to raise a laugh at an increase in rates or rents, but, on the other hand, the story about the first orange to be grown in a certain council orangery for one hundred years went round the world. The orange was stolen the day the Press came to take pictures of it!

The result: some excellent light-hearted publicity for one of the council's historic buildings.

The normal rules for the writing of news releases and the holding of press conferences apply, although it is worth emphasizing that it is essential to ensure for the latter that members and officers who will be attending the conference are properly briefed beforehand.

It is also worth bearing in mind the usefulness of photocalls. A minor news story can be frequently turned into a good picture by the simple expedient of applying imagination. There is little news, for example, in the Chairman or Leader of the council cutting a ribbon to open a new road, but give him a six foot pair of scissors with which to do the cutting and good picture coverage may follow (see Figure 12).

The good local government public relations practitioner will seek every opportunity to obtain picture coverage, and will be on the look-out for subjects suitable for press photographs. This certainly means unusual or 'action' pictures. The 'still life' of the mayor and other members in their robes of office may be impressive to the mayor, but they are singularly unimpressive to the Press unless, of course, they illustrate a story suggesting that the robes are to be replaced at a somewhat high cost to the ratepayer.

Last, but not least, an efficient press office contains an up-to-date mailing list without which the whole operation fails.

Information Services

Local government public relations is probably divided equally between press services on the one hand and all other publicity services on the other.

Some authorities, particularly those covering widespread areas, have opened information centres in shopping precincts; others have made use of mobile centres: caravans equipped with minor exhibitions and helpful staff thus bringing the Town Hall to the people. Others operate telephone information services, so that the public can receive immediate advice for the cost of a telephone call.

Other authorities have bookshops which sell, or give away, not only publications about the council's affairs, but sell books commercially published about the town or locality.

The centres and shops should not be overlooked when a particular public relations exercise is undertaken. Proposals for a new road, for example, can be shown at these centres and the staff, properly briefed or drawn temporarily from the appropriate Department, can answer questions. The telephone information service can also be briefed on the subject and explanatory leaflets can be distributed to each householder likely to be affected. Combine this with advertisements in and press notices to newspapers, local radio and television and a campaign begins to take shape.

There are two important considerations to be borne in mind: a centre is valueless unless it is sited where there are crowds; the staff must be carefully selected and trained.

The public relations officer working in a local authority responsible for library services will not, of course, overlook the value of the library as an outlet for information or the distribution of literature.

Publications and Graphic Design

Publications, ranging from the glossy booklet to the Green Paper, are again methods of communication which are under the council's control. Too often too little thought is given either to content or design. The committee document may be fine for those members well versed in committee affairs. To the public who are not, they merely confuse the issue. Considerable effort should be taken to ensure that all publications are written in 'layman's language' avoiding the use of jargon. The phrase 'population density' may mean one thing to Members and officers, but it could mean quite another (like 'people with thick heads') to the public.

No publication should be issued unless the council can take pride in it, since it may influence public attitude to the council itself. A slovenly produced booklet creates the impression of a slovenly organization. Good graphic design, reflecting the business-like approach of the modern authority, is essential and, if good graphic designers are not available on the staff, then the public relations officer should seek to use a consultant.

While the council's annual report to the public may be considerably more up-market in appearance than a Green Paper seeking the public's views on a particular project, they both merit the same attention to detail.

This thinking should apply also to exhibitions and to advertisements, whether these are recruitment advertisements or announcements about entertainment. The public will judge the council by what they see. But a word of caution about exhibitions. The object of an exhibition is to convey a message. It is not produced to act as free display of the designer's art. The most brilliantly designed exhibition is a failure if no one knows why it was held.

Public meetings, much in vogue with the coming of public participation, have their advantages and disadvantages. The advantages, of course, are that they give the council an opportunity to face the public directly with proposals, answer questions and to gauge public feeling. Too often, however, they attract people with problems not related to the subject and the discussion becomes wide-ranging and inconclusive. Particular attention to detail is necessary for such meetings, if they are to stand a chance of success, and public relations officers should ensure that they conform to an established pattern. This is best achieved by devising a checklist which is used on each occasion and should include such items as the need for hand microphones, nameplates and other obvious, but sometimes overlooked, matters.

Public meetings, or any other project, can be advertised by press releases, posters, advertisements, supported by direct mailing to homes within the area concerned. However, unless direct mailing can be arranged 'in house', the employment of an outside agency can be expensive and difficulties experienced in ensuring that the mailing remains within specific boundaries. The cost may be found to outweigh the benefit.

Visits and Visitors

Every effort should be made to show the public what Members and officers are doing. Organized visits to the Town Hall or Civic Centre should be encouraged and staff should be trained to handle such visits and to give explanatory talks. Equally, the public relations officer should be prepared to talk about the council's work to meetings of clubs and associations organized outside the Town Hall. For both purposes he should be armed with film, slides or other audio-visual aids.

Arrangements for VIP visits, normally including civic entertainment, are frequently handled by the office of the mayor or chairman, since they involve considerable knowledge of protocol. Even here the public relations officer should ensure that he is kept advised so that he may take whatever action he may think necessary from a public relations viewpoint.

Measuring success

Too few local authorities make effective attempts to measure the progress, successfully or otherwise, of their public relations campaigns and too many rely on the number of column inches of coverage appearing in the Press, or number of seconds coverage on radio or television. This is no measurement at all. It cannot indicate how many read or heard the story and, what is more, how many understood, remembered it or what influence it had upon them.

The only effective measurement is by public opinion survey. The cost is off-putting to local authorities in today's economic climate, but much time and money could be saved by such expenditure. A survey before and during a campaign might well indicate the need for a change in direction or even the dropping of the campaign altogether.

Staff public relations officers sometimes look askance at the use of public relations consultants, but there seems no reason why, assuming there are no union or other problems, a local authority with a small public relations unit should not use a consultancy to handle a specific campaign, leaving the staff man to act as co-ordinator between council and consultancy and to get on with the general day-to-day work. The spread and effectiveness of the council's public relations can thus be increased without employing staff to match the peak periods with little to do during slack times.

Internal communication with staff is usually the responsibility of Establishment or personnel officers, but the public relations officer should be ready to advise or assist, either during training courses, or with the planning and editing of house magazines or bulletins. With the proper tact and right approach, any suggestions which will improve staff communications are usually welcomed.

Finances

A word or two about finance. The cost of public relations is as much or as little as one wishes to make it but, clearly, there cannot be exceptional results from unexceptional expenditure. A large authority with a large area and population faces a more difficult public relations problem than a small authority communicating with a small population.

The sensible method of calculating costs is to meet officers from the council's various Departments at the time when estimates are being drawn up to discover what proposals are being planned for the coming year which are likely to require public relations action. From this the public relations officer can obtain some idea of the costs he may have to meet and make his bid accordingly, not forgetting to include in his estimates a sum for those unexpected items which Members so enjoy launching at the last moment.

In these days of economic restraint, however, it is not unusual to be told that next year's budget will be either the same as last year's, or the same plus 'X' per cent to cover inflation which is equal either to cutting back, or at least to standing still. In which case the public relations officer, knowing the Departmental proposals, will have to spend some time working out priorities based on his awareness of the political desires.

All in all, the local government public relations officer may not know in detail any particular aspect of his council's work, but his general knowledge about the council must be supreme.

Note. The views expressed are those of the author and are not necessarily shared by the Greater London Council.

9

Public Relations and Voluntary Movements

Philip Barron

The importance of public relations to charities and other voluntary movements can hardly be overestimated. They are in the market-place of ideas rather than that of goods (though with the spread of charity trading they may be there, too). Usually they wish to alter attitudes and change behaviour. People will not help a charity until they know about it and understand what it does, so good communication, and not in one direction only, is vital.

This is particularly true when the voluntary organization needs to raise money in the form of donations. The prospect is asked to part with his hard-earned cash — for what? Not to satisfy his own material needs or the kind of psychological needs to which purveyors of products usually appeal, although fund-raisers speak of 'the need to give'. Not only does he have to be convinced that the cause put before him deserves an altruistic response, he must believe that it is *more* worthy of that response than many others.

So we are in a situation as competitive in its own way as that of the supermarket, yet there are some important differences between *this* battle for hearts and minds and those being waged in the worlds of commerce and politics.

To start with an obvious one, the funds available for fighting the battle are likely to be far more limited than those available to PR practitioners in these other areas. This means, usually, that the charity PRO is short of munitions and objectives take longer to achieve.

Even where substantial resources have been built up, one has to bear in mind that the British tend to react against a charity that is seen to be too overtly business-like. 'On the one hand, the public expects its money to be efficiently spent; on the other, it overwhelmingly prefers "small, homely charities", in spite of a suspicion that they are inefficient. They have the underdog's appeal, and are supposed (quite wrongly) to spend a smaller proportion on administration.'[12]

[12] Benedict Nightingale, *Charities* (Allen Lane, London, 1973)

Another problem for the PRO of a registered charity may be the fact that while education is a charitable activity, 'propaganda' is not. The Charity Commissioners, interpreting ancient and confusing charity law, have refused charity status to many 'pressure groups' seeking reforms with which few would quarrel. Some existing charities have been warned for straying into the 'political' area and campaigners must bear in mind that a charity's trustees can be held personally liable for funds spent on activities judged by the Commissioners not to be charitable. It could be argued that intervention of this kind is itself a political act on behalf of the *status quo*, so it is not surprising that there have been calls for reform of the charity law.

The Message

Voluntary organizations have a marked tendency to be woolly about the essential message they want to communicate. This is often a reflection of uncertainty about their objectives, about which there may be differences of opinion among supporters and even among the leaders.

Whether the PRO is given a brief or invited to write his own, he should ensure that the resulting statement of objectives is endorsed by a representative sample of the membership, or by an authoritative group of leaders. A message based on such a consensus will carry much more conviction and will provide a firm base for the campaign.

Defining the publics

Even when a charity looks to virtually the entire population for support (e.g. Oxfam), it is advisable for practical purposes to break that vast public down into smaller sections, just as a commercial firm would do. When a charity's message is less universal than Oxfam's, it is even more necessary to see in one's mind's eye exactly who the target audiences are.

To take just one example, a body such as the British Trust for Conservation Volunteers could define its publics to include all the following:

1 Young people aged 17–35 (those most likely to come forward as volunteers).
2 Land-owners (who stand to benefit from work done). It is noteworthy here that land-owners today are more likely to be corporate bodies than individuals — some of the largest are nationalized industries.
3 Central Government.
4 Local authorities/councillors.
5 Commercial firms.
6 Charitable trusts.

7 Other bodies involved in, or likely to be concerned about, conservation, e.g.:
   a Society for the Promotion of Nature Conservation.
   b Individual county naturalists' trusts.
   c Countryside Commission.
   d Council for Environmental Education.
   e Land Decade 1980–90 Movement.
   f Watch Trust for Environmental Education.
   g Soil Association.
   h Civic Trust.
   i Nature Conservancy Council.
   j National Trust Groups.
   k Ramblers' Association.
   l Country-Wide Holidays Association (CHA).
   m Holiday Fellowship.
   n Youth Hostels Association.
   o Lawyers' Ecology Group.
   p Inland Waterways Association.
   q Country Gentlemen's Association.
   r Country Landowners' Association.

A good deal of research may be necessary to trace all the groups worthy of inclusion in such a list.

Charities and the Media

It is a temptation, when liaising with the media on behalf of a charity, to try to trade on the goodwill that some journalists naturally have towards a good cause. However, professional objectivity is just as important in this area as it is in other fields.

Moreover, one cannot assume that goodwill is universally present. Many journalists react warily to an approach from a charity, perhaps being anxious not to be thought of as a 'soft touch'. A minority show signs of a definite anti-charity prejudice; some believe that the existence of 'charity' helps to perpetuate social evils that would otherwise be removed by political action, while others are simply suspicious about the way charities are run.

Building a media list

Just as the potential sources of support for a voluntary agency will vary according to the nature of its work, so will the media that are likely to take an interest.

If the cause you are promoting is a national one, its work will probably have ramifications providing points of contact with a number of special-interest groups and thence with the journals published by or for those groups. Having analysed one's publics, it is in fact a relatively simple matter to work out the relevant media categories.

Let us take it for granted that the national Press, radio and TV are already on the media list. You will get in touch with them selectively, as and when you have a story that is strong enough.

For purposes of illustration, let us imagine (as before) that the organization 'employing' you is engaged in conservation of the environment. What other media should be added to your list?

First, one might think of national magazines whose audiences are not categorized by profession, but by what one might loosely call 'life style'. Readers of *Country Life* and *The Field* are likely, for obvious reasons, to be sympathetic to conservation activity.

So would ramblers and canal-lovers, so one might also include the journals of such bodies as the Ramblers' Association and the Inland Waterways Association (to name but two).

Next one might add the various magazines concerned with local government (councillors and municipal staff being concerned with the protection of amenities) and the professional journals covering estate management. A story about tools used in conservation work could even be of interest to a trade magazine like the *Hardware Trade Journal*, not to mention the house journal of the firm that makes the tools.

Provided that one has the resources and is prepared to take the trouble to produce material geared to their readerships, specialized media are more often able to devote space to relevant causes than are daily newspapers or mass-circulation magazines. They constitute the 'bread and butter' of press relations, with the occasional mention in nationals providing the 'jam'.

A particularly important media sector for voluntary movements is the provincial daily and weekly newspaper sector. Some regional dailies consistently give substantial coverage to matters of social concern. Unlike the nationals, local papers do not have to squeeze the whole world's news into their pages and if the press officer can give his story a local angle, the chances of its being used are very high.

There are just under 120 regional dailies and about 800 weekly titles in the United Kingdom, so mailing the lot is a costly operation. One of the specialist PR mailing firms, however, can reduce the postage and stationery costs by using, when appropriate, a list in which weekly titles that are published as a group are treated as one (this reduces the 800 to something like 157).

In practice, there is rarely justification for sending an identical release to all these local newspapers. It is more rewarding, in the long run, to work one's way gradually through the list and provide a local angle for each title or group.

Local organizations

When acting for a purely local voluntary agency, the Press officer will of course need a different kind of media list, extending it 'downwards' to include parish magazines and, for example, the house journals of companies based in the area. Local radio and TV will be important, but there is no reason why even such humble media as the shop-window postcard should not be considered.

Partnership with commerce

There are a number of ways in which commercial companies can help voluntary organizations (and themselves at the same time) apart from allocating a donation from the annual charity budget.

On-pack Offers

One of the most familiar forms of collaboration is the on-pack offer in which a firm undertakes to give money or goods to a deserving cause in proportion to the number of tokens or coupons sent in by purchasers of a product. Although in marketing terms it is basically a form of sales promotion, this technique has important public relations aspects.

There is no doubt that the association of the name of a popular charity with a product promotion can be a major factor in its success. For this reason, and in return for exclusivity, the charity should insist that there is a guaranteed minimum return to it from the deal, regardless of the redemption rate.

From the charity's point of view, the publicity value of having its name displayed in thousands of shops, and the educational effect of the message carried on so many packets, is immense. Sadly, it is too often the charities with a name already well-known that are selected for this favour.

Pioneers in the field of commercial charity campaigns were the Royal National Lifeboat Institution, who did a deal with Birds Eye in 1969.

Purchasers of Birds Eye fish fingers were invited to return a coupon from the pack, each coupon representing a donation of 8d or 4d (depending on pack size) which the company would pay to the RNLI. Birds Eye supported the promotion with considerable TV, press and point-of-sale advertising. The result was over £30,000 for the RNLI and the highest sales for fish fingers ever achieved in the summer months.

The money raised purchased a new lifeboat (named *Birds Eye*) which is stationed at New Quay (Cardiganshire). The following year the promotion was repeated, again raising £30,000 which went towards the cost of another boat. Over ten million packs carried the 'Help launch another lifeboat' message and the same number of leaflets were distributed door-to-door throughout the country. Birds Eye also produced full-colour display material for over 90,000 shops.

It makes good sense for manufacturers of branded goods to spread an on-pack promotion right across a product range and this was done in a 1979/80 tie-up between Dr Barnardo's and Cadbury-Schweppes. Buyers of nine grocery lines contributed towards a target of ten mini-buses, five of which the firm guaranteed to provide whatever the rate of redemption. In return for this guarantee, Cadbury-Schweppes had exclusive use of the Barnardo name in the grocery sector for nine months.

A special 16mm film was made about this promotion, simply to motivate the Cadbury-Schweppes sales force. Retailers were encouraged to tack schemes of their own on to the main promotion; these local schemes, not based on pack redemption, raised funds for a year's supply of petrol, roof racks and other items relevant to the core project.

There are, of course, many more subtle ways in which the PR department of a commercial firm can co-operate with a charity. Duckhams, who provide lubricants for RNLI lifeboats, sponsored a set of four educational posters in 1972. These have been in great demand; after a schools TV programme on lifeboats, 3,000 sets were sent out in two months.

The posters were designed specifically for schools, but were often used in exhibitions, displays and at fund-raising events. Subsequently Duckhams produced a new set, based on the originals, but scaled down to reduce postage costs and packaging problems.

Award Schemes

An industrial firm, or a professional institution, may find that one good way of expressing its sense of social responsibility is to sponsor, in conjunction with a voluntary agency, a competition for school or college students, or another of its publics. This will often be done in collaboration with a national or regional newspaper; a radio or TV company might also be willing to co-sponsor.

Events and Other Promotions

Promotional projects involving charities are legion and we have space here only to cite a handful of examples. The point I want to stress is that those charities who find partners for their promotions invariably do better than they would have done by going it alone.

The partners may be other charities (Oxfam and UNICEF very sensibly got together during the International Year of the Child in 1980) and/or commercial firms.

An enormous success for Dr Barnardo's has been the annual 'Champion

Children' promotion, run for two years in conjunction with Nationwide (BBC TV) and in 1979 with the *Daily Mirror*. This media participation was vital because of the on-the-spot investigation that is necessary all over the country.

Nominations were invited from the public of children considered outstanding in various fields (sport, art, etc.). After the written evidence supporting nominations had been sifted, there were preliminary investigations leading to a short list in each category. All the organizing costs had been underwritten by a business firm, leaving as clear profit the proceeds of programme advertising and ticket sales for the London luncheon at which the 'champions' were announced.

For several successive years the British Heart Foundation has run a national Sponsored Slim (friends of slimmers promise to subscribe a certain amount for each pound of weight shed). The income from this scheme grew from £14,000 in 1974 to £75,000 in 1979. It has been launched each year on the eve of St. Valentine's Day. To create a picture-story, representatives of a particular occupation (policemen and chefs are two groups already featured) are presented with a monster Valentine card by a well-known personality.

In an event of this nature a charity that has a network of regional organizers is, of course, in a better position to capitalize on the PR opportunities. In the case of the Heart Foundation, a letter is sent to all local newspapers, radio and TV stations, suggesting possible angles and giving the name and address of the nearest regional organizer. He then acts as 'local PRO' to assist the media.

In June the slimmers on whom most money has been put (not necessarily those who have lost the most weight) come to London to receive prizes donated by the firm backing the Slim, e.g. the 'Marvel' division of Cadbury.

Sometimes it is only the co-operation of several parties that makes a charity promotion viable, as in the case of Save the Children Fund's Jumbly ('the world's biggest jumble sale') held at Olympia first in 1978 and repeated in 1979. Success was ensured by the involvement of *Woman's Own* and by the agreement of the Post Office to waive charges on parcels.

Structure of the PR Department in Voluntary Movements

As in commerce, the ways in which charities seek to structure their PR operation can vary enormously. Some will rely on outside consultancy, some will set up a department in-house; others, of course, use a mixture of staff and consultancy service.

In some charities the chief executive will be a public relations officer in all but name, taking to himself the task of communicating. There may be no-one else to do it.

Rarely will a charity employ the same number of people to cover the various public relations functions as a commercial enterprise of similar size (in terms of annual turnover). This often means under-manning, which is a pity when one remembers what a central role PR plays in the life of a voluntary movement.

However, it is interesting to see how the PR function has evolved in some of the charities that are large enough to employ more than a one-man band.

Christian Aid

The history of the handling of Christian Aid's public relations is unusual in that throughout its formation and major growth-stages, virtually all its publicity work was carried out under contract by an external consultancy; then, after over twenty years, Christian Aid established its own PR staff structure. Both the external and, later, the internal systems were operated by the same person — Hugh Samson.

Samson, who had been in daily journalism for seven years when he entered PR via a large West End agency, set up as an independent consultant in 1956 with Christian Aid as his first client.

In a field notoriously fickle, where PR clients normally change hands every few years, how did he retain the Christian Aid account for twenty-one years? He attributes this to good relationships, cemented by professional competence which earned him the confidence of his client. 'But this was due,' he says 'to the respect which Janet Lacey — Christian Aid's Director from the early 'fifties until 1968 — had for all professionals: writers, artists, designers, film producers, musicians, the lot. She put their advice and abilities above those of the well-intentioned amateurs, to whom — sometimes unwisely — she turned a deaf ear.'

Samson started in the PR business as a one-man band plus a secretary and for the first two years rented an office from Christian Aid. So he, and they, had the best of both worlds: an economical deal with a free-lance operator fresh from the wider world of commercial promotion and marketing, detached from their staff structure, yet physically located on the premises.

In those first two years Janet Lacey and Hugh Samson introduced many innovations to what was then a small, little known charity with a staff of under twenty and an income of around £70,000. It was the beginning of growth into a major overseas agency with a £10 million income, and being associated with that growth the PR *modus operandi* was proven and secure enough to be maintained long after Samson moved out of his client's offices to facilitate their and his expansion.

By the 'seventies his agency, Noble & Samson Ltd, besides handling a variety of other accounts, was employing five people exclusively for Christian Aid work. They provided a full service in media relations, print, and publishing, while Samson himself personally acted as a consultant to Christian Aid's Director and Board, did a fair amount of creative writing, and took responsibility for the advertising and other contracted services such as film production, photography and design.

By 1974 Christian Aid's own staff numbered around 120 and there were some who felt, understandably, that a multi-million pound charity ought to have its own in-house PR capability. After much internal debate, Hugh Samson moved four members of his agency staff into Christian Aid's headquarters. These constituted an Information Unit which carried out all media work and also wrote and produced most of the charity's literature. Samson himself directed it, but remained outside as consultant to the Directorate and Board.

Early in 1977 it was decided that what appeared to be a structural anomaly should be ended by absorbing the Unit into headquarters staff, each member being given the option to transfer to Christian Aid's payroll. Later, when Hugh Samson's business partner reached retirement age, Samson was invited to join Christian Aid and create a Communications Department. Starting with the Information Unit as a nucleus, a department of some twenty-five people was built up, drawn from various sections of Christian Aid's staff and outside sources.

The Department is made up of the Information Unit (writers and journalists), an Audio-Visual Aids Section, a library (daily cutting of newspapers and periodicals), a Films and Publications Section dealing with all requests for materials, a Records Section handling data for an outside computer bureau, a Projects Focus section and the 'Christian Aid Week' campaign office.

'It's working out very well,' says Samson. 'I still do all the things I did before from outside, plus administering a department of some complexity. I can see how internal PR departments get over-involved in their own little world, so we make a conscious effort not to lose the professional standards which those who work in the open market have to maintain, or go out of business. Today's social climate demands the involvement of people at all levels in matters having any bearing on the fortunes of their organization. The consultation which this entails slows down the process of decision-making, though it sometimes improves the quality of decisions taken. Even where it doesn't, it invests them with the benefit of consensus, so that they are implemented with greater conviction.'

Dr Barnardo's

The growth of Dr Barnardo's into Britain's leading child care charity owes a great deal to the public relations genius of Dr Thomas Barnardo himself.

In 1977 Barnardo's management brought the three communications sections: photography, press and graphic design into a co-ordinating body: the

Creative Group. In 1983 the interdependency of function was acknowledged by strengthening the Group and making it a full head-office department. Now its task is to provide Dr Barnardo's with integrated and cost-effective communications. This means 'one stop' shopping for communications by Appeals and Child Care departments alike.

Of the three sections, the one of main interest is the Public Affairs Office. It currently has a staff of six and is based at Barnardo's head office in Barkingside. It is a resource which can be used by anyone in the organization, whether they are involved in appeals, child care, or any other activity.

Its main areas of work are:

1 *Press Relations* — dealing with press inquiries, and also going out to the press trying to get more coverage, using editorial space to help publicise the work, for instance by writing articles for other publications or by issuing press releases.

2 *Publicity* — contributing to the production of leaflets, posters, advertisements, exhibitions, publications, etc., in support both of appeals staff and child care staff.

3 *Public Relations* — with other organizations, businesses and individuals, including schoolchildren.

4 *Information to Staff* — e.g. through *Barnardo News* and other all-staff or selected staff bulletins.

The Public Affairs Office, as part of the Creative Group, works closely with the Graphic Design team and the Photographic Studio. Staff needing guidance or practical help with publicity or public relations are encouraged to use the facilities which the Creative Group has to offer. In particular the Public Affairs Office produces and issues press releases and writes copy for newspaper and magazine articles, advertising, leaflets, etc.

The Public Affairs Office is also charged with the responsibility of advising the Senior Director on press and public relations matters.

Age Concern England

Age Concern England is the co-ordinating body for over 1,100 local groups, each of which is autonomous. This means that while ACE can suggest topics which could do with publicity, and sometimes circulates specimen press releases, it is up to the organizing secretary of each group to decide whether and how to approach the local media.

Age Concern has found it worthwhile to employ two people in its press office. On national campaigns — such as that seeking to extend pedestrian time on Pelican crossings — the Age Concern headquarters press office will take the initiative with *national* media and encourage local groups to support the campaign. The press office is now part of a newly created Public Relations Department, which has three further staff working on issue-based publicity campaigns, promotional literature and audio-visual aids, a photo library, organising speakers and exhibitions, and advising the Age Concern movement on all aspects of its public relations.

Three people are responsible for producing the charity's publications, including two periodicals. There is also an in-house printer. The Head of Fund-Raising deals with money raised by donation, while the Head of Marketing and his assistant handle fund-raising through the sale of goods and publications.

Age Concern is a good example of a charity that has identified its opportunities in the communications area and been prepared to invest resources in the necessary staff.

Figure 6 A corporate sign in the public concourse at Waterloo Station.

Figure 7 (*below*)   Sea City, a model that predicts the future, was produced for the Pilkington Glass Age Development Committee.

Figure 9 (*above*)   The Central Office of Information's Exhibitions Division designed this stand for a careers exhibition. (Reproduced courtesy of the Central Office of Information.)

Figure 12 (*below*)   How to make a non-newsworthy picture of an opening ceremony newsworthy — add a pair of six foot scissors. (Reproduced courtesy of the Greater London Council.)

10

Parliamentary Public Relations

Bridgett Shearer

The right to be able to make representations to Parliament, like the right to vote, is one of the basic prerogatives of our democracy. But, in the same way that many people contest the value of a single vote in a first-past-the-post electoral system, many teachers and students of politics nowadays tend to underestimate the power of Parliament and to regard it as largely window dressing — the sop to the masses. Instead they tend to place more emphasis on direct access to the Government, their political advisers and the civil service.

In a complex society like our own, there are many levels of the decision-making process; routine questions decided by civil servants in the light of existing legislation, or accepted administrative practice; new legislation, drafted by civil servants on the instructions of Ministers, which can be amended or rejected by Parliament; and issues which are decided in Cabinet, with the aid of civil service briefs before or after having been put to Parliament.

Anyone who wants to influence the decision-making process should not ignore any of these levels. Certainly most organized groups will try to establish regular contact with the relevant civil service department. However, at the end of the day, it is Ministers who are responsible for the decisions made by their Departments and who are accountable to Parliament. Whether or not Parliament always makes the best use of its powers, it nevertheless remains the sovereign body.

In their 1979 manifesto, in a section headed 'The Supremacy of Parliament', the Conservatives commit themselves to 'see that Parliament and no other body stands at the centre of the nation's life and decisions, and to seek to make it effective in its job of controlling the Executive.'

The fact that a number of public relations agencies now offer advice on Parliamentary affairs to their clients shows an increasing realization that what is debated and decided in Parliament can have a very great effect on all our lives, as well as on our business and professional interests.

Indeed, many public relations campaigns now are aimed principally at

171

seeking the support of Parliament for a particular cause, e.g. to achieve legislative change or to maintain a legislative *status quo*.

What can actually be achieved in Parliament depends very much on the nature of the issue and on the make-up of the political parties in the Commons at any one time. Yet certainly any Minister will tell you that his civil servants do take note of and pay careful attention to anything that is raised or that may be raised in Parliament which concerns him and his Department.

When one party has a substantial majority, it is unrealistic to expect to be able to defeat a major legislative proposal on the floor of the House — although this could happen on very rare occasions. It is more usually at the consultation stage before the introduction of legislation into Parliament that most alterations are made, or concessions gained. However when a Bill is subjected to vigorous Parliamentary scrutiny during its passage through the Commons and Lords, Governments can also be persuaded to accept important amendments.

House of Commons 1974–9

In the 1974–9 'hung' Parliament, when there was a tiny Labour majority, which eventually disappeared, and as a result brought about the advent of the Lib-Lab pact, the opportunities for effecting major changes on the floor of the House or in Committee were obviously much greater. There was, for instance, the Rooker-Wise amendment to the 1977 Finance Bill, which introduced index-linking of personal allowances. On this occasion, in an unusual alliance of forces, the amendment tabled by two left-wing Labour backbenchers, Jeff Rooker and Audrey Wise, during the Committee stage upstairs of the Bill, was passed against the Government's wishes, due to Opposition support.

There was the emasculation of the Dock Work Regulation Bill in the form that it had originally been introduced into the Commons. During the passage of the Bill rebel Labour MPs, joining forces with the Opposition, succeeded in severely weakening one of the major provisions of the Bill by reducing a definable dock area from five miles from high water mark to within half a mile of a harbour. And again, when, under the terms of the Act, the Secretary of State introduced the new Dock Labour Scheme, it was defeated on the floor of the House.

Perhaps one of the most notable achievements was the success of Bristol Channel Ship Repairers in managing to escape nationalization when the Examiners of Private Bills in the House of Lords declared the Aircraft and Shipbuilding Industries Bill 'hybrid'. A hybrid Bill is a Public Bill which affects a particular private interest, or in this case firm, differently from the interest of others in the same category or class. Where hybridity is established, Parliament provides through the Select Committee procedure a right to aggrieved people to state their case. This can be lengthy and, in view of the strong demands not to prolong any further the already extended proceedings on this Bill, the Government agreed to delete ship-repairing altogether from its provisions.

Position of the House of Lords in the 1974–9 Parliament

It was mainly due to Opposition tactics in the House of Lords over the Aircraft and Shipbuilding Industries Bill that the Labour Government had to invoke the provisions of the Parliament Act, under which a Bill which is passed by the House of Commons in two successive Sessions may acquire the force of law without passing the House of Lords.

However, the leader of the Conservative Peers, Lord Carrington, and his whips had to be careful not to over-use the power that their majority gave them to wreak havoc with the Government's programme. For fear of encouraging further demand for complete abolition of the House of Lords they tended, on the whole, to follow a policy of protesting compliance. For the main part they kept to the convention, sometimes referred to as 'the Salisbury convention', whereby the unelected House tries to improve legislation in detail or lessen its ill effects, but does not use its one-party majority to deny a Labour House of Commons its mandate.

They put down amendments and provided further time for discussion on matters which had not been fully debated in the Commons and many of these amendments were in fact accepted by the Government. However, if the Commons disagreed with the amendments, in most cases in the end the Opposition Peers did not insist on them.

The fact that it was the will of the *Commons* rather than the will of the *Government* which the Opposition in the Lords thought best not to defy became significant during the passage of the Price Commission Amendment Bill. The Food Manufacturers' Federation was anxious to write in an amendment to the Bill to allow for automatic price rises in their products when there had been a substantial rise in the cost of imported raw materials.

They talked to all the minority parties — the Liberals, the Scottish and Welsh Nationalists and the Ulster Unionists, as well as the Conservatives, and received support from them all. The Scottish Nationalists agreed to put down an amendment, but it was declared out of order by the Chair and not called. The Federation then talked to the Liberal and Conservative spokesmen in the House of Lords, who recognized that the Federation had had the support of all the Opposition parties in the Commons and agreed to table a similar amendment. The amendment was duly put down, but withdrawn when the Government itself tabled an amendment, which although slightly weaker in effect, went a good way to meet the point.

It is however on many of the less political issues which are constantly before

Parliament, many of which are not written about in the Press at all, that influence can be more effective, and whilst not so dramatic as the major coups, these technical improvements in legislation can be of great importance to an individual interest and represent much of the bread and butter work of any parliamentary consultant.

The first essential to success in parliamentary consultancy is knowledge — knowledge of the functioning and potentials of the parliamentary process, knowledge of which MPs would be interested in a particular case, and when is the opportune moment to begin discussions and how best to continue.

Contact at local level

A natural starting point for any company wishing to make its views known to Parliament is its own constituency MPs. Whatever the political complexion of any MP, he will probably want to be informed about anything that could affect a factory in his constituency. In many cases, however, although there may be contact at grass roots between the MP and the local factory manager, this is often not properly co-ordinated at company level and certainly very rarely at trade association level. Thus the opportunity for invoking parliamentary help at the right moment is lost.

In addition to being invited for a tour of a factory in the constituency and hearing about its local problems, many MPs would probably welcome an invitation to meet some of the top management of the company. After all, the company's welfare, prospects and future plans are of prime importance to both employment and the environment in his constituency. If these relations are properly maintained, the company should then keep its constituency MPs informed of its views on any impending legislation it feels may affect it.

Industry and Parliament Trust

It was due to a feeling that there was a fundamental lack of understanding of the problems and working of industry among many politicians that the Industry and Parliament Trust was started on the initiative of a number of British manufacturing companies in 1977.

Initially, thirty-four MPs (fifteen Conservative, fifteen Labour and four from the minority parties) enrolled as Fellows and after the General Election in May 1979 a further forty-three (twenty-three Conservative and twenty Labour) were enrolled. Two MPs, usually one Government and one Opposition, are attached to each of the member companies and they undertake to spend twenty-five days with the company learning in some depth the way the company operates at all levels. The overall objective is to improve mutual understanding between industry and MPs, informing MPs about industry and informing industrialists more about Parliament and the way it works.

The Organized Lobby

The existence of more general and regular parliamentary liaison by individual companies would create a better informed and more sympathetic climate of opinion in which trade associations could then operate on matters of specific importance to their members.

The National Farmers Union is generally recognized as one of the most influential pressure groups on Parliament. In a country where only 2–3 per cent of the population are farmers, this has been achieved through hard work and effective organization. The NFU has very active local roots throughout the country, but is also well co-ordinated from the top, where there is a very lively appreciation of the importance of good parliamentary relations.

For a trade association or a pressure group, the natural starting points for communication with Parliament are the relevant Conservative and Labour backbench committees and the All-Party Committees. Both the major parties have between twenty-five to thirty backbench committees on major subjects, such as Agriculture, Fisheries and Food, Industry, Trade, Energy, Employment, Environment, etc. The All-Party Committees are numerous and varied as any MP is entitled to form a Committee. Committees can be found on such diverse subjects as the All-Party Management Group, the Motor Industry Group, the Franco-British Parliamentary Relations Committee, the Anglo-Cuban Group, the Animal Welfare Group, the Migraine Group, the Committee for the release of Soviet Jewry and so on.

These Committees and All-Party Groups will always welcome any input from responsible outside bodies on current issues, as they need up-to-date, well-researched information in order to be able to carry out effectively their function as a check on the Government and Civil Service, about which they often have deep suspicions.

The Departmental Select Committee System

The fourteen Departmental Select Committees were set up by the Leader of the House after the 1979 election to monitor the various Government Departments. They have become a natural target for those seeking to influence Government policy, but how influential they will be in the long run will depend to a large extent on the membership of the Committees and particularly on their Chairmen and their relationships with the Ministers concerned. The members have been chosen by the Committee of Selection, but evidently the Committee has not been allowed a completely free hand by the whips.

Preliminary identification of obvious areas of access to Members of Parliament through constituency interest or formal groups is relatively simple, but effective use can only be made of such access and other areas of access, if there is detailed and sophisticated knowledge of what is going on in Parliament at the time.

The Retained MP

One obvious way of obtaining this knowledge is to employ an MP as an adviser and many companies and trade associations now do this. However, the success of such a relationship must largely depend on the MP and the firm and on what the client actually wants from the MP.

As regards actually putting forward a client's views in the House, there are limitations to how far a retained MP can actively pursue a matter without infringing what is regarded as proper parliamentary practice (see Erskine May's *Parliamentary Practice*, 18th edition, p. 74, for the conclusions of the Committee of Privileges on the case of Mr Brown and the Civil Service Clerical Association). Members of the Institute of Public Relations and of the Public Relations Consultants Association who retain Members of the House of Commons or House of Lords have, under their professional codes of conduct, to declare the fact and register the object of their retainer in books which are filed each year in the library of the House.

As regards information that a client wants from his MP, certainly the MP can be usefully informative about the feeling amongst his colleagues or in the House generally on a particular issue, but very rarely do MPs really have the time to scour the massive parliamentary papers, Order papers, Hansards of both the Commons and Lords, etc, or attend committees on which they are not sitting in order to keep his client up-to-date and fully informed.

Parliamentary Consultants

Hence the growth in recent years of the parliamentary expert. This is someone who studies the mysterious ways of Parliament and specializes in giving information and advice about Parliament and parliamentary affairs.

Clients' demands vary — some only want an information service, some want advice on contacts and meetings and others may want to mount a full-scale campaign. However, a parliamentary consultant's first requirement is to be able to give up-to-date information on what is happening or likely to happen in both Houses of Parliament that might affect his client's interests.

The parliamentary papers are essential reading. Advance warning of any relevant parliamentary question, statement or debate can be crucial to any organization that might be asked to comment once an announcement is made in the House. Equally, some companies or trade associations are in the position where, with advance warning, they can contact the appropriate Government Department and offer the necessary information to help the civil servant draft the reply.

In addition, the consultant must know how matters raised in the House are likely to develop and how legislation progresses. He must know what it means when the 2nd Reading of a Bill is called for tomorrow, which does not mean tomorrow, or this time six months, which does not mean six months, but never; how and at what stages amendments may be moved and the distinction between a Private Members Bill introduced under the Ballot and one introduced under the Ten Minute Rule. It is based on all this kind of specialized information that a consultant advises his clients on lobbying or presenting a case to Parliament or Ministers.

When advising on how to present a case to Parliament, the consultant must try to make his client see his case in the perspective of all the other matters Parliament is considering at the time. MPs have so many different subjects to deal with that timing is crucial.

Often MPs find it impractical to inform themselves adequately until only very shortly before an issue is debated in the House, or becomes the subject of current legislative proposals. Briefings, meetings and letters on a particular subject are therefore often most effective when linked to something that is about to happen in the House.

A parliamentary consultant must be aware of and sympathetic to the physical limitations on MPs and the fact that most of them have incredibly limited office space with little room for a sophisticated filing system and that many of them only have a part-time secretary.

A parliamentary consultant should study the viewpoint of individual MPs and as a result be aware of what it is they want in the way of information and data to help them in debate or committee, or in supplementary oral questions, etc. In sending any written material it is important that it should always be clear and brief; if one is sending detailed technical information, a summary is essential.

The tone of any campaign is also of great importance. Documents should be drafted with a sense of proportion and with due regard for other aspects of the matter which Parliament may have to consider. Bias, hysteria and exaggeration must be avoided if Parliament is to have any respect for the views of an organization over any length of time. Equally, lavish expenditure of money on hospitality to MPs is not necessarily the prerequisite to a successful lobby and stunts such as mass telegrams tend to be viewed rather cynically as gimmicky. The essential is to direct the campaign to the right people at the right time with correct factual information.

Defensive Action

Parliamentary lobbying can be divided into two categories — defensive action or initiating action. Defensive action means presenting a case against something which has been introduced in Parliament or is going to be introduced in Parliament, which you either want abolished or amended. In the 1974–9 Parliament industry and commerce found themselves fighting a continual list of Labour legislation they deemed to be detrimental to their interests — the Industry Act, the Oil Taxation Act, the Petroleum Revenue Act, the Employment Protection Act, the Sex Discrimination Act, etc.

Although none of these Bills were defeated a number of amendments and concessions were achieved. The main tactic of the antagonists was to try and create a tide of public feeling against this flood of legislation. So, detailed parliamentary lobbying had to be supported by a large press and media campaign.

At the time of the Oil Taxation Bill, Amoco ran a series of full-page advertisements in the Press, stating its position in the North Sea, to back up its direct lobbying of the Government and MPs, and finally succeeded in getting the Government to agree to the exemption of gas from Petroleum Revenue Tax.

Another campaign designed to frustrate or delay legislation was mounted by all the interested parties of private medicine against the Health Services Bill, enabling the Government to phase out pay beds from NHS hospitals. The idea of the 'Campaign for Independence in Medicine', as it was known, was to encourage a groundswell of opinion against the proposal and to arm the Opposition spokesmen in the House of Commons with all the relevant facts and figures undermining the Government's case. A great deal of printed material was produced — leaflets, pamphlets, car stickers, lapel badges, etc, as well as detailed briefs and amendments for the MPs. After some delay the Bill did finally go through, but with some important amendments.

Initiating Campaigning

Initiating campaigning, on the other hand, is when an organization wants to stimulate action in Parliament, as for instance the Animal Welfare lobby, who have long been active and in many respects quite successful. There are a wide range of animal welfare organizations; some are very extreme, advocating the complete abolition of vivisection, battery hens, hunting of all kinds, etc., whilst others are in general more moderate, concentrating on the achievement of reasonable reforms.

The best example of the latter is the RSPCA, which has always maintained close touch with Parliament and has had an unusual record of success in getting its policy translated into legislation through the Private Members Bill procedure.

In the last fifty years such legislation has included Acts of Parliament dealing with the humane slaughter of animals, the protection of dogs, the conduct of pet shops, the docking of horses' tails and the well-being of circus animals, to mention only a selection.

The RSPCA has at times also combined with other organizations as, for instance, over legislation dealing with the protection of birds and the conduct of riding establishments. However, on the more controversial issues in which it has become involved recently, such as the abolition of hare coursing and all forms of hunting, it has had no success, partly because of the well-organized lobby of the British Field Sports Society and similar bodies.

Such has been the pressure of the Animal Welfare interests that both the Conservative and Labour Parties gave pledges in their manifesto for the May 1979 Election to legislate on certain matters, such as the revision of the Cruelty to Animals Act 1876, which deals with the control of experiments on animals in research laboratories.

In the 1979–80 session two Private Members Bills relating to this subject were introduced: one in the House of Lords by Lord Halsbury, President of the Research Defence Society; the other in the House of Commons by Peter Fry MP, who had been advised by several animal welfare organizations, including the RSPCA.

In the event, although much time was spent in discussion, both Bills 'died' as the Government was reluctant to anticipate the EEC's forthcoming legislation on the subject. It is interesting to note, however, that in the 2nd Reading debate on his Bill Mr Fry said, 'I pay tribute to the staff of the Royal Society for the Prevention of Cruelty to Animals, who have given me enormous and invaluable assistance in producing this legislation. . .'

Very often those MPs who come out top in the ballot for Private Members Bills do not have a clearly defined view of what they want to introduce and may well be prepared to adopt a cause put forward by some outside organization.

Sometimes, there is an advantage in introducing a Private Members Bill in the House of Lords rather than in the House of Commons, especially if the Bill is technical and not politically contentious. With all the far-ranging expertise existing in the Lords the details can be worked out and the Bill amended there, if that should be necessary, and it might then pass quickly through the Commons where time for Private Members Bills is at a premium.

Parliamentary public relations is a subject which it is impossible to cover in its entirety because we are dealing in an area which is surrounded by tradition and customs and privileges, the bible of which, Erskine May's *Parliamentary Practice*, stretches to over 1,000 pages. For instance, there is a whole range of items in the parliamentary field which have a bearing on any parliamentary campaign which have not yet been mentioned, such as: the rules and practice relating to questions; the procedure with regard to Statutory Instruments, by either a positive or negative resolution; the different kinds of motions on the Order Paper and the facilities for debating them; adjournment debates; Consolidated Fund debates, and so on.

The EEC

However, no chapter on parliamentary public relations nowadays can be complete without mentioning the EEC.

A whole new dimension has been introduced to parliamentary public relations since Britain joined the EEC in 1973 and found herself having to comply with legislation emanating from the European Commission and the Council of Ministers.

The EEC legislative system is different from the British parliamentary system, the most important difference being that the European Parliament is advisory, it is not the final arbiter on legislation, although it does have certain powers under the Treaty of Rome. The path of legislation there is that the Commission initiates draft legislation, Parliament advises and the Council of Ministers decides.

One of the Commission's objectives in drawing up its programme of proposed legislation has been to harmonize legislation in order to try and ensure greater protection for the consumer. It is therefore our consumer goods industries which have been the foreleaders in fighting these endless regulations, many of which appeared to them to be harmonization for harmonization's sake and gave little recognition to the fact that our existing system of controls and regulations are, on the whole, a good deal more sophisticated than those of the other Member countries.

Companies and trade associations have been gradually coming to the realization that they can make their representations direct to the Commission in Brussels, but the tendency has still been to direct themselves to our Parliament and Government and rely on our Ministers to fight in defence of British interests in Council meetings, e.g. the fights for preservation of the Milk Marketing Board, the pint of beer, the twelve-mile fishing limit, etc., and the fight against the introduction of the tachograph.

The main complaint has been the failure of the Government to provide enough time on the floor of the House of Commons for the debating of European legislation and that when time has been found it has usually been very late at night when attendance is low. In the circumstances, the work of the Select Committee on European legislation of both Houses of Parliament has been extremely important. It is their duty to sift through all the draft directives and regulations and decide which ones are of a contentious nature and so should be recommended for debate in their House. Both Committees welcome evidence from interested organizations, but it is, in fact, the House of Lords' Committee, with its seven sub-committees specializing in different subject areas, which has powers to criticize the EEC proposals and suggest detailed amendments. The first step for any organization wishing to give evidence to either of the Committees is to contact its clerk.

The European Parliament

The eighty-one British Members of the European Parliament are normally receptive to any input from British organizations. Much of what has already been said about the general method of making representations at Westminster will also apply to the European Parliament (i.e. providing the right person at the right time with correct factual information) but the rules and procedure that govern their business are very different from those at Westminster.

One of the main tasks of the European Parliament is to scrutinize the work of the Commission and the Council of Ministers. Much of this work is carried out in the fourteen subject committees (e.g. the Agriculture Committee, Transport Committee) which produce reports on those Commission proposals which fall within their subject area. The report incorporates a draft resolution and this is then considered in full session of the Parliament. It may be amended by the Commission before the Parliament's opinions are formally transmitted to the Council.

The alignment of the political groups within the Parliament must also be taken into consideration when representations are made by UK interests seeking to influence or alter the pattern of legislation, since Members of the European Parliament sit according to political groups rather than as representatives of their national Parliament.

Their actual power may be limited, but the European MPs are in a position to be able to question and criticize the Commission's thinking. We can be certain that the national interests of Member States such as France and Germany will always be strongly represented in the European Parliament and it is therefore in the best interests of the UK that British organizations should take the time and trouble to gain an understanding of the European system and make their representations there, as well as to Brussels and Westminster.

On the whole Members of Parliament, both Westminster and European, are anxious to help not only their own constituents but any persons or organization who have some serious contribution to make towards solving current problems with which Parliament is or may be concerned.

If any case of reasonable importance fails to get a fair hearing in Parliament, it is generally sensible to assume that it is a bad case in itself, that it has already been fully thrashed out, or that it has been presented to Parliamentarians in an incompetent way.

11

The Ethics of Public Relations

Kenneth Cook

All professional bodies observe ethical standards and invariably they have an established code of conduct setting out the essential disciplines for good behaviour by members, whether individuals or organizations.

Those engaged in such a fast-growing profession as public relations, which is so closely associated with the changing standards of society, find that set rules of conduct do not remain rigid or unchanged for long. But that makes it even more essential that PR maintains high standards and principles.

The Institute of Public Relations

To guide everyone in PR the Institute of Public Relations has devised a Code of Conduct which, when followed, offers a guarantee of reputable business dealing.

The code contains sixteen clauses. These are reproduced here, each accompanied by explanatory notes provided by the Institute, to enable every public relations practitioner to interpret and uphold its precepts:

Clause 1 Standards of professional conduct

'A member, in the conduct of his professional activities, shall respect the public interest and the dignity of the individual. It is his personal responsibility at all times to deal fairly and honestly with his client or employer, past or present, with his fellow members, with the media of communications and with the public.'

Clause 1 is intentionally drawn in broad terms. The expression 'the public interest' is used in statute law and the term 'the dignity of the individual' echoes wording used in the Universal Declaration of Human Rights. Both phrases have yet to be interpreted formally in a public relations context, but there are few members who would not in practice recognize any flagrant violation of the principles which they express.

'The public interest' can be assumed to mean the interest of the public as a whole, as opposed to the sectional interest of a public relations practitioner's employer or client, or indeed his own.

Which of us can claim to judge what is or is not in the interest of the public at large? It is, in theory, possible that the Institute might one day have to decide whether public relations action in support of some particular cause was promoting, say, immorality. In so unlikely a case, the Institute would certainly be guided by the climate of public opinion and the law in force at the time.

In practice, the more likely danger is the use of methods which are against the interests of the public. It is possible to envisage an unscrupulous practitioner lending himself to the fostering of ill-will between racial communities, or trying to conceal the future ill effects of an industrial process known to cause pollution. Such conduct would be contrary to Clause 1.

The 'dignity of the individual', if taken in its fullest sense, is equally a matter which can be judged only subjectively. Yet members in the National Health Service, for instance, will have no doubt of their obligation to respect the privacy and feelings of a patient or his relatives.

At a lesser level, perhaps, no member who respects the dignity of the individual would contrive a situation — perhaps in a press or radio interview — where a person was artificially held up to ridicule.

Dealing 'fairly and honestly' with clients, employers, fellow-members, the media of communication and the public is an all-embracing requirement. It applies particularly to consultants' public relations proposals, plans and reports.

Fairness and honesty must run through all public relations practice, from the way in which information is given to the financial world, to the manner in which the employee communications aspects of redundancy are handled.

Clause 2 Dissemination of information

'A member shall not knowingly or recklessly disseminate false or misleading information, and shall use proper care to avoid doing so inadvertently. He has a positive duty to maintain integrity and accuracy.'

The object of this clause is to make it plain that not only is it the member's moral duty to be honest and accurate, but that it must be his positive concern to ensure that all information issued, whether by himself or by those who work for him, is correct.

It forbids any form of deception in the issue of information and also lays upon the member the responsibility to ensure that no unchecked or unconfirmed material is released. This responsibility can range from avoiding misleading phraseology in financial documents to not stating as facts unproved claims for the performance of consumer goods.

Clause 3 Media of communication

'A member shall not engage in any practice which tends to corrupt the integrity of the media of communications.'

This clause is aimed at protecting the freedom of the Press, including radio and television, to publish news and views as they think fit. Any influence, or attempted influence, on the decision-making processes of the Press is expressly forbidden. This is one of the most serious forms of professional misconduct, whether it takes the form of straight or disguised bribery or hints of 'advertising considerations'.

Commonsense should rule the provision of entertainment for the Press, which can rarely be criticized as applying undue pressure. A meeting over drinks to get to know a specialist writer and his requirements is as acceptable as providing lunch during a press facility visit; on the other hand, a case of whisky for an editor before — or after — he has published a story is not permissible.

Clause 4 Undisclosed interests

'A member shall not be a party to any activity which deliberately seeks to dissemble or mislead by promoting a disguised or undisclosed interest, while appearing to further another. It is his duty to ensure that the actual interest of any organization with which he may be professionally concerned is adequately declared.'

The main purpose of this clause is to prevent the formation of 'front' organizations which appear to have a particular — and usually apparently laudable — objective, while in fact concealing vested interests of one kind or another.

An example would be the setting up of a body to campaign for more relaxed gaming laws on a social reform basis without revealing that the sponsors were running a chain of gambling casinos. A less extreme example would be an information bureau appearing to deal with a particular raw material, but which was covertly sponsored by one company and acted in its interests rather than those of the industry as a whole.

Actual cases of deception on similar lines have occurred and there are various situations in which the temptation to set up a 'front' organization might exist.

Disclosure of interest is a necessity in any body which seeks to impose professional standards and perhaps particularly in public relations, where accusations of misrepresentation are not unknown.

There are, of course, numerous promotional associations which set out quite openly to publicize a variety of products or services. Because the objects of these associations are clearly defined — often in the titles — and their sponsorship is made plain, there is no doubt of their aims and backing. Normally, the test is simple: is the interest which it is designed to further clearly and specifically identified?

Clause 5 Confidential information

'A member shall not disclose (except upon the order of a court of competent jurisdiction) or make use of information given or obtained in confidence from his employer or client, past, present or potential, for personal gain or otherwise, without express consent.'

Any professional adviser, if his advice is to be of value, must receive the full confidence of his client. Public relations practitioners in the financial field are entrusted with figures and information which could make them a fortune on the Stock Exchange. Those concerned with marketing — and indeed almost all public relations practitioners in some degree — hold information which competitors of their employer or client would wish to obtain. It is not merely ethically right, but a practical necessity, for practitioners to respect these confidences, if public relations is to hold the status the Institute believes it should.

It may well be that confidential information is obtained during the preliminary stages of negotiation with a client; the word 'potential' covers this phase. It is essential that confidential information obtained prior to there being a contract, or if no contract develops, must be subject to the same security.

In practice this means keeping a constant watch on security in the office. At least one financial public relations consultancy requires every executive and secretary to read and acknowledge a formal letter of warning regarding the buying or selling of personal shareholdings in client companies. If a practitioner changes employment, or takes on a new client whose business competes with that of a former client, great care must be taken to distinguish between what is useful experience in the field and what is information received in confidence by virtue of the public relations man's professional status. The bracketed phrase 'except upon the order of a court of competent jurisdiction' distinguishes the professional position of the public relations man from the position taken up by journalists, who have a traditional obligation — not, of course, recognized by the law — never to disclose their sources. The Institute does not ask or wish its members to defy the law, and their position in this matter is exactly the same as that of doctors or lawyers.

Clause 6 *Conflict of interests*

'A member shall not represent conflicting or competing interests without the express consent of the parties concerned after full disclosure of the facts.'

The question of conflicting or competing interests is one which affects every consultant. Competition needs no clarification. Conflict is perhaps rather less obvious, but could arise if, for instance, a practitioner were to be retained by a local authority and by an organization campaigning for improvement of amenities in the same area; or by a trade association of manufacturers and another of retailers in the same industry.

There is no rule that members may not represent conflicting or competing interests, only that they may not do so without the consent of those concerned, after full disclosure of the facts.

In some fields, clients often feel that the consultancy's special knowledge of their needs outweighs any danger caused by sharing its service with other organizations of the same type. This is so, for example, in the City, where merchant banks and others are themselves familiar with conflict situations, and where a highly confidential relationship between consultant and client is normal practice. In the context of consumer marketing, on the other hand, clients usually dislike their consultancy to represent a competitor.

Although the bigger the consultancy, the more frequent are the possible clashes of interest, it is easier for a large consultancy to ensure that a different team works for each client. This, of course, is the way in which firms in other professions deal with this problem.

Clause 7 *Sources of payment*

'A member, in the course of his professional services to his employer or client, shall not accept payment either in cash or in kind in connection with those services from any other source without the express consent of his employer or client.'

As a public relations man is paid by his client for writing and issuing a feature it would be wrong for him to accept an author's fee from a paper which publishes it. That is the simplest example of the malpractice against which this clause is aimed.

However, it does not preclude a consultancy, for example, receiving a trade discount from a supplier, such as a printer or photographer, provided that acceptance of this discount is approved by the client. If it is not agreed by the client, then the discount must be passed on.

This clause, however, does forbid the member from receiving rewards from suppliers or others as an inducement to place his employer's or client's business with them.

In Clauses 5, 6 and 7 the words 'express consent' are used. To say 'I know my client would not mind' or 'he is aware of the situation and did not object' is not enough, either ethically or as a defence against any complaint that the Code has been breached in this respect. The practitioner's client or employer must be made aware of the facts and formally accept the situation.

Clause 8 Disclosure of financial interests

'A member having a financial interest in an organization shall not recommend the use of that organization, nor make use of its services on behalf of his client or employer, without declaring his interest.'

This is an extension of Clause 7 to cover the situation in which, for instance, a consultant has an associated graphic design studio or photographic or model agency; or in which a staff public relations man is privately a partner in a printing or catering concern.

There is nothing wrong in the member having such an outside interest, but it is improper for him to use it or recommend its use without, firstly, disclosure of the interest and, secondly, the client's or employer's specific agreement.

Clause 9 Payment contingent upon achievements

'A member shall not negotiate or agree terms with a prospective employer or client on the basis of payment contingent upon specific future public relations achievements.'

One of the most discussed problems in the profession is the evaluation of the results of public relations activity. If there is any broad agreement on this, it is that the basic need, in an ideal situation, is for sophisticated research to check regularly on changes in attitude among the audience concerned. The problem affects all practitioners, but only consultants are likely to face it in the context of payment.

Confusing the situation is the ghost of the old-time press agent, who often charged his clients per column inch of press mentions obtained on their behalf. Even today it is not unknown for some form of payment by results to be suggested. The basic argument against this is that the client is buying the professional skill and knowledge of the consultant. The success of the wide range of methods used to further the client's interests cannot fairly be judged by specific results over a given period; nor do corporate public relations campaigns, for example, depend for their success solely upon specific achievements. A further point is that many outside factors may be involved in determining whether the intended results are realized. Moreover, a payment-by-results basis of operation is a potential inducement or corruption of the media.

Of course, at the end of the day the client has to decide whether he is getting value for money. This assessment is likely to depend upon the attainment of a variety of objectives ranging, perhaps, from improved employee relations to a defence against a takeover bid. The results which have been obtained need to be evaluated and management decisions made on future action and expenditure. This cannot sensibly be done on the basis of a prior agreement to pay a fixed amount for the achievement of such results as can be physically measured.

Members of the IPR are as much professional in their own field as are accountants and solicitors. A client in the UK does not arrange to pay a solicitor an agreed portion of the damages he might obtain in a court action, he pays for skilled work, having initially agreed what needs to be done. The purpose of Clause 9 is that this should also happen in public relations.

Clause 10 *Rewards to holders of public office*

'A member shall not, with intent to further his interests (or those of his client or employer), offer or give any reward to a person holding public office if such action is inconsistent with the public interest.'

Clause 10 simply reflects the fact that Institute members are citizens before they are public relations practitioners and must not improperly make use of the services of a public office-holder.

That does not mean that it is never proper to employ, or pay a fee to, a public office-holder; there are many respectable precedents for this both in and out of public relations.

For example, if an employer has premises which cause pollution or a consultant specializes in environmental problems, then to engage as an adviser an MP or a member of a local authority who has particular knowledge of such matters would not be improper, provided the public interest was not put at risk.

If, however, that adviser were then asked to be concerned with a specific issue with which he had to deal in the course of his public duties, there would be a clear risk of his acting in a manner inconsistent with his public responsibilities.

The moral problem facing both the Institute member and the office-holder may not be resolved by a simple declaration of the interests involved. It would clearly be wrong, for instance, to offer to pay the chairman of a planning committee for advice on a client's planning problems, if eventually he were likely to hear an application from that client; nor would it be an adequate defence to say that it was the chairman's duty to declare his interest.

An Institute member does not breach the Code simply by employing or retaining a public office-holder, but he would do so if he tried to persuade that individual to act in his employer's or client's interests contrary to the public interest.

Clause 11 Employment of Members of Parliament

'A member who employs a Member of Parliament, of either House, whether in a consultative or executive capacity, shall disclose this fact, and also the object of the employment, to the Director of the Institute, who shall enter it in a register kept for the purpose. A member of the Institute who is himself a Member of Parliament shall be directly responsible for disclosing or causing to be disclosed to the Director any such information as may relate to himself. (The register referred to in this clause shall be open to public inspection at the offices of the Institute during office hours.)'

Clause 11 simply requires an Institute member who employs or retains a Member of Parliament, of either House, to register the fact formally with the Institute. If the member is himself an MP or peer, he has a personal responsibility for registering.

The Institute is thus provided with a register which reveals to the public the names of Members of Parliament involved directly or indirectly in public relations practice. In other words, professional conduct in this sphere must not only be good, but be seen to be good!

It is hardly necessary to add that this in no way diminishes the traditional responsibility of a Member of Parliament to declare any personal interest which may have a bearing on his public duties.

Clause 12 Injury to other members

'A member shall not maliciously injure the professional reputation or practice of another member.'

Injury to the professional reputation or practice of a member is most likely to arise in practice under the temptation provided by competition between consultants: for instance, by informing a member's client of any real or imagined shortcomings in the member's practice of public relations.

Similarly the taking of unreasonable steps to secure another member's business (by making improper, extravagant or untrue claims for example) could constitute a breach of this Clause. While fair competition is a basic feature of a free society, attempts improperly to supplant another member may be considered to breach this Clause.

In any written approach for new business, it is recommended that a disclaimer be added to the effect that the solicitation be disregarded should the organisation already employ public relations services and is satisfied with these.

It is probable that 'maliciously' in the context of Clause 12 could be proved by any such behaviour carried out with an improper motive; indeed, an improper motive could often be inferred from the circumstances.

Clause 13 Instruction of others

'A member who knowingly causes or permits another person or organization to act in a manner inconsistent with this Code, or is party to such action, shall himself be deemed to be in breach of it.'

Clause 13 is an important safeguard to professional standards. No member can excuse breaches of the Code by pleading that they were committed by, for instance, a member of his staff, who might not be a member and by reason of his subordinate position might in any case be under pressure to comply with his client's instructions.

A member must not be a 'party to' a breach of Code. He must resist it and dissent from it. For example, a member who is a director of a consultancy must not acquiesce or join in any decision of the board which is in contravention of the Code.

If this were not so, a member would have the excuse that the breach was carried out by a corporate body which would not, of course, be amenable to the Institute's discipline.

Clause 14 Reputation of the profession

'A member shall not conduct himself in any manner detrimental to the reputation of the Institute or the profession of public relations.'

Clause 14 applies to all forms of behaviour which could harm the reputation of the Institute or the profession.

Certain jobs, estimable in themselves, may not be easily compatible with professional status. A member is unlikely to be able to hold a position on the staff of a newspaper or other medium without harming the reputation of journalism for objective assessment.

However, there is no 'black list' and each case must be decided on its merits.

The reputation of the profession could also suffer from the unreasonable solicitation of business as specified in Clause 12 already handled by another consultant. While Clause 12 is specifically concerned with injuring other members, maintenance of the Institute's good reputation outside its own membership is an important responsibility of all members.

Many other circumstances are covered by the clause. Reasoned criticism of the profession may sometimes be justified, but a member who writes an article or makes a speech in which he seriously denigrates the profession, or the Institute which represents it, would be in breach of Clause 14. So would any member who was found guilty of a major criminal offence.

Clause 14, in fact, is designed to protect the profession and Institute in all matters which, not part of public relations practice, reflect on their collective good name.

Clause 15 Upholding the Code

'A member shall uphold this Code, shall co-operate with fellow members in so doing and in enforcing decisions on any matter arising from its application. If a member has reason to believe that another member has been engaged in practices which may be in breach of this Code, it shall be his duty to inform the Institute. It is the duty of all members to assist the Institute to implement this Code, and the Institute will support any member so doing.'

Clause 15 requires members to uphold the Code, and — as a duty — to help the Institute to deal with possible breaches. The Institute has an effective procedure on disciplinary matters, but in the last resort it is helpless without members' co-operation. The Professional Practices Committee can often give guidance to members which — if they follow it — will ensure they keep within the Code.

Where disciplinary proceedings have to be taken, the Institute must depend on the co-operation of everyone concerned: it does not possess the powers of a court of law to compel witnesses, and without evidence the Institute may be rendered powerless against an individual who has harmed the profession by his conduct.

Clause 16 Other professions

'A member shall, when acting for a client or employer who belongs to a profession, respect the code of ethics of that other profession and shall not knowingly be party to any breach of such a code.'

This clause in the Code recognizes the public relations practitioner's responsibility for understanding and respecting the code of ethics applicable to a client or employer who is a member of one of the established professions.

It is specifically aimed at ensuring that members of the professions are not aided or persuaded to act in breach of their own ethical codes by the application of public relations techniques. The restraint laid upon doctors, architects and others over the use of publicity to attract business is an example of a likely area of difficulty.

The Public Relations Consultants Association

The Public Relations Consultants Association, which was formed in 1969, has a close practical relationship with the Institute of Public Relations. One of its principal objectives is to raise and maintain professional standards in consultancy practice. Members must comply with a Code of Consultancy Practice, which, though drawn up in slightly more general terms than that of the Institute's code, as befits a trade association, applies the same broad principles to member companies' work. There are fifteen clauses in the PRCA Code, as follows:

1 A member firm has a general duty of fair dealing towards its clients, past and present, fellow members and the public.

2 A member firm shall be free to represent its capabilities and services to any potential client, either on its own initiative or at the behest of the client, provided in so doing it does not seek to persuade the client to break any existing contract or detract from the reputation or capabilities of any consultancy already serving that client.

3 A member firm shall cause all its clients to be listed in the Annual Register of the Public Relations Consultants Association.

4 A member firm shall cause all its directors, executives and retained consultants who hold public office, are members of either House of Parliament, are members of local authorities or any statutory organization

or body, to be recorded in the relevant sections of the Annual Register of the Public Relations Consultants Association.

5 A member firm shall not offer to give nor cause a client to offer or give any inducement to such persons as described in Article 4 above who are not directors, executives or retained consultants with intent to further the interest of the member or of the client if such action is inconsistent with the public interest.

6 A member firm shall not engage in any practice which tends to corrupt the integrity of channels of public communication or legislation.

7 A member firm shall negotiate, propose or agree terms with a client or prospective client on the basis of the resources than can reasonably be expected to be applied.

8 A member firm shall not propose to clients any action which would constitute an improper influence on organs of government or legislation.

9 A member firm shall not engage in practice, nor be seen to conduct itself in any manner detrimental to the reputation of the Public Relations Consultants Association or the reputation and the interests of public relations consultancy.

10 A member firm shall not intentionally disseminate false or misleading information and is under an obligation to use reasonable care to avoid dissemination of false or misleading information.

11 A member firm shall not purport to serve some announced cause while actually serving an undisclosed special or private interest.

12 A member firm shall safeguard the confidence of both present and former clients and shall not disclose or use these confidences to the disadvantage or prejudice of such clients or to the financial advantage of the member firm.

13 A member firm shall only represent competing interests with the consent of all those concerned.

14 A member firm shall be free to accept fees, commissions or other valuable consideration from persons other than the client, in connection with services for that client, provided such consideration is disclosed to the client.

15 A member firm shall inform a client of any shareholding or financial interest held by that firm in any company, firm or person whose services it recommends.

The Public Relations Society of America

The Code of Professional Standards of the Public Relations Society of America follows similar lines. It differs however in one important respect from the British IPR Code, in that it is accompanied by a number of 'official interpretations' of several clauses. For example, the Code lays down that a member shall conduct his or her professional life in accord with the public interest. The interpretation defines 'the public interest' primarily as comprising respect for and enforcement of the rights guaranteed by the Constitution of the United States of America.

Again, the article of safeguarding client and employer confidences does not prohibit a member who has knowledge of client or employer activities which are illegal from making such disclosures to the proper authorities as he or she believe are legally required. This point is built differently into the Code for British practitioners, who are only bound to disclose such confidential information 'upon the order of a court of competent jurisdiction'.

The American article on corruption of the channels of communication also includes corruption of the processes of government, which in the British Code is covered by special clauses. It also spells out in more detail, in its interpretation of the article, what is meant by practices which tend to corrupt integrity. Banned practices include 'providing trips for media representatives which are unrelated to legitimate news interests' and 'the use by a member of an advertising commitment . . . to obtain preferential or guaranteed coverage in the medium'.

The American Code is also accompanied by two specialized official interpretations, one dealing with political public relations, the other with financial public relations, both of them in fact longer than the basic code.

The Code of Athens

The General Assembly of the International Public Relations Association meeting in Athens on 12th August 1965, drew up a code of Ethics. As modified subsequently at a General Assembly in Tehran in 1968, this Code, known as the 'Code of Athens', lays down the principles of a strict moral code for every practitioner. It reads as follows:

'Each Member of these Associations:

SHALL ENDEAVOUR:

1 To contribute to the achievement of the moral and cultural conditions enabling human beings to reach their full stature and enjoy the indefeasible rights to which they are entitled under the 'Universal Declaration of Human Rights'.

2 To establish communication patterns and channels which, by fostering the free flow of essential information, will make each member of the society in which he lives feel that he is being kept informed, and also give him an awareness of his own personal involvement and responsibility, and of his solidarity with other members.

3 To bear in mind that, because of the relationship between his profession and the public, his conduct — even in private — will have an impact on the way in which the profession as a whole is appraised.

4 To respect, in the course of his professional duties, the moral principles and rules of the 'Universal Declaration of Human Rights'.

5 To pay due regard to, and uphold, human dignity, and to recognize the right of each individual to judge for himself.

6 To encourage the moral, psychological and intellectual conditions for dialogue in its true sense, and to recognize the right of the parties involved to state their case and express their views.

SHALL UNDERTAKE:

7 To conduct himself always and in all circumstances in such a manner as to deserve and secure the confidence of those with whom he comes into contact.

8 To act, in all circumstances, in such a manner as to take account of the respective interests of the parties involved: both the interests of the organization which he serves and the interests of the publics concerned.

9 To carry out his duties with integrity, avoiding language likely to lead to ambiguity or misunderstanding, and to maintain loyalty to his clients or employers, whether past or present.

SHALL REFRAIN FROM:

10 Subordinating the truth to other requirements.

11 Circulating information which is not based on established and ascertainable facts.

12 Taking part in any venture or undertaking which is unethical or dishonest, or capable of impairing human dignity and integrity.

13 Using any 'manipulative' methods or techniques designed to create

subconscious motivations which the individual cannot control of his own free will and so cannot be held accountable for the action taken on them.

The Code of Athens is accompanied by the IPRA Code of Conduct, adopted in Venice in 1961. This is very similar to the British Code.

12

The Law and Public Relations

James Derriman

You don't have to be a lawyer to be a good public relations man, but some knowledge of the law will help you to be a better one. There are three reasons for this:

1   The practice of public relations, like any other professional, business or even social activity, has to be carried out within its own legal context. This context comprises both areas of law which are of wide general application (the law of contracts, company law and so on) and law which has special relevance to public relations work (for instance, the law of libel and copyright law).

2   In advising his client or employer, the public relations man will often be concerned with 'legal' situations. A factory is being closed — what is the law on redundancy? A share issue is to be made — what are the legal requirements on disclosure? No matter that these are the responsibility of the client and his lawyers; the public relations adviser is at a disadvantage unless he himself knows (or knows how to find) the elements of the law on such matters. At the least he will then be able to give advice which is within the limits of practicability, and be able to 'speak the same language' as his fellow-advisers of other professions. At the most he may find increased opportunities for public relations initiative.

3   The logical analysis of problems and situations which is used by lawyers can be an extremely useful discipline for the public relations man. However creative the thought put into a public relations programme, it will be convincing in proportion to the degree of orderly thought and clarity of expression with which it is presented. The same point applies with even greater force to a preliminary assessment of, and report upon, a public relations situation.

People who know nothing of the law — except perhaps that litigation is apt to be costly — tend to fight shy of it. If this were ever a sensible approach, it is an impossible one today. The ever-increasing flow of new legislation has seen to that. Not even the greatest lawyer can hope to know the whole of the law — but anyone can learn the general principles and a little of specialist areas which concern him.

The law of England and Wales (with which for most purposes goes the law of Northern Ireland) is different in a number of ways from Scottish law. Scotland has its own legal profession and its own law courts; it jealously guards its own legal traditions, which — like those of Continental countries — have their roots in Roman Law. We will deal here basically with English law, pointing out some of the differences in Scotland. If you are practising north of the Border, you may need to go into the Scottish system more fully than we can do here.

There is, of course, a basic distinction between criminal law (matters which are punishable as offences) and civil law (matters which can be the subject of legal claims by one person or organization against another). Here we shall mainly be concerned with civil law, though certain areas such as consumer protection and employee protection may involve either civil claims or criminal prosecutions, or both.

The rest of this chapter is intended to give a bird's eye view of some widely relevant aspects. More specialized fields cannot be covered, but may seem less daunting when general principles are known.

Contracts

A contract is a legally binding agreement. This simple and seemingly obvious definition is subject to a number of exceptions, but it is adequate for most purposes. In everyday life we make contracts every day (for instance, whenever we buy a bus or train ticket, or make a purchase in a shop). A contract does not have to be in the form of a written document in legal language, or be sealed and witnessed, though in some circumstances the law will not enforce a contract which is not made without such formalities: conveying land is an example.

Probably the two types of contract which most concern public relations people professionally are contracts with suppliers, and contracts of employment. It is surprisingly common in our profession for these types of contract to be made informally, by 'friendly' letters, or even by telephone. There is a tendency to feel that to use anything like a legal document indicates a rigid, unfriendly attitude, and suggests one party is seeking to 'pin down' the other for his own advantage. While it is often unnecessary to use a document in legal phraseology, if you do not do so you must accept a more difficult task in ensuring you state precisely what has been agreed. As we all know, the time when this matters is when something goes wrong, and then it is too late.

In English law, the rules concerning contracts by deed — such as conveyances or those setting up a trust — are different in some ways from those concerning 'simple' or ordinary contracts, and it is the latter we are dealing with here.

To be legally binding, a simple contract must:

1 Be intended to create legal relations (and be capable of doing so). An agreement for a lunch date, for example, is not normally an enforceable contract!
2 Made by people who have legal capacity to contract (a minor cannot make certain types of contract; an employee cannot bind his company by contract unless he is authorized to do so, and so on).
3 Be based on an agreement between two or more parties, reached by an offer and an acceptance of that offer.
4 Be supported by 'consideration'. This means that something of value — however small, and not necessarily in money or goods — must pass from each party to the other.
5 In certain instances be in a specific form required by law (these are unlikely to come the way of a public relations practitioner in his professional work).

Agreement

An agreement may be expressed, as when you agree with a client to provide him with services, or implied, as when you board a bus and pay your fare. In either case, there must be an offer on one side and acceptance on the other.

An offer must be distinguished from an invitation to make an offer. If a consultancy advertises its services, it is merely inviting potential clients to offer an assignment. If a company advertises a job, it is merely inviting potential employees to apply. The consultancy need not take an assignment offered to it, and the company need not employ an applicant. Only when an actual offer is made and accepted — when the parties are agreed — is there actually a contract.

At the same time, an offer need not be made to a specific person or company: it can be made to people in general. In a famous case in Victorian times a company advertised that they would pay £100 to anyone who caught influenza after using their product; the plaintiff bought and used the product, thus accepting the offer, but did catch 'flu. She sued for the £100, and won.

Even when an offer is made, it can be revoked at any time before it has been accepted. Sometimes the exact time of acceptance can be important. Suppose you write to a supplier ordering goods, then — perhaps because of a change in your PR programme — you wish to cancel. If the supplier has already accepted your order (that is your offer to purchase), you can cancel it only at your peril — the supplier can hold you to your bargain. In a case like this, the exact time of acceptance can be important. The acceptance must have been communicated to you before you withdraw (the law presumes that where acceptance is contemplated by post, acceptance is made when the letter of acceptance is posted).

For an agreement to be binding, the parties must be at one on all essential points, so it is sensible to spell out these points clearly and ensure that the person with whom you are contracting accepts them. If you are ordering artwork, for instance, make it clear whether you wish to buy the copyright, or merely the right to reproduce on a single occasion — or just the physical drawing or painting. Too often these things are left unsaid, or dealt with vaguely by telephone. There is no substitute for putting an agreement in writing, or confirming by letter, and getting a written acknowledgement.

Consideration

You can enforce a contract (other than a deed) at law only if you can show that you have provided some 'consideration'. This need not take the form of payment. It can be any benefit which you provide to the other party, or something which you agree to give up or forego: the value need bear no relation to what is given in return. In many cases the consideration will be a promise to do something (employ a person, supply goods or services for example) in exchange for another promise (to work for the employer, pay for the goods or services).

Acceptance can, however, be implied. If you pay your fare on a bus, you are accepting by implication the bus company's (equally implied) offer to take you on your journey. If you allow an employee to start work without making a specific agreement to employ him, you will be bound by implication to pay him for what he does.

Terms

The terms of a contract, like the offer and acceptance, may be written or implied. If they are broken by either side, the aggrieved party can sue for damages and if they go to the root of the agreement he can claim that the contract is at an end.

In the case of an agreement for public relations consultancy, it obviously avoids problems if the parties contract on the basis of detailed written terms or conditions. (The Public Relations Consultants Association provides model terms for inclusion in consultancy contracts, and CERP, the European Public Relations Confederation, supplies a model form of agreement.) Such terms, including such matters as notice periods, payment of out-of-pocket expenses, and indemnity against claims by third parties, can either be part of a formal contract or 'built in' to a contract made by letter — so long as it is made quite clear that they are to be regarded as part of the agreement, and accepted as such. A supplier or consultant may print such terms or conditions on his order form, and if the order is accepted the contract will be on this basis of those conditions, unless there is any agreement to the contrary.

Where a term of the contract is not covered by written 'conditions', it may be implied by law or by the custom of the trade. Long before modern consumer protection legislation, the Sale of Goods Act 1893 established basic implied terms for sale of goods. The Act covers three principal points:

1 Sale by description, where goods must correspond with the description.
2 Condition of fitness for the purpose for which goods are normally intended
3 Merchantable quality, i.e. that goods are basically of a quality which is suitable for those goods.

Human nature being what it is, people or companies making contracts will attempt to by-pass legal restrictions by 'contracting-out' of them if they can. Two recent Acts have stopped up loopholes of this kind. The Supply of Goods (Implied Terms) Act 1973 forbids contracting out of the conditions on description, 'merchantability' and fitness in sales to consumers. The Unfair Contract Terms Act 1977 made illegal in certain circumstances exemption clauses which seek to exclude liability by one party to the other for negligence, or for breach of contract.

Mistake

If a party to a contract entered the agreement under a mistake of fact on an essential matter, the contract will be held void, simply because the offer and acceptance did not correspond. If a client enters a contract for public relations services with X and Associates, a small and not very efficient firm, believing that he is dealing with a big and highly expert firm with a slightly similar name, it could be held that he need not carry out the agreement: though if the case came to court, he would have to show that had he known the identity of the firm he would not have contracted with it.

It is commonsense to read, and make sure you understand, a written contract before you sign it. Normally you will be bound by the terms of the contract even if you have not read it; the exception is the unlikely case where you sign a contract believing it to be a different type of agreement altogether.

Misrepresentation

A 'representation' is a statement made by one person which induces another to enter a contract with him. If the statement is false — a 'misrepresentation' — the law will provide a remedy for the party who has acted on it to his detriment.

The familiar rule *caveat emptor* — let the buyer beware — lives on, even though modified by much recent legislation. Under the general law, no one is bound to make any 'representation' at all. A seller does not have to tell a buyer of defects in the article he is selling: it is up to the buyer to find out. But if he is asked, or chooses to describe the goods, he must be truthful, or he will be liable for the result of his misrepresentation. This is so even if the statement was true when he made it, but later became false. Suppose that you, as a consultant, tell a potential client that his account will be handled by a well-known and highly skilled member of your staff. That member of your staff leaves, but you enter a contract with the client without disclosing the changed situation. If the client was led to make the contract on the basis of your representation, he will have a valid claim against you.

Misrepresentation may, of course, be either fraudulent or innocent. In either case the injured party may choose to set aside the contract, or to sue for damages; but if the defendant can show that he believed on reasonable grounds *up to the time of the contract* that the statement was true, he can escape damages.

There are various situations where disclosure is specifically required. Apart from modern consumer protection law, the commonest example is that of insurance; if the party seeking to be insured does not disclose all material facts, the insuror can rescind the contract. Contracts between partners likewise require full disclosure.

Contracts in restraint of trade

Certain types of contract are by their nature illegal. One of the most important of these is the contract 'in restraint of trade', because it can often apply to employment situations. In contracts for senior and specialist posts, the employer often wishes to impose restrictions on the employee even after he has left the company. A consultancy, for instance, may wish to include a term in its directors' contracts binding them not to approach the firm's clients for some fixed period after the director has left the firm. To be upheld by the courts, a restriction like this must be shown to be reasonably necessary to protect the interests of the employer, and not unreasonable as regards the employee or the public. (The length of period will be one of the factors taken into account here; the extent of the restriction will be another.) Contracts of this kind which do not meet these conditions are held illegal, as being 'in restraint of trade' and therefore contrary to public policy, though if a contract is valid apart from the restrictive clause, the remainder will be enforced.

How does a contract come to an end?

There are five ways in which a valid contract comes to an end:

1 Performance — when it has been carried out. This need not be a fixed term but, as with contracts of employment, can continue until the expiry of notice.
2 Agreement — if both parties wish to end (or change) the contract, they can agree to do so. If one party has carried out his obligations, the other one must give 'consideration' in exchange for his release, unless the waiver is made by deed.
3 By operation of law. A contract for personal services, for example, ends with the death of either party.
4 Frustration. If circumstances have changed radically so that the contract cannot be performed in its original form, it is at an end. Example: a pop singer was engaged to play seven nights a week, but following a nervous breakdown was fit only to play for four nights a week. The contract (and perhaps the audience!) was held to be 'frustrated'.
5 Breach of contract. If a contract is broken in such a way that it is useless to continue it, it is at an end.

A 'simple' contract can be enforced by legal action only up to six years after the contract is entered into; a deed is enforceable up to twelve years. These are periods to remember when destroying letters, invoices or other papers which could be evidence in any dispute. (However, if the debtor acknowledges his debt in writing or makes part-payment, the time starts to run again from the date of these events.)

Remedies for breach

If a breach of contract occurs, the other party can, as an alternative or in addition to suing for damages, ask the court to order the party in breach to carry out his agreement. He can also ask for an injunction to prevent further breaches.

Assignment

The benefits of a contract can be assigned to a third party, under certain conditions, but not the liabilities. You can for instance assign the fees you receive for your public relations work — but you cannot (without first agreeing with the client) assign the legal responsibility of carrying out the work to another consultant or firm. You may be able to sub-contract, but this will depend on the terms of the contract, stated or implied.

Careless Mis-statement

Any contract (whether written or not) for the provision of advice — such as by a public relations consultant — has an implied duty of care owed to the client, unless that condition is expressly excluded or limited. Even where there is no contract a professional person owes a duty of care to people who can be expected to rely upon his skill (doctors frequently insure against claims on this score).

It was made clear in the important *Hedley Byrne* case in 1964 that this duty of reasonable care extends to voluntary statements made by anyone to someone else who can be expected to rely on their truth, unless liability is expressly excluded. The most obvious example of this is where — as in the Hedley Byrne case itself — a misleading reference is given. There is no obligation to give a reference, on an employee or a business, for instance, at all; but if you do so, you must take reasonable care that it is accurate and sufficiently complete. You can, however, exclude liability by stating specifically that you give the reference 'without responsibility'.

Agency and Vicarious Liability

An aspect of the law which is often of great importance to professional people, such as public relations practitioners, is: how far am I responsible in law for someone else's act? The rules on this differ according to whether we are considering contracts, torts (civil wrongs not based on contract) or criminal offences.

Agency

An agent is a person given authority by another (called the principal) to do something on his behalf, such as enter a contract.

In public relations consultancy it is important, for reasons which will appear, to be clear about when the consultant is acting directly and when he is acting as an agent for his client. This point arises whenever, for instance, he books a room for a Press conference or orders printwork in the course of his assignment.

If the consultant is acting as a principal, the buck stops with him. Any claim by the supplier for payment, etc., can only be made against him and whether or not he can recover from his client is his problem, not the supplier's. If the consultant is openly acting as the client's agent, the supplier must normally claim against the client (the consultant's principal) and not against the consultant; moreover, only the client can sue the supplier if necessary. If, however, the consultant has not disclosed the fact that he is acting as agent, the supplier can claim against him, though provided he has acted within the client's actual authority the client can ratify the contract.

The agency situation can arise merely by implication. If the client puts the consultant in a position where the consultant appears to have authority to act for him, he cannot afterwards deny that he was so authorized (even if, for instance, unknown to the supplier he had forbidden the consultant to place the order).

It is important to note that it is a criminal offence, under the Prevention of Corruption Act 1906, for an agent to take any undisclosed commission or other reward in connection with the client's business. An agent who makes any undisclosed profit can be sued in the civil courts and made to hand it over.

Generally it is more satisfactory, in public relations consultancy, for the consultant to make it clear to all parties that he is acting as principal, and re-charge the client as necessary. For this reason, it is sensible to avoid referring to a public relations 'agency' or 'agent'. This could lead to legal problems; although the 'custom of the trade' in advertising regards advertising agencies as principals, it is doubtful whether the courts would apply the same 'custom' to public relations consultancy.

Vicarious Liability — Tort

An employer is liable for torts committed by his employees or agents in the course of their employment. This means that if a member of your staff is (for example) negligent, causing damage to a third party, *you* can be sued as well as the employee. Generally speaking, employers have more money than employees, so they are more worthwhile suing! This liability arises only if the tort was committed in the course of employment; the courts interpret this quite widely, and the test is really whether the employee was doing what he was employed to do — even if, as will usually be the case, the employer would not have wished him to carry out his duties in a harmful way. We have taken negligence as an example, but the same rule applies to all torts: including, for instance, defamation or passing-off, which we shall look at later in this chapter.

This 'vicarious liability', as lawyers call it, applies in the case of employees but not normally in the case of an independent contractor, such as a freelance or a design firm, or printer with whom you contract to do work for you. The important difference is that an employee is subject to the employer's control not only on what he does, but how he is to do it: the fact that he disobeys his instructions is unfortunately irrelevant, unless he goes (in the words of a famous judgement) 'on a frolic of his own'.

An employer is liable for the torts of an independent contractor only if he has chosen the contractor negligently, or if he has given instructions not only on what work is to be done, but how it is to be done, or otherwise interfered, in effect assuming the sort of control he is presumed to have over an employee. An independent contractor, by definition, has a contract to perform *services*, as distinct from the contract of *service* which creates the relationship of employer and employee with the control that that implies.

Vicarious Liability — Criminal Offences

If an employee commits a criminal offence, the basic rule is that the employer is not liable — even if the offence is committed in the course of employment — unless it is done on his instructions, or with his assistance. This rule, however, is subject to many exceptions arising from Acts which prohibit certain actions absolutely.

In this latter case — an example is offences relating to the sale of food and drugs — the employer is liable even if the offence is committed without his authority and even contrary to his instructions. In some cases the employee may be liable in addition. A company for these purposes is liable to the same extent as any other employer.

Employment Law

In practice, the law cannot be divided into neat packages like 'Employment Law' or 'Consumer Protection Law'. A great deal of the law has general application, though strengthened and supplemented in particular fields by specialized Acts of Parliament. Employment law is a good example.

Trade Unions

The idea of special employment law largely dates from the rise of the trade unions, many of whose rights and powers have legal backing. Since the Employment Act 1982 unions no longer have immunity from liability for tort in respect of industrial action, unless that action is in furtherance of an industrial dispute between members and their employers. Other important provisions on trade unions and union membership are contained both in the 1982 Act and in the Employment Protection (Consolidation) Act 1978. The requirements for disclosure of certain information to unions contained in this statute and in the Industry Act 1975 can be of relevance to public – especially internal — relations.

Contracts of Employment

We have seen the distinction between a contract for services (such as consultancy agreement or a contract with a freelance) and a contract fo service, i.e. employment (between employer and employee). Contracts c employment basically follow the same rules as contracts in general, but ar affected by special legislation. Although a contract of employment can b implied (the employee working, the employer paying wages), or merel verbal, the Employee Protection (Consolidation) Act 1978, requires th employer to give the employee a written statement of the terms and condition on which he is employed. These must comprise certain specific items including the date on which 'continuous employment' began — a matte relevant to such claims as those for unfair dismissal, maternity rights an redundancy compensation.

Action for *wrongful* dismissal has always been possible, because it amount to breach of contract by the employer. *Unfair* dismissal is a new and fairl specific concept introduced by statute in 1971, and is the subject of hearings b Industrial Tribunals. The Industrial Tribunals, which have developed a larg case law of their own, deal with a variety of matters contained in recen statutes, all of which can be important in public relations: the Redundanc Payments Act 1965; Equal Pay Act 1970; Trade Union and Labour Relation Act 1974; Sex Discrimination Act 1975; and Employment Protection (Con solidation) Act 1978; and Employment Act 1982.

In addition to all these Acts, which it would be impossible to summariz here, the Health and Safety at Work, etc. Act 1974 is of importance to man public relations people. So, of course, is the Race Relations Act 1976. Codes o practice issued under various Acts, especially those produced by ACAS, th Arbitration, Conciliation and Advisory Service, do not have the force of law but it necessary to have at least some acquaintance with them.

Companies, and Related Matters

From the PRO's point of view, business organizations come in two sizes, as i were. Public relations consultancies, and many of the suppliers with whicl they deal, tend to be (in industrial terms) small. They may be privat companies, partnerships, or one or two individuals trading under a busines name. On the other hand, businesses which employ public relations staff o retain consultants are more often public companies quoted on the Stocl Exchange.

The financial public relations specialist needs to be familiar with company law in technical detail, but the general principles are straightforward and important to all practitioners.

The underlying concept of company law is that of the corporation. A corporation, in legal terminology, means simply a succession or collection of persons which has a legal existence, rights and duties of its own. It is a legal 'person', quite separate from the individuals of which in human terms it is composed. Apart from companies, there are several other types of corporation — in local government we still talk of the 'Mayor and Corporation', statutory corporations such as British Rail, even successive holders of an office, such as Archbishop of Canterbury.

What is a Company?

A company is an association of persons formed for the purpose of some business or undertaking carried on in a corporate name, and incorporated by law. To carry on its business, every company needs money — its capital — provided by its members, each of whom in the normal case holds one or more shares in the enterprise, in proportion to the amount he has subscribed. The money subscribed for those shares cannot by law be repaid until the company is wound up, because it must be kept to meet any debts which the company may incur, but the shares may be sold by any member who wishes to realize his investment. The company, being a separate legal entity, can own property in its own name, sue or be sued, owe money or be owed it by others, and even be convicted of certain criminal offences.

A group of persons formed for the purpose of trading would, without further formalities, be simply a partnership in the eyes of the law. Each of its members would be fully liable for the debts of the group, as partners are. By taking the formal steps to become incorporated under the Companies Acts as a company limited by shares, the group gains a very considerable advantage: the liability of each member is then restricted to the amount of his shares. This is the normal form of business company in Britain, but there are also certain other specialized forms of companies. One is the company limited by guarantee, but not by shares: a form often used for associations which are not primarily trading bodies. The Institute of Public Relations is an example. Members of the Institute do not hold shares, but if the IPR were to be dissolved each member would be liable to outsiders for a maximum of £5 (the sum set by its Memorandum of Association). It is also possible, but unusual, to have an *un*limited company, in which the liability of members is not limited.

The main body of law on companies in the United Kingdom is still contained in the Companies Act 1948, although this act has been modified and strengthened by further Companies Acts in 1967, 1976, 1980 and 1981. The purpose of the basic Act was to protect the public from abuse of the great privilege of limited liability and the subsequent Acts have endeavoured to increase this protection particularly through the increased disclosure of relevant information. Moreover, the EEC has paid much attention to company law, calling for further requirements to be adopted nationally.

There are two main types of limited companies: the private company and the public company (many companies begin life as private companies, seeking public status when they become big enough to need more capital).

A company of either type must have at least two members (shareholders), at least one director, and a secretary. It may have as many more members or directors as it wishes. A private company must not offer its shares or debentures to the public, whereas a public may (but need not) do so. A public company must end its name with the words 'Public Limited Company' (instead of just 'Limited'), or the equivalent in Welsh. Since the 1980 Companies Act these are the main differences between the two types of limited company.

Private companies — which are by far the most numerous — are subject to less exacting rules than are public companies, because there is not the same need to protect the investing public. Nevertheless, even here the law has been growing tighter.

Note that a public company need not offer its shares or debentures to the public, and it is possible (though unusual) for a public company not to be a 'quoted' company, that is not to have applied for its shares to be quoted on The Stock Exchange. If a Stock Exchange quotation is sought, the company will have to comply with the Stock Exchange's own rules, which are even more stringent than those of the law.

Forming a Company

To form a company, certain documents — notably a Memorandum of Association and Articles of Association — must be submitted to the Registrar of Companies in Cardiff for companies incorporated in England or Wales, or his opposite numbers in Edinburgh or Belfast. Even before this, the name of the new company will have been chosen. Permission will not be given for any name too similar to that of an existing unconnected company, nor for certain other types of name which are considered undesirable or misleading (such as those using the word 'Royal' or even 'British' — existing companies with titles of this kind were formed before the rules were tightened). Basic rules on company names are now set out in Part II of the Companies Act 1982. Previous enquiry of the Companies Registry will give an indication of whether a proposed name is likely to be approved.

The Memorandum and Articles together form the constitution of the company, and — once settled — can be altered only upon certain limited grounds by a general meeting of the company. The Memorandum gives basic information on the external aspects of the company, such as the types of business it is empowered to run. Objects are normally drawn very widely, because anything done by the company beyond these powers is *ultra vires* and in certain circumstances void. Since the European Communities Act 1972, however, a transaction between the compaɴy and an innocent outsider remains valid in favour of that person, even if *ultra vires* so far as the company is concerned, provided the transaction is made after a decision of the directors.

The Articles regulate the internal affairs of the company — the rights of shareholders, powers of directors, and so on.

Once the Memorandum and Articles, and other documentation, have been approved and fees paid, the Registrar issues a certificate of incorporation and the company may commence business.

Whenever a company — either at its formation or later — invites the public to subscribe for shares or debentures (a debenture is an interest-bearing loan, normally on security), it must in most circumstances issue a prospectus. This is a document giving full information, on lines laid down by the Companies Acts, and is defined very widely as 'any prospectus, notice, circular, advertisement or other invitation. . .' — even a press release could fall into this category. Fraudulent and misleading statements, concealments or reckless promises or forecasts in prospectuses are criminal offences by the Prevention of Frauds (Investments) Act 1958.

Every company is required to make an annual return to the Registrar, including a list of its shareholders and/or changes in shareholdings since the last return, particulars of directors and secretary, a balance sheet, profit and loss account, and directors' report. All these items, together with the Memorandum and Articles, may be inspected at the Companies Registry offices (nowadays on microfiche).

The accounts and directors' report must be put before shareholders in advance of the annual general meeting required by law, and the details of this and other procedures are laid down in the Acts. See especially the Companies Act 1981 (Pt. I and Schedules), which sets out requirements on company accounts and the directors' report.

The company's 'nominal' capital need not be issued all at once, and the 'issued' capital may therefore be a smaller figure. Different classes of shares may be issued, with different rights attaching to each. Preference shares entitle their holders to a fixed amount of dividend (share-out profits) payable before any dividend is payable to the Ordinary shareholders — whose dividend is variable, depending on what profit, if any, the company has made, and on the amount which the directors consider it wise to keep back for the company's business needs. In America the words 'stock' and 'stockholders' are used as synonymous with 'shares' and 'shareholders'. In the United Kingdom, however, 'stock' is, as it were, a bundle of shares. Shares are of fixed amounts

— say £1 each — but 'stock' can be issued in odd sums, according to the wish of the purchaser. (We are, of course, speaking of the nominal value, or price of the shares or stock when issued — the price at which they are bought and sold is controlled solely by market forces.)

Dividends are paid to shareholders in proportion to the nominal value of their shares. Shareholders cannot insist on the payment of a dividend, unless fraud is involved, but once a dividend has been declared its payment can be enforced like any other debt. Every trading company has an implied power to borrow and give security for the loan, unless prohibited by its Memorandum and Articles, and the issue of debentures is a frequent method used. Interest on debentures must be paid before any dividend, and debentures — unlike shares — may be redeemable. They are usually secured on the company's assets.

Directors are appointed by the members (shareholders) of a company, and can be removed by them. They need not necessarily be shareholders themselves, but their powers and duties are considerable, governed by law and by the company's Memorandum and Articles.

Two points on company meetings useful to the public relations practitioner are worth mentioning here, if only because they are seldom mentioned. The first is that the Press and public may be admitted to a general meeting, and in the case of a public company, normally are: but the decision whether they shall remain is entirely one for the meeting itself, and if necessary a vote is taken. Secondly, a speech by a shareholder defamatory of the directors has qualified privilege provided it is on a matter affecting the interests of the shareholders — but if the shareholder himself expressly invites the public or Press to be present, he forfeits the privilege.

Company Letter-headings, etc.

Certain information must, by the Companies Acts and the European Communities Act 1972, appear on the company letter-head and trade literature. Subject to certain exceptions, the names of all directors must appear, together with the nationality of any director not a national of a Common Market country. The registered number of the company must be given, the place of registration, and the address of the registered office. The words 'Limited' or 'Public Limited Company' must form part of the title of a limited company and be shown as such (apart from rare exceptions, and even then the fact that liability is limited must still be stated). Breach of these provisions is a criminal offence, and designers have to live with them!

Dissolution of Companies

Dissolution of a company may be carried out in several ways. If a company has been inactive for some time, the Registrar of Companies may — after giving an opportunity to the company to object — simply strike it from the register, as a sort of housekeeping operation. Apart from this, dissolution takes the form of 'winding up', which may take place on any of several grounds. One of these is inability of the company to pay its debts, in which case a creditor may apply to the court to have the company wound up compulsorily; a liquidator is then appointed to realise the company's assets and share it out proportionately among the creditors — he may, if necessary, carry on the business temporarily. When the company's affairs are completely wound up, the liquidator applies to the court for it to be dissolved. It is also possible for the company to be wound up voluntarily, appointing its own liquidator, and in some cases the court will order that the winding up continues under court supervision.

Partnership

Most of the law on partnerships is set out in the Partnership Act 1890, which defines a partnership simply as the 'relationship which subsists between persons carrying on a business in common with a view of profit'. So a partnership may be implied by the law, but usually the relationship is set out in a formal agreement. There is no legal maximum number of partners. Companies may be partners, because they are legal 'persons', but the partnership itself is not a 'person' or corporate entity. The basic rule is that each partner is individually liable for the whole debts of the partnership without limit, though there are exceptions to this. There is also a form of 'limited' partnership, but even here at least one of the partners is required to have unlimited liability.

Business Names

It is often convenient for an individual, or for that matter a company, to trade under a name which is not its own — perhaps the name of a product, or the service which it offers. The law requires that any such title must be registered as a 'business name'. The choice of name is restricted in much the same way as a company name, and similarly it is possible to inquire in advance whether a particular name is likely to be accepted. It is not, however, possible to use a business name to disguise the underlying identity of the business: the law requires that the registered proprietor of the name be stated on the letter-head, catalogues, etc.

Defamation: Libel and Slander

When I lectured to public relations students on this subject, I used to remind them that Labouchère, the celebrated editor of *Truth*, is said to have so thrived on libel actions that he had a special letter-box at his office marked 'writs'. I added rather obviously that public relations does not thrive on such things — even though it is not hard to think of some modern editors who might carry on the Labouchère tradition. Apart from the fact that attacks on people's good names are the opposite of good public relations, an action for defamation can be very costly, even if you are a successful defendant.

National newspapers employ lawyers to read in proof every word that is printed, to avoid legal trouble before it starts. Public relations people (and for that matter, most advertising people) have to do it themselves. So a knowledge of this branch of the law is vital.

Defamation has been defined as the publication of a statement which tends to lower a person in the estimation of right-thinking members of society generally; or which tends to make them shun or avoid that person. English law divides defamation into libel, which covers statements in written or other permanent form (supposedly worse) and slander, covering statements which are spoken or otherwise transitory. The rules on these two broad classes are slightly different. In Scottish law there is no distinction.

English law presumes that a libel causes damage — an action can be brought without the need to prove any quantified damage. Not so in the case of slander, where special damage must be proved except in certain definite instances, including slanderous statements imputing a criminal offence (punishable by more than simply a fine), or of unfitness, dishonesty or incompetence in the plaintiff's carrying out of his office, profession or business.

Recognising a Libel or Slander

How can you recognize a libel or slander? Four elements must always be present:

1 A defamatory statement,
2 which is false (*but* the law presumes falsity until the contrary is proved),
3 which is understood to refer to the plaintiff,
4 and which has been published (made known) to a third party.

Clearly there are all sorts of ways in which a statement can be defamatory, within the definition given earlier. Apart from the obvious ones such as implication that the person concerned is in financial difficulties, has committed an offence, or is dishonest or immoral, the law has held that it is defamatory to say that someone is insane (if he is not), or suffering from some unpleasant disease (if he is not) because these things would tend to make him 'shunned or avoided' by other people.

At this point we must mention 'innuendo', a word which though popularly used or misused has a specific legal meaning. A statement which on the face of it is not defamatory may be so by innuendo: that is in the light of knowledge possessed by the third party to whom it is published.

In a famous case, an advertisement for chocolate featuring a star golfer was held defamatory because people who knew the golfer was an amateur would believe he had given permission in return for a cash payment (which in fact he had not). This example — and one could give many others — indicates how careful it is necessary to be.

We have mentioned that the law presumes a statement claimed as defamatory to be false unless proved otherwise. The point here is that *proving* the truth of something in court is not always easy. The statement must be understood to refer to the plaintiff even if it was not intended to do so. Unlike some other countries, civil law in Britain does not provide a remedy for libel on a large class of people (such as Catholics, Communists, or tax-collectors). Anyone can say with impunity 'all public relations people are dishonest', but if a similar statement were made about 'all directors of X company' any one of those directors could sue, because they are clearly identifiable individuals whose reputation has been aspersed.

Finally, there is the question of publication. This, too, has a legal meaning; the statement must have been communicated to at least one other person other than the plaintiff or his or her spouse. The person to whom the statement is published must be in a position to understand its defamatory nature.

A moment's thought will show that a defamatory statement can be published in all sorts of ways — once made it is not so easy to stop it. A Press release containing a defamatory statement is sent to a news agency (publication 1), which then sends it to a newspaper (publication 2), which then prints it and sells the newspaper (publication 3). Each person or firm along this chain can be sued by the defamed person — there is a legal let-out for the luckless newsagent who sells the paper, provided he has no knowledge that it contains a libel and could not be expected to know that this was the case. A defamatory speech is heard by an audience, broadcast, reported, and so on — a similar chain of publications and resulting liability. Publication can even be unintentional: a libel on a postcard is presumed to be published, because it can be read in the course of the post.

To complete the guidelines, and to balance the picture, here are possible defences to an action for defamation:

1 Assent: if the plaintiff has agreed, directly or by implication, to publication of a statement about himself which is true on the face of it, the defendant is not liable. An instance (not so impossible as it might seem) is a Press release, the text of which was approved by an individual referred to in it, who later decides it is defamatory of him.

2 'Unintentional Defamation', under the Defamation Act 1952. Until this law was passed, one of the biggest dangers arose when a fictional name was used — say in an advertisement — whereupon someone who actually had that name claimed that people understood the item to refer to him, and that it was defamatory. The 1952 Act provides that if the defendant can show that he published the words innocently, offers to publish a reasonable correction and apology and pays the plaintiff's costs, he is not liable for damages. This applies when *either* the defendant did not intend the statement to refer to the plaintiff, *or* it was not defamatory on the face of it and he did not know it could have a defamatory meaning. Reasonable care must have been taken in either case.

3 Justification — that is, truth. The law will not protect a reputation which is not deserved, so if the defendant can prove that the statement he has made is true, he will not be liable. Proving the truth in court is often far from easy, and the statement (including any hidden meaning) must be proved true in substance. Merely to prove that it is a correct report of someone else's statement (except in some special cases which are privileged) is not enough.

4 Fair comment. If the statement is fair comment (not factual but based on true facts) on a matter of public interest, the defendant is not liable.

5 Privilege. This covers certain specified circumstances in which the law allows defamatory statements to be made without liability. Privilege comes in two kinds: absolute, and qualified. Absolute privilege provides complete immunity in certain limited situations, such as statements made in Parliament or parliamentary papers, or in the course of judicial proceedings. Qualified privilege gives exemption in a number of other situations, *provided* the statement is made honestly as to what is said and the means by which it is said. Fair and accurate reports of parliamentary proceedings or judicial proceedings open to the public come in this category. Certain other newspaper or broadcast reports have qualified privilege subject to the publication of explanation and contradiction: among these are reports of the findings of professional bodies in relation to their members (the IPR Council, for example). Qualified privilege also attaches to a statement made by a person who had a duty to make it to another person with a coresponding interest to receive it; examples are the giving of references on former employees, and legitimate complaints to people in authority.

Qualified privilege is valid only if there is no malice or spite involved. If you issue a defamatory statement on behalf of your client or employer, it is 'his' privilege which normally counts — if he is actuated by malice, you are liable as much as he is, even though you have acted innocently: though, of course, you may be able to claim against him in turn.

In addition to damages, a plaintiff in a defamation case can also seek an injunction, temporary or permanent, to stop further publication.

In rare circumstances, libel can be a criminal offence. Different conditions then apply, including the fact that a dead person, or a class of people, can be the subject of a criminal (but not a civil) libel. Truth is no defence, unless the statement can be shown to be in the public interest.

Slander of Title

This term is misleading, because it has little to do with the ordinary kind of slander. A better name is 'injurious falsehood'.

Defamation is essentially an attack on someone's personal reputation. Equally damaging, if not more so, can be statements which harm his business or other material interests. Under certain conditions, such statements — whether oral or in writing — are actionable. The statement must be made to some person other than the plaintiff, and there must be some indirect, dishonest or other improper motive. Recklessness may qualify, but not mere carelessness.

Moreover, with certain exceptions, the plaintiff must prove special damage. The exceptions, under the Defamation Act 1952, are when the false statement is in writing or other permanent form and calculated to cause pecuniary damage to the plaintiff; or when, whether it is in permanent form or not, it is calculated to cause pecuniary damage to the plaintiff in respect of his office, or profession, etc.

To say that your (or your client's or employer's) goods are better than those of someone else is not actionable as slander of title, though consumer legislation may, of course, apply. It is important, however, to be as alert to avoiding slander of title as ordinary defamation, and to consider the possible effect of any statement you make, especially in writing. For instance, to state falsely that a firm is no longer in existence, or no longer trading, can clearly harm the firm concerned, and could be actionable. So could the classic example of a notice stating that a certain garage is 'the last for ten miles', when in fact someone else's garage is within that distance.

Copyright, Registered Designs and Patents

Anyone concerned with public relations, communications, or any other activity with a creative element, will sooner or later need to know how far the law will protect the results of his creative thought from being pirated by others.

The first thing to realize is that, except in the case of patents, the law does not (and could not practicably) protect *ideas*. All it can do is to protect the expression of those ideas in written, artistic or other form. The second is that in this field, perhaps more than any other we are discussing, it is very easy for legal rights to be lost on the one hand, or infringed on the other, by default. Alertness pays.

Copyright

This is the most widely applicable form of protecting original work, and the most frequently misunderstood. It is governed in the United Kingdom almost entirely by the Copyright Act 1956, and internationally by the Universal Copyright Convention of 1952 (signed by almost every important country except the Chinese Republic).

Copyright means the right, for a stated period, to prevent any other person (without permission of the copyright owner) from copying or using in various other ways the work concerned.

In Britain, copyright exists automatically (that is without any need to claim it or for legal registration) in — for all practical purposes — every original literary, dramatic, artistic or musical work. The word 'original' in this sense means simply that the work must have been created by the author, not copied from someone else's work: if two people produce a virtually identical drawing quite independently, each drawing will have copyright. Because, as we have said, copyright protects the expression of ideas, it is not confined to words, pictures or music as such. There is copyright in a compilation, such as a timetable. In the case of a book, there is copyright not only in the text, but also separately in the typographical design of the book.

Ownership

The copyright of an original work is normally held by the author — the person who used his creative thought to produce it. There are, however, important exceptions. When work is produced in the course of employment, the copyright normally belongs to the employer, not the employee. (But although a newspaper proprietor has the right to use articles written by his staff in his newspaper, all other rights, such as the right to reprint them in book form, for instance, remain with the journalists who wrote them. This is a special case.)

A second exception is equally important for public relations people: photography. Copyright in photographs which are *commissioned* is held by the person or company who commissioned them. You should, however, beware of one point in this regard. Even though you have commissioned a photograph, the negative remains the property of the photographer, unless you specifically arrange to buy it — so he can make his own terms with you for supplying prints, though he has no right to supply prints to anyone else.

Copyright in a cinema film is owned by the maker of the film, and although this is defined as 'the person by whom the arrangements for the making of the film is undertaken', this is normally assumed to be the film company. When commissioning a film, it is usual to provide in the contract that the copyright shall be automatically assigned to the company or person who has commissioned it.

Copyright in television broadcasts (as distinct from the material they contain) is held by the BBC or the IBA as the case may be.

Although copyright of Government documents and publications is held by the Crown, there is normally no objection made to reproducing parliamentary papers such as Bills, Acts, Statutory Rules and Orders, reports of Select Committees, or items in Hansard (the latter may not be used in advertising).

Performers' rights are a separate though related subject, and are now governed by the Dramatic and Musical Performers Protection Act 1958 and the Performers Protection Act 1963.

What copyright protects

Despite its name, copyright protects work not merely against being reproduced, in any material form, but against such uses as translations, adaptations, or being performed or broadcast. It is sensible to assume, as a starting-point, that you can make *no* use without permission of any work in which you do not own the copyright.

Nevertheless, there are certain practical exceptions. The law allows 'fair dealing' with a copyright work for research or private study or for criticism or review (provided there is proper acknowledgement), and in various other circumstances. Certain uses by libraries are allowed, and also use for educational purposes. Records of musical works may be made under certain conditions where a fixed royalty is paid. Sound recordings of films or broadcasts may be made for private purposes. And so on — the only safe thing to do is to check the Act or, where there is doubt, get an expert view.

How long does copyright protection last?

In literary, dramatic and musical works copyright continues for the lifetime of the author of the work, plus fifty years from the end of the year in which he dies — but if the author dies before the work is published, the copyright runs for fifty years from the end of the year in which the work is first published (which may, of course, be a long time after his death — and then it may be difficult to discover the owner).

Copyright in artistic works, including photographs, continues for fifty years from the date of first publication, and the same thing applies to sound recordings and to films (except that with films other than newsreels, advertising films and some education films, the period runs from the date of registration).

No permission is needed to reproduce a work not published within one hundred years, fortunately; and copyright in the typographical arrangements of a book lasts only for twenty-five years.

International Copyright

The Geneva Convention, which provides international copyright protection, requires as a condition of that protection that published works bear the letter 'C' in a circle, accompanied by the name of the owner of the copyright and the year of first publication. Whether or not you have international circulation in mind, it is always a wise precaution to take this simple step.

Remedies for infringement

A plaintiff who proves that his copyright has been infringed can ask the court:

1 To grant an injunction to forbid any further infringement, temporarily (pending trial of the action) or permanently.
2 To award damages.
3 To order the defendant to render an account of the profits he has made through the infringement.
4 To order infringing copies to be delivered up.

An action for infringement must be brought within six years of the act complained of. In some circumstances a breach of copyright law may be a criminal offence. Merely to possess a sound recording or film known to infringe copyright is, for instance, an offence under the Copyright Act 1956 (Amendment) Act 1982.

Defences

Anyone sued for breach of copyright can claim in defence:

1 That there is no copyright in the work.
2 That the plaintiff is not the owner of the copyright.
3 That the material copied is not a substantial part of the work.
4 That the act complained of falls within the 'fair dealing' exceptions.

Registered Designs

Copyright, although it arises automatically on the creation of a work, applies only if the work is 'original'. Certain types of design can be registered under the Registered Designs Act 1949. Registration is a kind of guarantee that the design *is* original: any infringement of a registered design is actionable, and it is no defence to say that the infringer thought up the same design independently. Moreover, the mere fact of making known that the design is registered can put people on notice that the owner intends to protect it.

Registration is available only for designs intended to be reproduced in more than fifty articles, which is regarded as the criterion for 'industrial' designs; and sculpture, wall plaques and medals, and printed matter are excluded. Although the application to designs of industrial products in the ordinary sense is obvious, the method can be used for (say) a character created for advertising which could be exploited in other forms, such as on T-shirts, toys and so on. Application for registration must be made before the design has been published (or publicly used) in any way. Protection lasts initially for five years, renewable for two further periods of five years.

Copyright protection for products produced industrially and based on copyright drawings which are registrable is provided for a fifteen-year period by the Design Copyright Act 1968.

Trade Marks

Trade marks used in relation to goods can be registered under the Trade Marks Act 1938, and the Trade Marks Rules of the same year, with subsequent amendments. Note that there is no provision for registered trade marks in relation to *services* — hence, for instance, the British Rail symbol is not, and could not be, registered in the UK.

A trade mark need not, of course, be a symbol; it can be an invented word or words, some other word (but not one having a direct reference to the character or quality of the goods, or a geographical name or surname, though it can be the name of a company, individual or firm represented in some special way), or 'any other distinctive mark'. Protection lasts initially for seven years, renewable for periods of fourteen years.

Many trade marks cannot be protected under the law of copyright, nor as registered designs. Trade mark registration fills the gap, though its limitation to use in relation to goods eliminates many 'corporate identity' symbols.

Patents

Patents really lie outside the scope of this chapter, but it may be noted that they differ in mind from the other ways of protecting 'intellectual property' mentioned, in that they do protect workable *ideas* capable of industrial application, rather than the *expression* of ideas. The law is now largely set out in the Patents Act 1977. New inventions for which a patent is granted are protected initially for four years, and the period can be extended up to a maximum of twenty years.

International protection is available in one form or another for registered designs, trade marks and patents.

All these forms of protection, like copyright, can be assigned complete, or licences may be granted by the holder to allow another party to use them for a period or in part.

It will be seen that the different forms of protection and also, to some extent, registration of company names and business names may overlap. It is sensible, when considering the protection of any 'intellectual property', to look at the whole range of possibilities and seek expert advice.

Passing Off

To pass off your goods or services as those of someone else is actionable. Recently the courts have tended to extend this protection to cover non-proprietary names such as 'champagne' (the only true champagne is that made in the Champagne area of France, and a French manufacturer successfully sued a Spanish firm which called its wine 'champagne'). It is fair to add that a name *can* become general property in time and lose this protection: Bath buns, for instance, can be made with impunity outside the City of Bath!

Passing off is often a possible alternative action to a claim for infringement of copyright: even if the copyright has not been infringed, a similar design or label could be held as 'passing off'. No actual damage need be proved — only a tendency to cause damage; and it is no defence to prove that the passing off was innocent or done without knowledge. Passing off could, of course, also constitute a criminal offence under the Trade Descriptions Act.

Breach of Confidence

Misuse of ideas or information, received in confidence from someone else, can be the subject of an action for breach of confidence. In public relations this may apply to material received in confidence from a client or employer. It could also apply to a consultant's plan 'pirated' by some other person or company, though a claim on this basis would not succeed unless it could be shown that the ideas were original and not simply derived from common professional knowledge. It has even been suggested that if a house journal is supplied to a newspaper editor on condition he does not publish certain marked stories, he could be sued for breach of confidence if he does so. In practice one feels public relations would not be helped by such a step!

The law on this matter is none too well defined, and it is unsafe to rely upon it as an alternative to any other method of protection available.

Consumer Protection Law

This is now a large field, which the public relations practitioner will do well to read up in one of the specialist books on the subject.

Consumer protection can be considered to have begun with the Sale of Goods Act 1893, which we have already mentioned above under Contracts. It still has a great deal of life in it, and has been strengthened by the Supply of Goods (Implied Terms) Act 1973, to which we have also referred.

The next most important Act is probably the Trade Descriptions Act 1968, which makes it an offence to describe inaccurately either goods or services. It sets out the various points which must be correctly described, and the definition of 'trade description' is extremely wide: a description used 'in any manner likely to be taken as referring to the goods' could well cover, for instance, a Press release or booklet. In relation to products the provisions of the Act forbidding some types of false price reductions should be noted.

The Food and Drugs Act 1955 also makes it an offence to mislead on the nature, substance, or quality — including the nutritional value — of foodstuffs, and there are regulations made under this Act covering food hygiene and food labelling.

The Fair Trading Act 1973 set up the Office of Fair Trading — incidentally a valuable source of information on this whole field — and gave its Director General power to take legal action against manufacturers or traders who harm consumers. The Office encourages trade associations to produce voluntary codes of practice in their fields.

The Consumer Credit Act 1974 applies to all kinds of credit and hire transactions, mainly involving sums of £5,000 or less. All businesses in this field now require a licence from the Director General of Fair Trading, and the Act requires full information to be given in advertisements.

Competitions

The organizing of competitions is something which comes the way of most public relations practitioners at one time or another. Despite a gradually growing number of exceptions, lotteries in general remain illegal in Britain. A competition which does not depend upon skill is likely to be held to be a lottery, and those who run it may be prosecuted under the Lotteries and Amusements Act 1976.

There must be sufficient skill in the competition to influence the result — even a 'tie-breaker' has been held insufficient, if the first stage of the competition is so simple that no real skill is required to get to the 'tie-breaker'.

Fortunately there are exemptions for charitable and private lotteries (under the Lotteries Act 1975), but unless you are certain that your competition falls into a permitted category it is sensible to make sure you are well within the law.

Quite apart from the lotteries question, the Act also forbids competitions in newspapers or magazines or in connection with trade, business or sale of any article to the public, in which prizes are offered for forecasting the result of events: football pools do not come into this category, because they are regarded as a form of betting, and separately regulated.

Free gifts are perfectly lawful, so long as everyone eligible gets an equal gift and there is, of course, no limitation on the kind or number of gifts which can be made to people who do not know they will be entitled to any!

Restrictive Trade Practices: Monopolies and Mergers

Agreements or arrangements made between suppliers of goods or services which restrict competition have to be registered with the Director of Fair Trading. The law on this subject is now mainly to be found in the Restrictive Trade Practices Acts 1976 and 1977 and the Restrictive Practices Court Act 1976. The types of agreement which must be registered are laid down in the Acts, and once registered any major agreement is referred to the Restrictive Practices Court for decision on whether it is contrary to the public interest.

The Treaty of Rome also contains provisions against agreements or arrangements which restrict competition, or restrict cross-frontier trade in the Common Market.

Monopolies and mergers are now covered by the Fair Trading Act 1973, and the Director General of Fair Trading has power to refer a monopoly situation to the Monopolies and Mergers Commission for investigation. Again, the EEC has rules against the 'abuse of dominant positions' which restrict competition.

The public relations implications of any of these situations can obviously be great, and any practitioner in the area of finance, major groups of companies or trade associations is particularly advised to know something of the relevant law.

Professional Discipline

The word 'profession' has two degrees of meaning in English. It is often used loosely as equivalent to 'occupation'. It also indicates a field of work with an advisory element, whose practitioners are members of a professional body which requires them to have certain qualifications and to observe a code of professional conduct enforced by a disciplinary procedure. Public relations in Britain can claim to be a profession in this latter sense, though there is no legal or other requirement confining the practice of public relations to members of the professional body, the Institute of Public Relations.

In a legal context it is of interest to know what power the IPR (or any similar body) has to maintain standards in its profession.

The relationship of members to a professional body is an unusual one. If the association is (like the IPR) a company, the members of the association are the members of the company, and the members of the association's governing body are the directors of the company, as we have seen above. But each member is also bound contractually to the association. By his membership, he agrees to abide by the association's rules and to pay his subscription, in return for the rights of membership. If (again the IPR is an example) those rules require him to observe a code of conduct and to submit to penalties, including expulsion, and if he fails to do so, he has in such circumstances no legal claim against the association for he has agreed to those rules. If the rules provide that decisions on disciplinary matters shall be announced publicly for the protection of the public, similarly he has no right of action, provided the announcement is not defamatory, and even if it is it may be privileged.

This is one way in which a professional body is enabled, under English law, to maintain standards. Another is by protecting the right to claim membership of the association, or the use of letters indicating qualifications or membership. If a person uses the letters MIPR (Member of the Institute of Public Relations) or Dip.CAM (Diploma of CAM), for instance, without being entitled to do so, the body concerned can take action against him in the courts for passing off.

Conclusion

Clearly it has not been possible to do more in this chapter than give a bird's-eye view of some areas of the law of importance to the public relations practitioner. Although it is hoped that the introduction may be useful, do not rely upon it to find the definitive answer to a legal situation: space makes it impossible to give all the details and qualifications necessary, and the law is constantly developing.

A few practical words of advice with which to conclude:

1 Check and re-check any statement made in the course of your work, for accuracy and for its likely effect on those who receive it, looking for the worst interpretation which could be placed upon it.
2 When you are doing business, placing orders, or getting into any other contractual situation, get the full details clear and stated (or confirmed) in

writing and accepted — preferably in writing — by the other party.
Example: if you order a photograph or artwork, settle at the outset what
rights you are buying.
3 Make sure you know a solicitor to whom you can turn for advice at short
notice. It is worth establishing a continuing relationship and taking trouble
to ensure that the solicitor knows what your work consists of — public
relations practice is not always understood.
4 Save yourself time and money when you do consult a solicitor by
marshalling all the facts and papers beforehand.
5 An ounce of care and commonsense at the time can save you the alternatives
of conceding a claim, with consequent loss to you or your company, or
having to oppose it legally at considerable cost.

FURTHER READING

Johnston, Dan *Design Protection*, Design Council (1978)
McNae, L. C. J. *Essential Law for Journalists*, National Council for the Training
of Journalists (8th edition 1982) Vol I
James, Philip S. *Introduction to English Law*, Butterworth (10th edition 1979)
Harvey, Brian W. *The Law of Consumer Protection and Fair Trading*, Butterworth
(2nd edition 1982)
Slade, Elizabeth *Tolley's Employment Handbook*, Tolley (3rd edition 1983)

There is no easy way to keep abreast of changes in the law overall, but in
individual fields such as Employment Law and Company Law there are
several useful bulletins, whose names can be found from the bodies concerned
with these areas, such as the Industrial Society or the Institute of Chartered
Secretaries and Administrators, or from one of the legal publishers. The *Night
Lawyer* articles in the UK Press Gazette are always worth reading. And make
sure you use the *latest* editions of your textbooks.

13

Professional Attitudes

Pat Bowman

Freedom of the Media

The concept of the freedom of the Press is generally held to be an essential element in a democratic society, yet it is seldom closely defined. For all the emotional words spoken and written against what are seen as attacks on press freedom — and here 'Press', of course, includes radio and television as well as newspapers, news agencies and magazines — little heed is paid to the various real constraints within which journalists have to work.

Indeed, the term 'freedom of the Press' has become devalued by its use in circumstances that have little to do with freedom, but more to do with disputes over who is to wield power in a newspaper office, radio station or publishing house.

The distinction can, of course, be plainly made between the degree of freedom accorded to the media in an essentially democratic country and the restrictions imposed by an authoritarian *régime*. This is not necessarily related to the political persuasion of the government of the land, but is determined by the extent to which that government controls the flow of information to its people and to which it is prepared to allow untrammelled comment upon the issues of the day.

It is widely believed that in Britain we have a free Press, yet there are at least half a dozen pressures on the media that limit freedom to a greater or lesser degree.

The most obvious and most severe of these is the law. The legal pressures on the media are considerable, and more restrictive than in most other democracies. The laws of libel, in particular, may sometimes inhibit publication even when an editor is convinced that his staff have incontrovertible evidence of, for example, the misdeeds of a politician or financier. A libel is basically the publication of a false statement about a person which is to

227

his discredit, and will expose him or her to hatred, ridicule and contempt. Even when the information is true, the classic plea of 'fair comment on a matter of public interest' is not always sufficient defence if not quite all the facts have been discovered or stated correctly.

Reputable papers have lawyers specializing in libel always available to advise on the risk involved in publishing a particular story, as well as to stop inadvertent libels slipping through. Yet each year large sums in damages are extracted by those who take to the courts their dislike of what has been written or said about them. The editor, or radio or television producer, has to judge whether or not the public interest is served, whether the matter is sufficiently important to go ahead. 'Publish and be damned' is a bold war-cry and not one to be used lightly.

In recent years, what has become known as 'the alternative Press' has provided an outlet for many stories that major publications dare not use, convinced as they may be of their truth or, at any rate, partial truth. Publication in periodicals that cheerfully live on their writs as much as their wits has often led to wider examination of some alleged scandal that has later been substantiated and, only then, covered in the conventional media.

The laws on contempt and the system of privilege by which the courts and Parliament defend their status also present problems that trouble every journalist, the more so because both law and precedents tend to be vague.

Governments, too, produce pressures upon the media that are not often recognized by the ordinary listener, viewer and reader. Direct censorship in this country is known only in time of war, but the Official Secrets Act hovers over a whole area of government topics, ranging from vitally important defence matters to trivial routines within the Civil Service.

Prosecutions for minor technical infringements seldom take place, but the decision on whether or not to prosecute is a political one, since it is made by the Attorney-General, who is a politician and a member of the government of the day. Not all Attorneys-General see the Official Secrets Act in the same way and they have in their hands a power that can be used to prevent on grounds of security the publication of information related to government affairs, past as well as present, that the media might well hold to be in the public interest.

So far as security in the sense of defence is concerned, there is an organization originally set up to guide editors and specialist correspondents, called the D Notice Committee. Put at its simplest, if a sensitive matter comes to the attention of the media its publication can be stopped by the issue of a D Notice. The Committee itself has representatives of the media on it, but effectively its executive operates a governmental control on what is published.

There are also other less formal, and even less noticeable, forms of political or Civil Service pressure on the media. Close relationships are often formed between journalists and politicians and senior civil servants, resulting in better understanding and more accurate interpretation of events. The threat of withdrawal of co-operation, made on a personal basis, may influence a journalist who has come across a story that might embarrass Westminster or Whitehall. Government links with both the British Broadcasting Corporation and the Independent Broadcasting Authority are close, through their statutory structure. Newspaper proprietors tend to be politically active men in whom a word of advice from a Cabinet Minister can produce a realization that publication of a particular story might be unwise.

Newspaper proprietors and editors have long been regarded as defenders of the freedom of the Press, and many have fulfilled that role energetically and effectively. Yet there are proprietors to whom freedom means simply the power to have what they wish published in their papers, with their influence extending to the selection and suppression of news and the tendency of comment, even into unlikely areas such as arts criticism and religious features.

The editor of a local newspaper or, for that matter, of a specialized magazine has to live and work among his readers. It is hardly surprising that sometimes personal pressures are brought to bear to keep information out of the paper or ensure that, for example, a court case involving a local notable receives the minimum of space. This can be held to be an abuse of responsibility, or simply social and commercial prudence.

The role of the advertiser in relation to the freedom of the media is often misunderstood. Although all newspapers and magazines depend far more on advertising than on circulation for their revenue, the extent to which an advertiser can influence any major publication is negligible. Even in minor specialist magazines and small-town weekly newspapers, the advertiser's influence over editorial content is small, certainly on any issue of importance. The reason may to some extent lie in a certain antipathy that many journalists feel for advertising and advertising people, in spite of the fact that advertising revenue pays their salaries. Also, they know that readers will soon recognize and derogate advertising-based items.

In independent radio and television, advertising is so separated from programme content that there is virtually no influence on editorial material whatever. Indeed, the non-commercial BBC is sometimes more lenient nowadays in its admittance of advertising references in programmes than are the commercial stations.

In recent years the growth of pressure groups of all kinds has affected the approach of the media to a variety of subjects, in effect forcing a more balanced treatment by making their voices heard in support of minority causes and contributing at the same time to the proliferation of the alternative Press. The BBC has responded positively to this by a very limited exercise of allowing such groups to make their own programmes for transmission in off-peak times.

A less welcome tendency in the past decade has been for employees in the media, notably in Fleet Street, to disrupt production when they disagree with some part of the content of a paper or, less frequently, radio or television programme. This has led to stories, pictures and even cartoons being omitted from newspapers, to whole editions being stopped, and to television programmes being blacked out. In Fleet Street this practice can perhaps be better understood when the items concerned relate to issues of disagreement between the management and the employees or their unions. It may then be felt that the newspaper is being used to make a case against its own workers, and this attitude is a partial response to those proprietors who cry 'abuse of the freedom of the Press' in the course of a dispute whenever production is threatened by industrial action. This approach is readily interpreted by employees as no more than a demand for unimpeded freedom to publish in any circumstances. Yet when the exponents of workers' control use their technical ability to interfere with the content of a paper on a matter in which they are not directly involved, a more real threat to freedom is involved.

Society and the Journalist

The emotion which surrounds most discussion of the freedom of the Press and the relationship of all the media to the fabric of modern society stems from two main causes: a false perception of the role of the journalist, and a failure to recognize the multi-faceted function of the newspaper, which has to a lesser extent devolved upon radio and television. The two are inextricably intertwined.

In the earliest days of the coffee shop journals published in eighteenth-century London, journalists were purveyors of political and social gossip, of scurrilous comment and innuendo — in other words, of entertainment. The responsible newspapers of the middle nineteenth century lifted journalism onto a higher plain of the provision of news and information, the writing of serious comment and criticism, the espousal of causes, and the creation of that forum for debate, the correspondence column.

The early twentieth century, with a combination of fast transmission of news and newer techniques to print words and pictures quickly and in quantity, saw the growth of the popular Press — still just a little scurrilous by comparison with its more respectable brethren — and the vast array of magazines and specialized periodicals now taken for granted.

Through all these years the image of the journalist as a scribbler, a hack, a menial fellow irresponsibly dedicated to any story for its own sake, has persisted in spite of the concurrent recognition of the social and political reforms engendered and encouraged by the great editors of the past, the amazing standards of literary skill displayed in a product that is yet produced each day, and the revelations of responsible investigative journalism that can bring down politicians into the morass of their own corruption.

This double vision of journalism arises from a lack of appreciation that a newspaper, a magazine or a radio or television station (other than the non-commercial BBC) has to sell itself to survive. It is a commercial entity just like any other business; it must attract sufficient readers, listeners or viewers for advertisers to find it worthwhile to buy space or time to promote their goods. To do that it has to entertain as well as inform, to make its news, comment and features palatable and comprehensible to its audience, to offer help and advice to guide its faithful followers through a complex society, to satisfy the minority who care about chess or country walks, as well as the majority who care about football and film stars.

This may sometimes seem to accord ill with leading articles calling doom down upon the United Nations, political profiles aimed at affecting votes in the next General Election, or features crusading against child prostitution in Asia. But the media is as it is because the typical viewer, listener or reader (who no more exists than 'the man in the street') wants something of everything — 'the whole of human life' as one paper's slogan puts it.

Part of the blame for society's imperfect view of the journalist lies with the profession itself, for few who practise it seem able to enunciate clearly how they see their own role. There is a generalized, unspoken understanding that news is what people want to read, that facts are sacred and comment is free, that anyone who tries to hide something is probably operating against the public good, that politicians and big businessmen would like to manipulate the media for their own ends, that all issues are better discussed openly rather than behind closed doors as a normal part of a democratic society.

Relatively few major journalists over the years have set their beliefs down and, for all the influence these men have had directly on their profession and indirectly on society, the impact on the public appreciation of journalism has been slight. The grubby man in a shabby raincoat with a notebook in his hand shouting 'hold the front page' lives on in the world of cheap drama and fiction, along with the comic clergyman, the lugubrious undertaker and the pompous lawyer.

The journalist sees himself as a representative of those for whom he writes. He feels free to comment on any topic under the sun, to criticize individuals or organizations, to investigate and to disclose, to find out first and let everyone know as quickly as possible. His life is governed by time constraints; there is seldom time to reflect and barely enough to check the facts. He may be irresponsible and working for an irresponsible paper, but that is a far greater rarity than critics of the media would have others believe. He will more likely be skilled, knowledgeable and balanced. He may be young and inexperienced or old and wise, but he will still know that it is his right and duty to ask questions, dig out facts and figures, observe trends and build words and pictures into a story — for a story is what all of his audience want to read, hear and see.

And he knows who his audience is. Whether he edits a national daily newspaper or a regional evening, a mass circulation magazine or a specialized quarterly, a local radio news feature or the networked television news, the journalist knows for whom he is writing and that will govern the way he works.

It is little wonder, then, that the media is the whipping boy of politicians and industrialists or trade union leaders and all others who see a threat to themselves in the fact that their actions are criticized, their motives questioned, or that a case other than their own has been well made. This part of the hurly-burly of media life and the friction that is generated is in itself a source of energy in society — although sometimes more of heat than of light.

Few areas create more friction than investigative journalism, and the heat of the respondents is usually in direct proportion to the nearness of the enquiry to their own doorsteps. An investigation over many months into the diversion of overseas relief funds into the pockets of some far-distant statesman produces commendation and, occasionally, international remedial action. An investigation into the relationship of a top politician and a leading criminal, with a string of Westminster and City figures involved along the way, produces allegations of muck-raking, character assassination, bias, inaccuracy, political motivation, anti-capitalism and so on. Yet either of these investigations, if they are responsibly conducted and reveal factual evidence of some kind of wrongdoing, may produce information that should be in the public domain — and which would not come into the public domain without the intervention of the media.

On the other hand, it would be naive to assert that all such investigations are initiated from entirely altruistic motives. There is nothing like a good scandal to increase sales or put up the viewing figures. This mixture of public service and commercial gain is inherent in the media system.

An attempt, not always successful, to police this ill-defined area has been made since 1953 by the Press Council, which has been defined as the 'journalists' court of honour'. It is a watchdog of standards of propriety to which complaints can be addressed. The council is composed of equal numbers of professional and lay members, with a lay chairman, usually an eminent lawyer.

The council's constitution lists its first two objectives as the preservation of the established freedom of the Press and the maintenance of the highest professional and commercial standards. Neither of these objectives has been fully defined, but through the accumulation of case law, the council has contributed to a recognition of values and has some effect on editorial behaviour through the power of publicly expressed disapproval. Many, however, regard it as a watchdog without teeth and debate about editorial standards in the media continues unabated.

Less controversial, but probably only because it is so much less noticed, is the growing role of the media as a third-party communicator, positively used by groups to speak to one another. The most common instance of this is the almost daily use of the Press by trade unions or employers' organizations to strike a stance before a negotiation, or during a pause in a dispute. Whatever they may say to one another in secret across the table, they may add to or subtract from it before the larger audience, including those whom they represent, at the press conference.

Companies can speak not only to shareholders, but to their competitors and their customers, when the chairman is interviewed on television or a financial editor writes a considered study. Most of all, governments speak to the world of commerce not merely through ministers' speeches at official functions, but through responses to journalists' questions about price rises, shortages, pay policy, import control or any other issue of the day.

The skilled public relations communicator can see this happening and may, sparingly, make use of this capacity himself, recognizing that while for the most part the media have no objection to conveying news and views if they believe them to be of interest to their audience, they naturally resent feeling used.

The Journalist and Public Relations

There is an inevitable conflict of interest between the journalist and the public relations man. The former is serving his audience and his paper or his programme as he perceives it and as it is expressed for him by his editor or producer. The latter is serving his employer or client.

Their relationship will vary from time to time and from circumstance to circumstance. There are occasions when the public relations man has information he wishes to be published that the journalist would like to have and, moreover, has it in the form and at the time the journalist would like it. Such occasions are rare. Not quite so rare are those times when the journalist has information the public relations man wishes not to publish, or is asking questions he is unwilling or unable to answer, or is pursuing a line of enquiry or comment contrary to the public relations man's appreciation of the facts. There is a large range of subtle variations from almost total co-operation to almost complete opposition.

Today the two functions are inter-dependent. They need one another, for all the Fleet Street hard cases who declare that they never get anything worthwhile from public relations sources and despite the few in public relations who relegate press relations to the bottom of their list of communications techniques.

Inter-dependence means mutual trust, and to achieve this requires understanding of, and respect for, the other man's point of view, objectives, and operational needs. There is no excuse for the public relations man who fails in his media relations tasks because he does not understand how newspapers and magazines work, how radio and television operate, their time constraints, their processes of selection and their methods of production. This is essential as a first step towards earning the journalist's confidence, and it can be acquired by study.

More difficult for those who have not worked as journalists themselves is to gain an appreciation of how a journalist's mind works: what is behind a particular line of questioning, for instance, or how a persistent emphasis in handling a given subject may relate to the paper's total policy. This may come from long experience, but it will come more quickly from personal contact, discussion of how and why a particular story came to be handled as it did, why one paper dismissed a major release in a single paragraph, while another made it a page lead, or why some relatively small story was built up into a networked radio or television item. Endless study and comparison of all the media is vital to the public relations man's understanding.

Obviously, trust must depend upon honesty. Apart from the ethical codes governing the practice of both journalism and public relations, a relationship of honesty is all-important. If the public relations man can give only part of what the journalist wants he must say so frankly. If he can give nothing, he must say so and, preferably, why. If he gives wrong information inadvertently, he must seek to have it corrected at once and admit his error. He must honour promises, whether to keep a story exclusive to one man or merely to telephone a progress report by a certain time. He may make a case for his employer or client as powerfully as he wishes, but he must recognize the journalist's responsibility to write a balanced story.

If he issues false or inaccurate information, if he lies or deceives by suppression of facts, then not only is he guilty of unethical conduct, but he will have destroyed a relationship and damaged his reputation. Unreliable sources of information soon become recognized in the media for what they are.

It is easy for people in public relations to congratulate themselves on the closeness of their relationship with some journalists, particularly specialist correspondents or editors of specialized periodicals. A form of over-dependence can develop in which the journalist too easily accepts and absorbs the information he is given, questions too little and forgets the sense of proportion that it is his duty to his audience to preserve. As the man in the middle between media and management or client, the public relations man must never ignore the value of healthy enquiry and criticism; after all, the employees, the shareholders, the customers and the suppliers are among the journalist's audience too.

A sad reflection of falling standards, particularly in the specialist Press, is over-reliance on public relations sources. The man who has issued a press release and sees it printed word for word in a trade magazine should, before he congratulates himself on getting his message across so well, think whether or not the reason is simply that the paper is run by an editor and a secretary. They may have no staff to go out and find news, or even time to take a press release and by shrewd questioning make it into something special to that paper. Readers soon detect a dull sameness of material, a lack of competitive edge, a form of journalism that merely processes words and figures. The public relations man should remember that if the reader is not interested in the paper, his story might as well not have been published at all.

In establishing his personal contacts with journalists the public relations man must have something to offer, not necessarily an immediate story, but maybe a feature or picture idea, the suggestion of an interview, the opportunity of a background briefing. At the very least he should set out to discover what the journalist needs from him. Entertainment in itself is not persuasion; a journalist wants to gain something practical from any meeting and is almost always a busy person, whose time should not be wasted.

Exclusivity is not the goal of all journalists. It matters far less in the world of daily newspapers than was once held to be the case. In television, however, an idea that may be used by someone else is all but useless. In radio, major ideas for national networks need to be exclusive, but the appetite of local radio for material is so vast that exclusivity is less vital than a local angle.

One of the biggest stumbling blocks in the relationship of journalists and public relations men is the handling of information or opinion 'off the record'. This usually arises from a failure to understand what this much abused term means. Broadly, 'on the record' material is for use freely and can be attributed to the speaker or his organization; information given 'off the record' is for use without attribution; and there is also information or opinon given in confidence, not for publication, but specifically to help journalists interpret correctly.

This is a subtle area of operation where the inexperienced public relations man would do well to move cautiously, always making sure that the journalists with whom he is dealing agree the basis on which information is being given. The man he is talking to may be inexperienced too.

Experienced journalists are sensitive to what has become known as news management, a term which attempts to cover the blatant manipulation of information for the benefit of, mostly, governments and politicians, but sometimes nationalized and private industry, the armed services, the police and aggressive pressure groups.

News can be held back expressly to create a favourable impression on a particular day, or to distract attention from an adverse story. Favourable stories about export orders can boost share prices at a crucial time, when only the board of directors know that a take-over bid is in the air. News of a new employee benefit may be discreetly leaked to take the edge off a forthcoming announcement of a reduction in the work force. Many such manœuvres are justified by political or commercial prudence, but the public relations man should be alert to the ethical dangers of the misuse of timing and make his judgements case by case.

Any journalist will state categorically that the protection of the reader against news management and other potential abuses lies in the ability and integrity of the editorial staff of the paper, the radio station or the television programme: the news judgement of experienced professionals will guard against the unscrupulous manipulator. This is undoubtedly true, but the public relations man also has a part to play in ensuring that the media which his employer or client need remain ethical, accurate, objective, critical and a true service to their audience. That is probably as near 'a free Press' as one can expect to get.

14

Routes to PR

Warren Newman

Public Relations is not one of the easiest occupations to enter because there is no established career path to follow. Yet at the same time there is a continuing moan from employers at how difficult it is to find and retain skilled public relations practitioners. The potential rewards from a career in PR are attractive both financially and in terms of job satisfaction. So the purpose of this chapter is to suggest ways in which you can prepare yourself to join this branch of the communications industry.

For most people public relations is a second career. It is virtually impossible to get a job straight from school and still pretty difficult to gain employment in the profession direct from university. There are signs that this is changing. The Public Relations Consultants Association now encourages member consultancies to include a proportion of trainees among new recruits — favouring those with a degree in the arts, marketing communications or allied fields.

We will be looking in detail at the arrangements made for training in public relations skills leading to qualifications recognized by the Institute of Public Relations. However it is unlikely that in the foreseeable future PR will become a profession which is restricted to those who have undergone apprenticeship and passed examinations. The current trend is for consultancies to want to recruit people with a specialist knowledge related to their clients' activities and to help the new recruit learn how to apply public relations principles. In other words, it is easier to teach an electronics graduate to write a news release than it is to teach a journalist to understand electronics.

Successful PR people have begun their working lives as barristers, civil servants, politicians or economists. They have come from backgrounds in general management or from marketing. Still the greatest recruiting ground for public relations people is journalism. Yet even here the chances are that the journalist will not have been a general reporter, but a specialist on a particular subject — anything from motoring to medicine.

Public relations practice covers a very wide range of specific activities carried out often by different staff within a department of an organization, or within a consultancy. The training experience needed to carry out these specialized tasks will be different. An account executive working on the production of company journals will have learnt his craft differently from the parliamentary affairs expert whose value to clients lies in his intimate knowledge of how the government machine functions and can be influenced.

This diversity of activity and sources of recruitment makes it particularly difficult to give an authoritative account of how PR skills are acquired. A body of academic knowledge about PR practice exists and is growing. Such material is the foundation of training courses and examinations. It provides a means of offering students 'accelerated experience'. Everybody working in public relations — whatever their speciality — should want to take examinations to prove that they understand the environment in which they are working. But unlike those in many professions the exams are something you *choose* to do rather than *have* to do.

The diversity of public relations recruitment is also one of its great strengths. It means that a wide range of different disciplines can be brought to bear on solving problems and developing plans for future action. Each profession tends to have its own way of looking at the world and the large public relations department or consultancy benefits from having a very wide perspective. The writer, designer, photographer, marketing man, researcher, film-maker, lawyer, advertising person, home economist and so on, come together and contribute to the development of creative strategies.

I have stressed the range of PR work because it is important to recognize that one of the routes to a career in public relations is a successful career elsewhere first. The most tried and trusted of those 'first steps' is journalism, but a young person with interests in any field would be well advised to follow that interest and convert to public relations in their late twenties and early thirties, when the maturity of judgement necessary to be successful has had a chance to develop. No earlier career will be wasted.

After establishing this base of experience it is possible for someone who aspires to join a consultancy to have a short note about their background circulated to members of the Public Relations Consultants Association. Application should be made to 37, Cadogan Street, Sloane Square, SW3 2PR.

Qualities Required

Before doing anything towards a career in public relations it would be sensible to look carefully at the kind of qualities a good PR person may be expected to have.

One quality has already been mentioned: judgement. It is so hard to define, but so vital. The PR person will be called on to absorb information, relate it to what he already knows, guess at the likely consequence of certain courses of action and advise on what to do. It is often not a question of right or wrong, but of one opinion versus another. The PR person must be able to make judgements quickly, under pressure, and his advice must be trusted.

The need to be trusted leads to another requirement from the PRO. He must have integrity and be honest in dealings with clients, journalists, members of Parliament and others whom he may meet in the course of his work.

Facility with language is another essential attribute. The PRO is a professional communicator and must be able to write and speak clearly and with respect for precision in the use of language. In sensitive situations he must be aware of the finest nuances in the meaning of words and phrases. He should be at home with arguments, able to assess a case and present it with clarity and impact. And his use of language should be flexible because one day he may be composing a news release: the next, a speech for a company chairman. He must have a natural feel for the kind of language which is appropriate for different people in different situations.

Such facility with language is commonly found among people who have had a very liberal education, are well read and have an insatiable curiosity. The PRO needs a wide general knowledge and to be deeply concerned with current affairs.

The public relations professional is more and more called on to predict the consequences of social trends which may have an impact on his employer or client. This requires great sensitivity and imagination and a 'feel' for current affairs, informed by a historical perspective.

Crisis management is part of the work of many PR people. In a crisis situation the ability to stay calm and think fast is invaluable. Equally important is the recognition that other people are under stress and need tactful assistance. In many other situations tact is an essential attribute of the good PRO.

The ability to form relationships with other people and earn their confidence is important. It requires some familiarity with the 'social graces', since you will be entertaining all kinds of people under different circumstances. Public relations is not really the ideal career for the shy, retiring type.

Perseverance is also needed. Your good ideas may not be self-evidently good to others. You will often have to fight to persuade others you are right and having embarked on a course of action you will need the courage to stick with it.

You will need to be a good listener — the kind of person that others feel able to talk to.

Finally, among this frightening list of virtues, you need to be able to administrate. Creativity is highly prized in the PR business but it does not replace concern for minute detail which makes the difference between success or failure.

Preparation for a Career

Education in public relations was, until recently, geared almost exclusively to teaching those who had already found themselves a job and wanted to improve their knowledge and skills by private study, evening classes or day release. It is now becoming possible to study public relations in preparation for a career.

Some students get their first brush with the subject at GCE A Level when they take the Associated Examinations Board Communications Studies examination. This covers the arts, practices and media of communication, and some psychology. Similar, but more advanced communications courses are available at some universities and polytechnics. They are unashamedly academic in approach and some practitioners feel they are not a good foundation for a career. Others believe the PR profession needs more people who have a deep understanding of the discoveries of psychology, sociology and related social sciences. Such courses can therefore be commended for those who wish to attend university, but have their eyes on a career in PR.

A current list of courses at degree or diploma level and useful to intended PROs can be obtained from the CAM Foundation, Abford House, 15 Wilton Road, SW1V 1NJ.

Less academically inclined students may prefer to take a course of studies in some aspect of journalism. For the school-leaver with A Levels there is a lot to be said for joining a local newspaper under indentures and studying to obtain the National Council for the Training of Journalists Proficiency Certificate. This not only gives a very sound grounding in the practice of journalism; it also teaches practical skills like shorthand which will be a very useful asset. So too will the instruction in interview technique. Most courses on PR are very short on practical skills and these technical abilities are much in demand.

Another good way of learning foundation skills would be to take a course intended for magazine and house journal reporters. Work on a house journal would be a very good 'first step' to a career in public relations and the British Association of Industrial Editors organizes its own examinations leading to membership. Full details of the syllabus, study arrangements and examinations can be obtained from: BAIE, 3 Locks Yard, High Street, Sevenoaks, Kent TN13 1LT. The National Council for the Training of Journalists runs courses which although not specific to house journals, will help you to pass the BAIE exams. Details are available from The Deputy Director (Training), NCTJ, Harp House, 179 High Street, Epping, CM16 4BJ.

The Business and Technical Education Council have a PR module for their Higher Certificate syllabus.

Anyone who has successfully passed any of the examinations mentioned so far will be well prepared for the studies which are recommended by the Institute of Public Relations — the CAM Certificate and Diploma. Many of the degree and diploma courses mentioned already earn exemption from the first stage of the CAM system and permit the candidate to move straight to the Diploma.

The CAM Education System

CAM is short for the Communications Advertising and Marketing Education Foundation. As the name implies it organizes examinations on behalf of the communications industry.

An important principle underlying early studies is that all students should be familiar with the basic principles of advertising, marketing and public relations. Specialization does not occur until the Diploma.

So the first step for the student is to study for the Certificate in Communications Studies. There is a choice of seven subjects of which six must be passed before the candidate is allowed to sit for a Diploma. As well as the three subjects mentioned, students may study media, research and behavioural studies, communications practice, and business and economic environment.

It takes a typical student two years to achieve passes in the six subjects. Then a further year is normally required to obtain a Diploma which is awarded for passes in three out of a selection of five subjects. These subjects are:

1 PR for commercial organizations.
2 PR for non-commercial organizations.
3 PR Strategy.
4 Market research.
5 Marketing strategy.

Successful candidates are then entitled to use the style: Dip CAM. They may also apply for membership of the CAM graduate society and if accepted may describe themselves as MCAM. The Institute of Public Relations encourages all those studying for the PR Diploma to take out student membership of the IPR and when qualified to apply for associate or full membership. This is important because people qualified to practise public relations by virtue of the CAM Diploma should recognize the importance of submitting to the high ethical standards and disciplinary procedures which the Institute applies to all its members.

Methods of Study

How you study is largely influenced by where you live. Full-time study at a college is only possible in London (at the Centre for Business Studies, Greenwich) and at Nottingham (where the Polytechnic combines a CAM and Institute of Marketing course).

Part-time and evening class study is offered at the following colleges subject to sufficient students enrolling:

In London

1 College for the Distributive Trades, WC2.
2 City of London Polytechnic, EC2.
3 The Centre for Business Studies, SE10.
4 City College of Management Studies, W1.
5 West London Business School, W3.
6 The Centre for Marketing and Management Studies, SW17.

If you are out of London CAM will advise you on your nearest tuition centre. It is only possible at the moment to attend Diploma classes in London at the College for the Distributive Trades.

For most students therefore study will be at home. *Correspondence courses* are organized by International Correspondence Schools, Intertext House, Stewarts Road, SW8 4UJ, and by Metropolitan College, Oxford OX2 6PR.

All students must anyway register with CAM before beginning their study course.

Even after obtaining a CAM diploma the keen practitioner will want to learn more about detailed aspects of PR practice. Regular seminars are held by both CAM and the Institute of Public Relations. The IPR also holds an annual conference where members can hear leading speakers and compare notes with colleagues.

London Chamber of Commerce and Industry

The London Chamber of Commerce and Industry holds certificate and diploma examinations in public relations which are particularly suited to overseas students with many questions related to practice in 'country of origin'. There is a Group Diploma in Public Relations for three subjects, of which Public Relations must be one, passed at the same time. The Diploma choices cover Advertising, Marketing and Sales Management. Distinctions earn exemptions from the equivalent CAM certificate subjects. Details from the London Chamber of Commerce and Industry Examinations Board,

Marlowe House, Station Road, Sidcup, Kent DA15 7BJ. A self-tuition course for this examination is run by the Frank Jefkins School of Public Relations, 84 Ballards Way, South Croydon, CR2 7LA. This school also runs a series of courses which are intended for practising PR personnel.

For young entrants to the profession the IPR has a careers counselling service — widely known as the 'uncle' scheme. Experienced PR people throughout the country have agreed to meet and talk to people who are considering a career in public relations or moving from one branch of PR to another. And the IPR also keeps a recruitment register listing the names of people who are considering changing jobs.

Advertisements for jobs in public relations appear regularly in *Campaign* and *UK Press Gazette*. Some national newspapers routinely carry media appointments — notably *The Guardian*. But the newly-qualified PRO need not wait for advertisements to appear. The larger consultancies are usually very willing to meet suitably qualified potential new recruits who write requesting an interview.

Towards the Future

The public relations profession has realized that improvements must be made to make it easier for people to decide they would like to join it. In particular the trends described at the beginning of this chapter make it inevitable that sooner rather than later there will be a high standard 'transfer' course aimed at people who realize that a career in public relations would suit them. Journalists are one group who need to build on their skills if they are to broaden out into PR.

Advertising executives often come to realize that they would be better suited temperamentally to working in PR and are sometimes asked to transfer to the PR subsidiary of an advertising agency.

People connected with the Stock Exchange are finding themselves attracted to the possibilities of working in financial public relations.

The police and armed services ask serving officers to spend a spell of time working in the units dealing with PR and on leaving the services such people may wish to stay in the field.

Large companies are increasingly choosing to put a senior executive in charge of their public relations and public affairs whose training has been in other fields.

For all these and the many others who will enter the public relations profession from all walks of life, it is almost certain that a course will be developed to help them make the switch.

Index

Charts, 59
Checklists, 10, 11
  exhibition, 74–5
  press conferences, 65–9
  special events, 64–5
  student factory visits, 72
Christian Aid, 167–8
City of London, 108, 111, 147
Civil Service, see Government
Clients,
  Annual Register of, 194
  competing interests of, 187
  confidentiality, 186, 194
  disclosure of interest to, 188, 195
  needs, 134
  payment not contingent on achievement, 188–9, 194
  relations, 10, 131, 133, 136–7, 167, 177, 194
Closed circuit television, 52, 86, 153
Code of Athens, 195–7
Code of Conduct
  IPR, 183–93
  IPRA, 197
Code of Consultancy Practice, 193–5
Code of Professional Standards (PRSA), 195
Colour magazines, 27–29
Column inches, 13, 153, 188
Communications audit, 2, 13
Communications, Advertising and Marketing Education Foundation (CAM), 7, 90–1, 93, 240–2
  Certificate, 241
  Diploma, 241
  methods of study, 242
Communications gap, 2
Community relations, 105, 108, 111, 132
Competitions, 5, 223–4
Confederation of British Industry, 19, 83, 106
Conferences, 63–9
  displays at, 60, 62, 65, 69
  overseas, 79
  report on, 12
  Press, 65–9
Confidential information, 186–7, 194, 195
Consultancy, 130–7
  advertising agency subsidiaries, 130–1
  agreement for, 201–2
  costs, 8, 134–6
  fees, 135–6
  independent, 131
  new business, 189–90
  Parliamentary, 171, 174, 176–7
  recruitment, 237
  role, 117, 131, 158, 166, 167
  specialist, 132
  structure, 10–11, 133–4

Consumerist, 105
Contact report, 12
Corporate design, 5, 112
Corporate identity, see Identity
Corporate image, see Image
Corporate PR responsibilities, 111–12, 116–17
Costing, 8, 134–6
Country Life, 163
Creative consultancies, 38
Customer, 105, 108, 223

Daily Express, 24, 26, 27, 29, 42
Daily Mail, 24, 26, 29, 42
Daily Mirror, 24, 26, 28, 166
Daily Star, 24, 27, 29, 42
Daily Telegraph, 24, 25, 28
Dates,
  article publication, 95, 96
  news release, 91, 93, 94
Deadlines, 88, 95, 231
Definition of PR practice, ii, 150
Demonstrations, 5, 68, 69
Design,
  briefing, 11
  company philosophy, 60, 112
  copyright, 218
  cost, 8
  exhibition stand, 6
  local government, 156–7
  Registered, 220–1
  staff, 169
  whom for, 5
Diagrams, 59
Dictating equipment, 11
Direct mail, 5, 11, 24, 37–8, 77, 80, 81, 157
Direct Mail Producers' Association, 38
Disclosure, 105
  failure in, 203
  financial information, 112, 210
  of interest, 185–6, 188, 194, 206
  to employees, 115, 207
Displays, 60, 61–2, 68, 73, 81
D-Notice Committee, 228
Doorstepping, 21
Dr Barnardo's, 165–6, 168–9
Drawings, 59
Drogheda, Earl of, 147
Duckhams, 165
Duplicators, 11

Editor,
  and embargoes, 94
  features, 95
  press freedom, 229
  public interest, 228
  time constraints, 92